Holt McDougal
Algebra 1

Practice and Problem Solving Workbook

Copyright © by Houghton Mifflin Harcourt Publishing Company

All rights reserved. No part of this work may be reproduced or transmitted in any form or by any means, electronic or mechanical, including photocopying or recording, or by any information storage or retrieval system, without the prior written permission of the copyright owner unless such copying is expressly permitted by federal copyright law.

Permission is hereby granted to individuals using the corresponding student's textbook or kit as the major vehicle for regular classroom instruction to photocopy entire pages from this publication in classroom quantities for instructional use and not for resale. Requests for information on other matters regarding duplication of this work should be addressed to Houghton Mifflin Harcourt Publishing Company, Attn: Contracts, Copyrights, and Licensing, 9400 South Park Center Loop, Orlando, Florida 32819.

Printed in the U.S.A.

ISBN 13: 978-0-55-402404-2

2 3 4 5 6 7 8 9 10   1409   18 17 16 15 14 13 12 11 10

4500244849

If you have received these materials as examination copies free of charge, Houghton Mifflin Harcourt Publishing Company retains title to the materials and they may not be resold. Resale of examination copies is strictly prohibited.

Possession of this publication in print format does not entitle users to convert this publication, or any portion of it, into electronic format.

Contents

Practice

Chapter 1 1
Chapter 2 9
Chapter 3 20
Chapter 4 27
Chapter 5 33
Chapter 6 43
Chapter 7 49
Chapter 8 58
Chapter 9 64
Chapter 10 73
Chapter 11 81
Chapter 12 90

Problem Solving

Chapter 1 97
Chapter 2 105
Chapter 3 116
Chapter 4 123
Chapter 5 129
Chapter 6 139
Chapter 7 145
Chapter 8 154
Chapter 9 160
Chapter 10 169
Chapter 11 177
Chapter 12 186

LESSON 1-1 Practice
Variables and Expressions

Give two ways to write each algebraic expression in words.

1. $15 - b$

2. $\dfrac{x}{16}$

3. $x + 9$

4. $(2)(t)$

5. $z - 7$

6. $4y$

7. Sophie's math class has 6 fewer boys than girls, and there are g girls. Write an expression for the number of boys.

8. A computer printer can print 10 pages per minute. Write an expression for the number of pages the printer can print in m minutes.

Evaluate each expression for $r = 8$, $s = 2$, and $t = 5$.

9. st

10. $r \div s$

11. $s + t$

12. $r - t$

13. $r \cdot s$

14. $t - s$

15. Paula always withdraws 20 dollars more than she needs from the bank.

   a. Write an expression for the amount of money Paula withdraws if she needs d dollars.

   b. Find the amount of money Paula withdraws if she needs 20, 60, and 75 dollars.

Name _____ Date _____ Class _____

LESSON 1-2

Practice
Adding and Subtracting Real Numbers

Add or subtract using a number line.

1. $-6 + (-8)$

2. $2 - (-8)$

3. $10 + (-4) =$

4. $-2 - (-6)$

5. $-7 + 7$

6. $-0.25 - 4$

Add.

7. $-5 + 23$

8. $-15 + (-9)$

9. $24.6 + (-45.5)$

10. $-\dfrac{3}{8} + 5$

11. $a + (-14)$ for $a = 16$

12. $-3.3 + x$ for $x = -9.1$

Subtract.

13. $-35 - (-80)$

14. $12 - (-16)$

15. $8.3 - 10.7$

16. $-\dfrac{2}{3} - 5\dfrac{1}{3}$

17. $15 - t$ for $t = -22$

18. $z - 3.5$ for $z = 1$

19. The record high temperature for Asheville, North Carolina was 99°F. The record low was −17°F. What is the difference between these two temperatures?

20. The balance in Mr. Sanchez's bank account was $293.74. He accidentally wrote a check for $300. What is his balance now?

Evaluate the expression $18 - n$ for each value of n.

21. $n = -13$

22. $n = 8.55$

23. $n = 20\dfrac{1}{5}$

LESSON 1-3 Practice
Multiplying and Dividing Real Numbers

Find the value of each expression.

1. $-24 \div -8$

2. $24(-5)$

3. $-96 \div 3$

4. $-6(20)$

5. $-7p$ for $p = -15$

6. $t \div (-1.5)$ for $t = 6$

Divide.

7. $-\dfrac{8}{9} \div \dfrac{2}{3}$

8. $-12 \div \left(-\dfrac{6}{25}\right)$

9. $2\dfrac{1}{4} \div \left(-5\dfrac{1}{3}\right)$

Multiply or divide.

10. $0 \cdot 4.75$

11. $0 \div 10$

12. $-\dfrac{1}{3} \div 0$

13. When Brianna's first CD sold a million copies, her record label gave her a $5000 bonus. She split the money evenly between herself, her agent, her producer, and her stylist. How much money did each person receive?

14. $(0.3)(-1.8)$

15. $\dfrac{2}{5}\left(-\dfrac{5}{2}\right)$

16. $-15 \div (-6)$

Evaluate each expression for $x = 16$, $y = -4$, and $z = -2$.

17. $y \div x$

18. $x \cdot y$

19. xz

20. $z \div y$

21. $(y)(z)$

22. $y \div z$

23. $x \div z$

24. $x \div y$

25. $z \div x$

Name _____ Date _____ Class _____

LESSON 1-4

Practice
Powers and Exponents

Write the power represented by each geometric model.

1.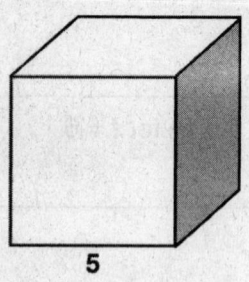
   5

   _____

2.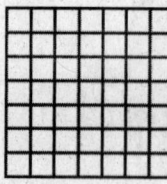

   _____

3.

   _____

Evaluate each expression.

4. 2^4

5. $(-3)^3$

6. $\left(\dfrac{2}{5}\right)^2$

_____   _____   _____

7. 3^5

8. $(-10)^4$

9. $\left(\dfrac{3}{4}\right)^2$

_____   _____   _____

Write each number as a power of the given base.

10. 16; base 2

11. 1,000,000; base 10

12. −216; base −6

_____   _____   _____

13. 2401; base 7

14. 256; base −4

15. $\dfrac{8}{27}$; base $\dfrac{2}{3}$

_____   _____   _____

16. Anna needed to let everyone in the music club know the time of its next meeting. She called two people and asked each of them to call two other people, and so on. If each phone call takes one minute, how many phone calls were made during the fifth minute?

_____

LESSON 1-5

Practice
Square Roots and Real Numbers

Find each square root.

1. $\sqrt{144}$

2. $-\sqrt{36}$

3. $\sqrt{\dfrac{1}{49}}$

4. $\sqrt{196}$

5. $-\sqrt{64}$

6. $-\sqrt{\dfrac{4}{25}}$

7. A contractor needs to cut a piece of glass to fit a square window. The area of the window is 12 ft². Find the length of the side of the window to the nearest tenth of a foot.

8. A piece of cloth must be cut to exactly cover a square table. The area of the table is 27 ft². Find the length of the side of the table to the nearest tenth of a foot.

Write all the classifications that apply to each real number.

9. $\sqrt{2}$

10. $\dfrac{2}{3}$

11. −10

12. $\sqrt{81}$

13. 0

14. 1

Name _____ Date _____ Class _____

LESSON 1-6 Practice
Order of Operations

Simplify each expression.

1. $18 - 12 + 4^2$

2. $5 \cdot 3 + 2(4)$

3. $-2[7 + 6(3 - 5)]$

4. $-7 - (2^4 \div 8)$

5. $-6 \cdot 3 + |-3(-4 + 2^3)|$

6. $\dfrac{-16 + 4}{2(\sqrt{13} - 4)}$

Evaluate each expression for the given value of the variable.

7. $3 - y^2 + 7$ for $y = 5$

8. $-3(x + 12 \cdot 2)$ for $x = -8$

9. $(m + 6) \div (2 - 5)$ for $m = 9$

10. $-5t + 12 - \dfrac{1}{2}t$ for $t = -10$

Translate each word phrase into a numerical or algebraic expression.

11. the product of 6 and the sum of 3 and 20

12. the absolute value of the difference of m and -15

13. the quotient of -18 and the sum of -2 and d

Degrees Fahrenheit *F* can be converted to degrees Celsius *C* using the expression $\dfrac{5}{9}(F - 32)$. Degrees Celsius can be converted to degrees Fahrenheit using the expression $\dfrac{5}{9}C + 32$.

14. The hottest recorded day in Florida history was 109°*F*, which occurred on June 29, 1931 in Monticello. Convert this temperature to degrees Celsius. Round your answer to the nearest tenth of a degree.

15. The coldest recorded day in Florida history was about −18.9°*C*, which occurred on February 13, 1899 in the city of Tallahassee. Convert this temperature to degrees Fahrenheit. Round your answer to the nearest tenth of a degree.

Name _____ Date _____ Class _____

LESSON 1-7
Practice
Simplifying Expressions

Simplify each expression.

1. $18 + 9 + 1 + 12$

2. $7 \cdot 15 \cdot 2$

3. $3 + 4\frac{1}{2} + 11 + 5\frac{1}{2}$

4. $-5 \cdot 7 \cdot 20$

5. $-12 + 3 + 12 + 19$

6. $-1 \cdot 5 \cdot 9 \cdot 2$

Write each product using the Distributive Property. Then simplify.

7. $14(12)$

8. $5(47)$

9. $4(106)$

Simplify each expression by combining like terms.

10. $16x + 27x$

11. $-4m + 12m$

12. $6t^2 - 2t^2$

13. $-5w^3 + 18w^3$

14. $4p + 7p^2$

15. $-2.6d - 3.4d$

Simplify each expression. Justify each step.

16. $4(x + 9) + 5x$

17. $-12d + 3 + 14d + 18$

Give an expression in simplified form for the perimeter of each figure.

18.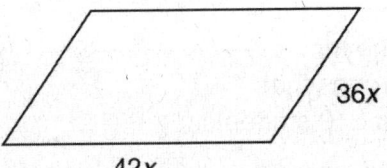

19.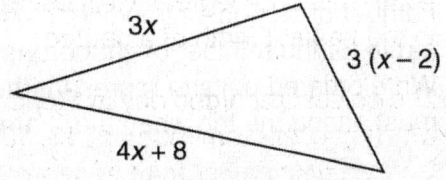

Original content Copyright © by Holt McDougal. Additions and changes to the original content are the responsibility of the instructor.

Holt McDougal Algebra 1

Name _____ Date _____ Class _____

LESSON 1-8

Practice
Introduction to Functions

Graph each point.

1. G (2, 2)
2. M (3, 8)
3. X (4, −7)
4. L (−6, −1)
5. K (8, 0)
6. T (−2, 5)

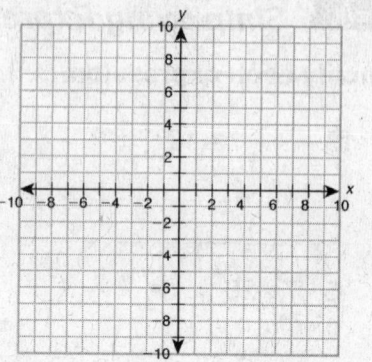

Name the quadrant in which each point lies.

7. A _____
8. B _____
9. C _____
10. D _____
11. E _____
12. F _____

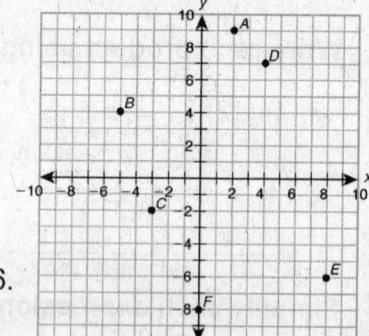

13. Generate ordered pairs for $y = |x - 4|$ using $x =$ 2, 3, 4, 5 and 6. Graph the ordered pairs and describe the pattern.

Input	Output	Ordered Pair
x	y	(x, y)

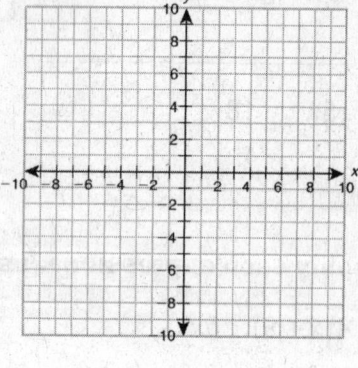

_____

14. The number of chaperones at a school field trip must be $\frac{1}{5}$ the number of students attending, plus the 2 teacher sponsors. Write a rule for the number of chaperones that must be on the trip. Write ordered pairs to represent the number of chaperones that must attend the trip when there are 120, 150, 200, and 210 students.

_____

Name _____ Date _____ Class _____

LESSON 2-1 Practice
Solving Equations by Adding or Subtracting

Solve each equation. Check your answers.

1. $g - 7 = 15$
2. $t + 4 = 6$
3. $13 = m - 7$

4. $x + 3.4 = 9.1$
5. $n - \dfrac{3}{8} = \dfrac{1}{8}$
6. $p - \dfrac{1}{3} = \dfrac{2}{3}$

7. $-6 + k = 32$
8. $7 = w + 9.3$
9. $8 = r + 12$

10. $y - 57 = -40$
11. $-5.1 + b = -7.1$
12. $a + 15 = 15$

13. Marietta was given a raise of $0.75 an hour, which brought her hourly wage to $12.25. Write and solve an equation to determine Marietta's hourly wage before her raise. Show that your answer is reasonable.

14. Brad grew $4\dfrac{1}{4}$ inches this year and is now $56\dfrac{7}{8}$ inches tall. Write and solve an equation to find Brad's height at the start of the year. Show that your answer is reasonable.

15. Heather finished a race in 58.4 seconds, which was 2.6 seconds less than her practice time. Write and solve an equation to find Heather's practice time. Show that your answer is reasonable.

16. The radius of Earth is 6378.1 km, which is 2981.1 km longer than the radius of Mars. Write and solve an equation to determine the radius of Mars. Show that your answer is reasonable.

Original content Copyright © by Holt McDougal. Additions and changes to the original content are the responsibility of the instructor.

Holt McDougal Algebra 1

Name _____ Date _____ Class _____

LESSON 2-2 Practice
Solving Equations by Multiplying or Dividing

Solve each equation. Check your answers.

1. $\dfrac{d}{8} = 6$

2. $-5 = \dfrac{n}{2}$

3. $2p = 54$

_____ _____ _____

4. $\dfrac{-t}{2} = 12$

5. $-40 = -4x$

6. $\dfrac{2r}{3} = 16$

_____ _____ _____

7. $-49 = 7y$

8. $-15 = -\dfrac{3n}{5}$

9. $9m = 6$

_____ _____ _____

10. $\dfrac{v}{-3} = -6$

11. $2.8 = \dfrac{b}{4}$

12. $\dfrac{3r}{4} = \dfrac{1}{8}$

_____ _____ _____

Answer each of the following.

13. The perimeter of a regular pentagon is 41.5 cm. Write and solve an equation to determine the length of each side of the pentagon.

_____

14. In June 2005, Peter mailed a package from his local post office in Fayetteville, North Carolina to a friend in Radford, Virginia for $2.07. The first-class rate at the time was $0.23 per ounce. Write and solve an equation to determine the weight of the package.

_____

15. Lola spends one-third of her allowance on movies. She spends $8 per week at the movies. Write and solve an equation to determine Lola's weekly allowance.

_____

LESSON 2-3 Practice
Solving Two-Step and Multi-Step Equations

Solve each equation. Check your answers.

1. $-4x + 7 = 11$

2. $17 = 5y - 3$

3. $-4 = 2p + 10$

4. $3m + 4 = 1$

5. $12.5 = 2g - 3.5$

6. $-13 = -h - 7$

7. $-6 = \dfrac{y}{5} + 4$

8. $\dfrac{7}{9} = 2n + \dfrac{1}{9}$

9. $-\dfrac{4}{5}t + \dfrac{2}{5} = \dfrac{2}{3}$

10. $-(x - 10) = 7$

11. $-2(b + 5) = -6$

12. $8 = 4(q - 2) + 4$

13. If $3x - 8 = -2$, find the value of $x - 6$. _____

14. If $-2(3y + 5) = -4$, find the value of $5y$. _____

Answer each of the following.

15. The two angles shown form a right angle. Write and solve an equation to find the value of x.

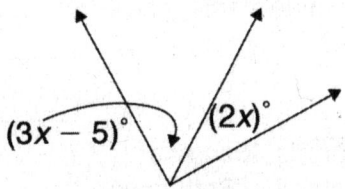

16. For her cellular phone service, Vera pays $32 a month, plus $0.75 for each minute over the allowed minutes in her plan. Vera received a bill for $47 last month. For how many minutes did she use her phone beyond the allowed minutes? _____

Name _____ Date _____ Class _____

LESSON 2-4 Practice
Solving Equations with Variables on Both Sides

Solve each equation. Check your answers.

1. $3d + 8 = 2d - 17$

2. $2n - 7 = 5n - 10$

3. $p - 15 = 13 - 6p$

_____ _____ _____

4. $-t + 5 = t - 19$

5. $15x - 10 = -9x + 2$

6. $1.8r + 9 = -5.7r - 6$

_____ _____ _____

7. $2y + 3 = 3(y + 7)$

8. $4n + 6 - 2n = 2(n + 3)$

9. $6m - 8 = 2 + 9m - 1$

_____ _____ _____

10. $-v + 5 + 6v = 1 + 5v + 3$

11. $2(3b - 4) = 8b - 11$

12. $5(r - 1) = 2(r - 4) - 6$

_____ _____ _____

Answer each of the following.

13. Janine has job offers at two companies. One company offers a starting salary of $28,000 with a raise of $3000 each year. The other company offers a starting salary of $36,000 with a raise of $2000 each year.

   a. After how many years would Janine's salary be the same with both companies? _____

   b. What would that salary be? _____

14. Xian and his cousin both collect stamps. Xian has 56 stamps, and his cousin has 80 stamps. Both have recently joined different stamp-collecting clubs. Xian's club will send him 12 new stamps per month, and his cousin's club will send him 8 new stamps per month.

   a. After how many months will Xian and his cousin have the same number of stamps? _____

   b. How many stamps will that be? _____

Name _____ Date _____ Class _____

LESSON 2-5

Practice
Solving for a Variable

Answer each of the following.

1. The formula $C = 2\pi r$ relates the radius r of a circle to its circumference C. Solve the formula for r.

   _____

2. The formula $y = mx + b$ is called the slope-intercept form of a line. Solve this formula for m.

   _____

Solve for the indicated variable.

3. $4c = d$ for c

4. $n - 6m = 8$ for n

5. $2p + 5r = q$ for p

6. $-10 = xy + z$ for x

7. $\dfrac{a}{b} = c$ for b

8. $\dfrac{h-4}{j} = k$ for j

Answer each of the following.

9. The formula $c = 5p + 215$ relates c, the total cost in dollars of hosting a birthday party at a skating rink, to p, the number of people attending.

   a. Solve the formula $c = 5p + 215$ for p. _____

   b. If Allie's parents are willing to spend $300 for a party, how many people can attend? _____

10. The formula for the area of a triangle is $A = \dfrac{1}{2}bh$, where b represents the length of the base and h represents the height.

    a. Solve the formula $A = \dfrac{1}{2}bh$ for b. _____

    b. If a triangle has an area of 192 mm², and the height measures 12 mm, what is the measure of the base? _____

LESSON 2-6

Practice
Solving Absolute-Value Equations

Solve each equation.

1. $|x| = 12$

2. $|x| = \dfrac{1}{2}$

3. $|x| - 6 = 4$

4. $5 + |x| = 14$

5. $3|x| = 24$

6. $|x + 3| = 10$

7. $|x - 1| = 2$

8. $4|x - 5| = 12$

9. $|x + 2| - 3 = 9$

10. $|6x| = 18$

11. $|x - 1| = 0$

12. $|x - 3| + 2 = 2$

13. How many solutions does the equation $|x + 7| = 1$ have? _____

14. How many solutions does the equation $|x + 7| = 0$ have? _____

15. How many solutions does the equation $|x + 7| = -1$ have? _____

Leticia sets the thermostat in her apartment to 68 degrees. The actual temperature in her apartment can vary from this by as much as 3.5 degrees.

16. Write an absolute-value equation that you can use to find the minimum and maximum temperature. _____

17. Solve the equation to find the minimum and maximum temperature. _____

Name _____ Date _____ Class _____

LESSON 2-7 Practice
Rates, Ratios, and Proportions

1. The ratio of freshman to sophomores in a drama club is 5:6. There are 18 sophomores in the drama club. How many freshmen are there? _____

Find each unit rate.

2. Four pounds of apples cost $1.96.

3. Sal washed 5 cars in 50 minutes.

_____   _____

4. A giraffe can run 32 miles per hour. What is this speed in feet per second? Round your answer to the nearest tenth. _____

Solve each proportion.

5. $\dfrac{y}{4} = \dfrac{10}{8}$

6. $\dfrac{2}{x} = \dfrac{30}{-6}$

7. $\dfrac{3}{12} = \dfrac{-24}{m}$

_____   _____   _____

8. $\dfrac{3t}{10} = \dfrac{1}{2}$

9. $\dfrac{32}{4} = \dfrac{b+4}{3}$

10. $\dfrac{7}{x} = \dfrac{1}{0.5}$

_____   _____   _____

11. Sam is building a model of an antique car. The scale of his model to the actual car is 1:10. His model is $18\dfrac{1}{2}$ inches long. How long is the actual car? _____

12. The scale on a map of Virginia shows that 1 centimeter represents 30 miles. The actual distance from Richmond, VA to Washington, DC is 110 miles. On the map, how many centimeters are between the two cities? Round your answer to the nearest tenth. _____

Name _____ Date _____ Class _____

LESSON 2-8
Practice
Applications of Proportions

Find the value of x in each diagram.

1. $\triangle ABC \sim \triangle DEF$

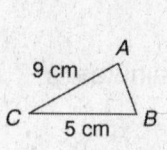 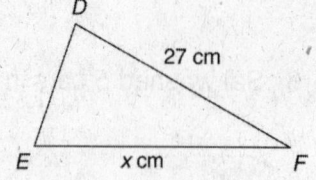

2. $FGHJK \sim MNPQR$

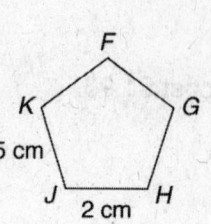 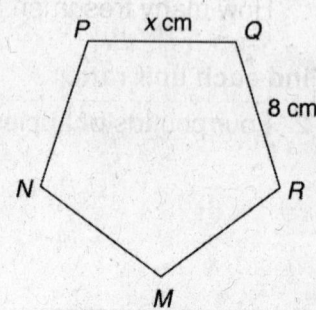

_____ _____

3. A utility worker is 5.5 feet tall and is casting a shadow 4 feet long. At the same time, a nearby utility pole casts a shadow 20 feet long. Write and solve a proportion to find the height of the utility pole. _____

4. A cylinder has a radius of 3 cm and a length of 10 cm. Every dimension of the cylinder is multiplied by 3 to form a new cylinder. How is the ratio of the volumes related to the ratio of corresponding dimensions?

_____

5. A rectangle has an area of 48 in². Every dimension of the rectangle is multiplied by a scale factor, and the new rectangle has an area of 12 in². What was the scale factor? _____

Name _____ Date _____ Class _____

LESSON 2-9 Practice
Percents

Write each percent as a decimal and as a fraction.

1. 17% 2. 22% 3. 68%

_____ _____ _____

_____ _____ _____

4. 2.5% 5. 140% 6. $\frac{1}{2}$%

_____ _____ _____

_____ _____ _____

Write each decimal or fraction as a percent.

7. 0.28 _____   8. $\frac{13}{50}$ _____   9. $\frac{19}{10}$ _____

Find each value. Round to the nearest tenth if necessary.

10. 3% of 100   11. 100% of 3

_____   _____

12. 80% of 120   13. 115% of 6

_____   _____

14. What percent of 128 is 32?   15. 3 is what percent of 36?

_____   _____

16. 23.7 is 30% of what number?   17. $7\frac{1}{2}$% of what number is 12?

_____   _____

18. According to the US Census, Virginia had about 7.1 million residents in 2000. Of those, 24.6% were under age 18. To the nearest tenth of a million, how many Virginia residents were under age 18 in 2000? _____

19. A CD-ROM has 700 megabytes of storage space. What percent of the space is used by a file that takes up 154 megabytes? _____

Original content Copyright © by Holt McDougal. Additions and changes to the original content are the responsibility of the instructor.

Holt McDougal Algebra 1

Name _____ Date _____ Class _____

LESSON 2-10
Practice
Applications of Percents

Solve each problem.

1. Mr. Holtzclaw sells his home for $240,000. He must pay the real estate agents a 5% commission. How much is the commission? _____

2. A textbook salesperson is paid a base salary of $35,000 plus a 3% commission on sales. Her total sales last year were $620,000. Find her total pay last year. _____

3. A music publisher earns a 6.75% commission on the money made from the use of a song on a CD. If the music publisher earns $84,375, how much money was made from the use of the song? _____

4. Find the simple interest earned after 5 years on $1200 invested at 2% annual interest rate. _____

5. After 6 months, $1.78 simple interest was earned on an investment of $890. Find the annual interest rate. _____

6. Ms. Pecho currently owes $637.50 simple interest on a loan of $2500 at an annual interest rate of 17%. How long has she had the loan? _____

7. The lunch check for Tawfiq and Helen is $16.98. Estimate the tip using a rate of 15%. _____

8. The state sales tax rate in North Carolina is 4.5%. Estimate the state sales tax on a model of the Wright Brothers' airplane that costs $139.99. _____

9. A wedding reception is held at a restaurant in Mississippi. The food and drinks cost $1492.50. The state sales tax rate is 7%, and the restaurant automatically adds a 20% tip for large parties.

   a. Estimate the state sales tax. _____

   b. Estimate the tip. _____

   c. Estimate the total bill for food, drinks, tax, and tip. _____

Original content Copyright © by Holt McDougal. Additions and changes to the original content are the responsibility of the instructor.

Holt McDougal Algebra 1

Name _____ Date _____ Class _____

LESSON 2-11

Practice
Percent Increase and Decrease

Find each percent change. Tell whether it is a percent increase or decrease.

1. 8 to 10

2. 50 to 20

3. 120 to 54

_____ _____ _____

4. 12 to 96

5. 72 to 108

6. 2 to 1.3

_____ _____ _____

Solve each problem.

7. Find the result when 20 is increased by 35%.

8. Find the result when 40 is increased by 64%.

_____ _____

9. Find the result when 68 is decreased by 25%.

10. Find the result when 120 is decreased by 15%.

_____ _____

11. A pharmacy discount card gives the user 40% off prescriptions. Mr. Allen's cholesterol medication normally costs $96.50. What is the final price with the discount card?

_____

12. A gas station purchases fuel at a wholesale price of $1.75 per gallon. The price is marked up 8%. What is the selling price per gallon?

_____

13. San Francisco's Bay Area Rapid Transit (BART) sells $48 tickets at a discount price of $45. What is the percent discount?

_____

14. A recording company sells a music CD for the wholesale price of $12.75. A record store marks up the price to $19.89. What is the markup as a percent?

_____

Find each missing number.

15. 50 increased by 20% is _____.

16. 10 increased by _____ % is 30.

17. 200 decreased by 55% is _____.

18. 60 decreased by _____ % is 45.

LESSON 3-1 Practice
Graphing and Writing Inequalities

Describe the solutions of each inequality in words.

1. $2m \geq 6$ _____

2. $t + 3 < 8$ _____

3. $1 < x - 5$ _____

4. $-10 \geq \frac{1}{2} c$ _____

Graph each inequality.

5. $x > -7$
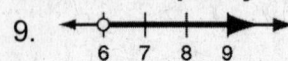

6. $p \geq 2^3$
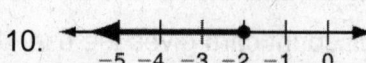

7. $4.5 \geq r$

8. $y < -\sqrt{14-5}$
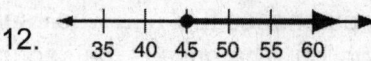

Write the inequality shown by each graph.

9. ![number line with open circle at 6, arrow right through 7, 8, 9]

10. ![number line from -5 to 0 with closed circle at -2, arrow left]

_____   _____

11. ![number line 7 to 9.5 with open circle at 8.5, arrow left]

12. ![number line 35 to 60 with closed circle at 45, arrow right]

_____   _____

Define a variable and write an inequality for each situation. Graph the solutions.

13. Josephine sleeps more than 7 hours each night.

_____

14. In 1955, the minimum wage in the U.S. was $0.75 per hour.

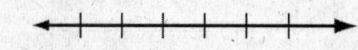

_____

LESSON 3-2 Practice
Solving Inequalities by Adding or Subtracting

Solve each inequality and graph the solutions.

1. $b + 8 > 15$

   _____
   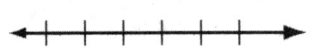

2. $t - 5 \geq -2$

   _____
   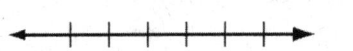

3. $-4 + x \geq 1$

   _____
   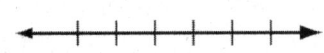

4. $g + 8 < 2$

   _____
   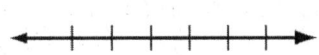

5. $-9 \geq m - 9$

   _____
   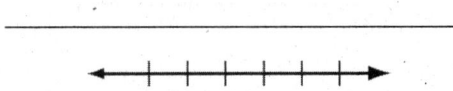

6. $15 > d + 19$

   _____
   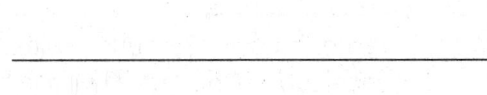

Answer each question.

7. Jessica makes overtime pay when she works more than 40 hours in a week. So far this week she has worked 29 hours. She will continue to work h hours this week. Write, solve, and graph an inequality to show the values of h that will allow Jessica to earn overtime pay.

   _____

8. Henry's MP3 player has 512MB of memory. He has already downloaded 287MB and will continue to download m more megabytes. Write and solve an inequality that shows how many more megabytes he can download.

   _____

9. Eleanor needs to read at least 97 pages of a book for homework. She has read 34 pages already. Write and solve an inequality that shows how many more pages p she must read.

   _____

Practice
LESSON 3-3
Solving Inequalities by Multiplying or Dividing

Solve each inequality and graph the solutions.

1. $4a > 32$

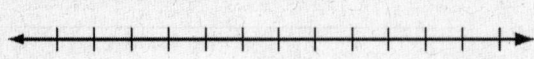

2. $-7y < 21$

3. $1.5n \leq -18$

4. $-\frac{3}{8}c \geq 9$

5. $\frac{y}{5} > 4$

6. $2s \leq -3$

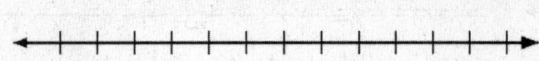

7. $-\frac{1}{3}b < -6$

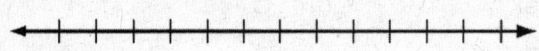

8. $\frac{z}{-8} \geq -0.25$

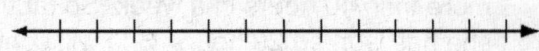

Write and solve an inequality for each problem.

9. Phil has a strip of wood trim that is 16 feet long. He needs 5-foot pieces to trim some windows. What are the possible numbers of pieces he can cut?

10. A teacher buys a 128-ounce bottle of juice and serves it in 5-ounce cups. What are the possible numbers of cups she can fill?

11. At an online bookstore, Kendra bought 4 copies of the same book for the members of her book club. She got free shipping because her total was at least $50. What was the minimum price of each book?

Name _____ Date _____ Class _____

LESSON 3-4 Practice
Solving Two-Step and Multi-Step Inequalities

Solve each inequality and graph the solutions.

1. $-3a + 10 < -11$

2. $4x - 12 \geq 20$

_____ _____

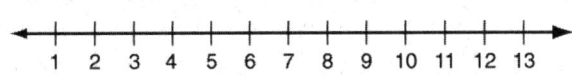 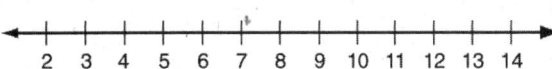

3. $\dfrac{2k - 3}{-5} > 7$

4. $-\dfrac{1}{5}z + \dfrac{2}{3} \leq 2$

_____ _____

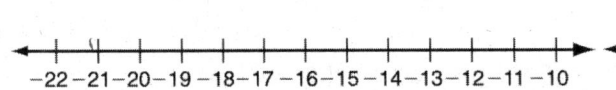 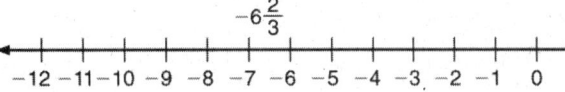

5. $6(n - 8) \geq -18$

6. $10 - 2(3x - 4) < 11$

_____ _____

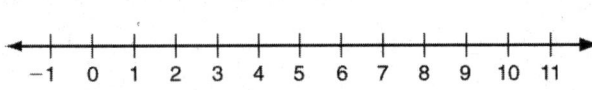 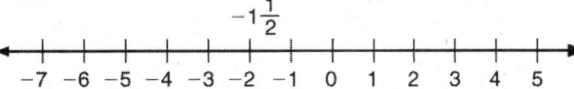

7. $7 + 2c - 4^2 \leq -9$

8. $15p + 3(p - 1) > 3(2^3)$

_____ _____

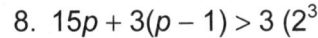

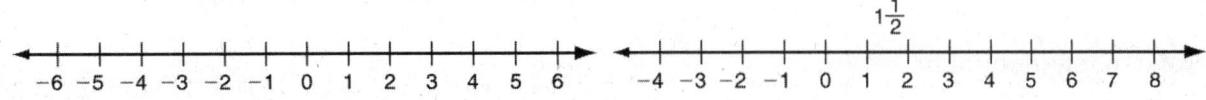

Write and solve an inequality for each problem.

9. A full-year membership to a gym costs $325 upfront with no monthly charge. A monthly membership costs $100 upfront and $30 per month. For what numbers of months is it less expensive to have a monthly membership?

_____

10. The sum of the lengths of any two sides of a triangle must be greater than the length of the third side. What are the possible values of x for this triangle?

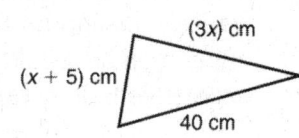

_____

Practice

LESSON 3-5: Solving Inequalities with Variables on Both Sides

Solve each inequality and graph the solutions.

1. $2x + 30 \geq 7x$

   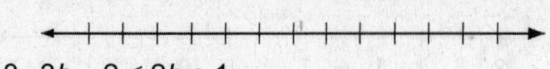

2. $2k + 6 < 5k - 3$

   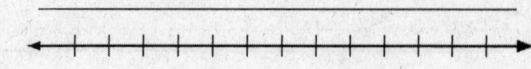

3. $3b - 2 \leq 2b + 1$

   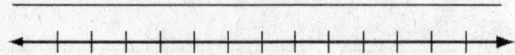

4. $2(3n + 7) > 5n$

   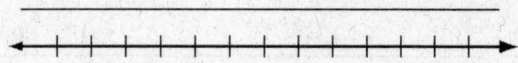

5. $5s - 9 < 2(s - 6)$

   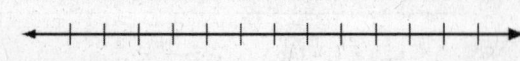

6. $-3(3x + 5) \geq -5(2x - 2)$

7. $1.4z + 2.2 > 2.6z - 0.2$

   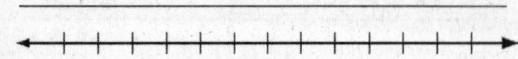

8. $\dfrac{7}{8}p - \dfrac{1}{4} \leq \dfrac{1}{2}p$

   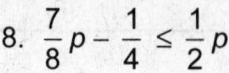

Solve each inequality.

9. $v + 1 > v - 6$

10. $3(x + 4) \leq 3x$

11. $-2(8 - 3x) \geq 6x + 2$

Write and solve an inequality for each problem.

12. Ian wants to promote his band on the Internet. Site A offers website hosting for $4.95 per month with a $49.95 startup fee. Site B offers website hosting for $9.95 per month with no startup fee. For how many months would Ian need to keep the website for Site B to be less expensive than Site A?

13. For what values of x is the area of the rectangle greater than the perimeter?

    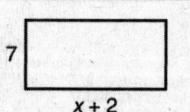

LESSON 3-6	**Practice**
	Solving Compound Inequalities

Write the compound inequality shown by each graph.

1.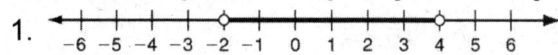

   _____

2.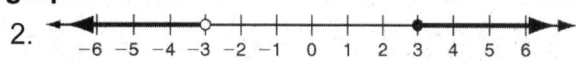

   _____

3.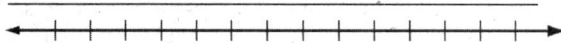

   _____

4.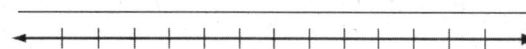

   _____

Solve each compound inequality and graph the solutions.

5. $-15 < x - 8 < -4$

   _____
   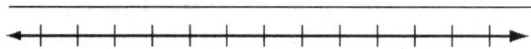

6. $12 \leq 4n < 28$

   _____
   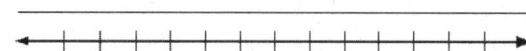

7. $-2 \leq 3b + 7 \leq 13$

   _____
   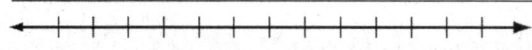

8. $x - 3 < -3$ OR $x - 3 \geq 3$

   _____
   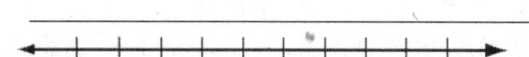

9. $5k \leq -20$ OR $2k \geq 8$

   _____
   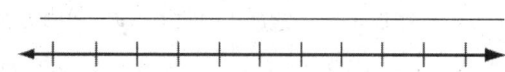

10. $2s + 3 \leq 7$ OR $3s + 5 > 26$

    _____
    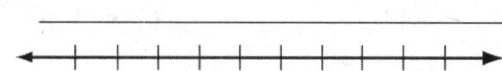

Write a compound inequality for each problem. Graph the solutions.

11. The human ear can distinguish sounds between 20 Hz and 20,000 Hz, inclusive.

12. For a man to box as a welterweight, he must weigh more than 140 lbs, but at most 147 lbs.

Practice

Solving Absolute-Value Inequalities

Solve each inequality and graph the solutions.

1. $|x| - 2 \leq 3$

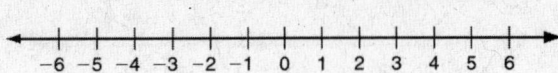

2. $|x + 1| + 5 < 7$

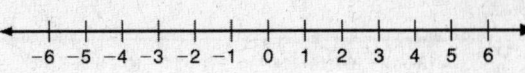

3. $3|x - 6| \leq 9$

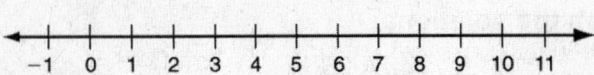

4. $|x + 3| - 1.5 < -2.5$

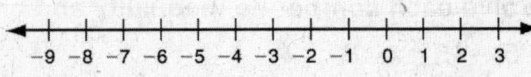

5. $|x| + 17 > 20$

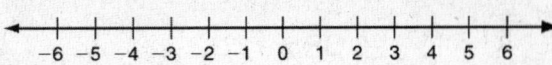

6. $|x - 6| - 7 > -3$

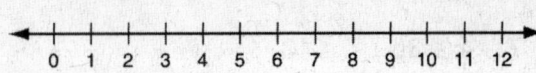

7. $\frac{1}{2}|x + 5| \geq 2$

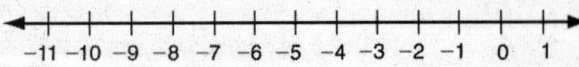

8. $2|x - 2| \geq 3$

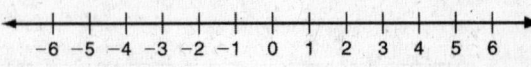

9. The organizers of a drama club wanted to sell 350 tickets to their show. The actual sales were no more than 35 tickets from this goal. Write and solve an absolute-value inequality to find the range of the number of tickets that may have been sold.

10. The temperature at noon in Los Angeles on a summer day was 88 °F. During the day, the temperature varied from this by as much as 7.5 °F. Write and solve an absolute-value inequality to find the range of possible temperatures for that day.

Practice

Graphing Relationships

LESSON 4-1

Choose the graph that best represents each situation.

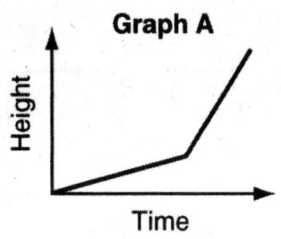 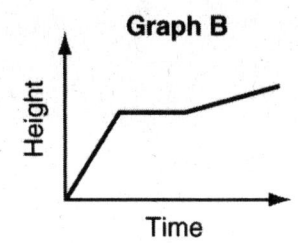 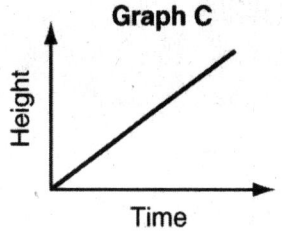

1. A tomato plant grows taller at a steady pace. _____

2. A tomato plant grows quickly at first, remains a constant height during a dry spell, then grows at a steady pace. _____

3. A tomato plant grows at a slow pace, then grows rapidly with more sun and water. _____

4. Lora has $15 to spend on movie rentals for the week. Each rental costs $3. Sketch a graph to show how much money she might spend on movies in a week. Tell whether the graph is continuous or discrete.

   _____

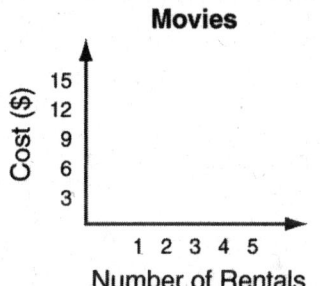

Write a possible situation for each graph.

5.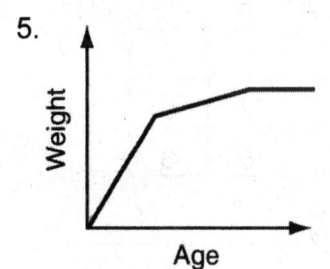

   _____
   _____
   _____
   _____

6.

   _____
   _____
   _____
   _____

Name _____ Date _____ Class _____

LESSON 4-2 Practice
Relations and Functions

Express each relation as a table, as a graph, and as a mapping diagram.

1. {(–5, 3), (–2, 1), (1, –1), (4, –3)}

x	y

2. {(4, 0) (4, 1), (4, 2), (4, 3), (4, 4), (4, 5)}

x	y

Give the domain and range of each relation. Tell whether the relation is a function. Explain.

3.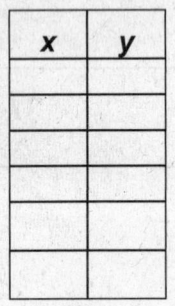

4.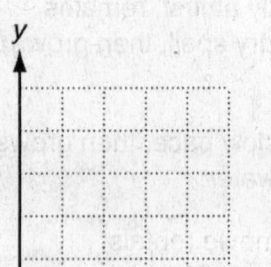

5.

x	y
8	8
6	6
4	4
2	6
0	8

D: _____   D: _____   D: _____

R: _____   R: _____   R: _____

Function? _____   Function? _____   Function? _____

Explain: _____   Explain: _____   Explain: _____

_____   _____   _____

_____   _____   _____

_____   _____   _____

Name _____ Date _____ Class _____

LESSON 4-3 Practice
Writing Functions

Determine a relationship between the x- and y-values. Write an equation.

1.

x	−4	−3	−2	−1
y	−1	0	1	2

_____

2. {(2, 3), (3, 5), (4, 7), (5, 9)}

_____

Identify the independent and dependent variables in each situation.

3. Ice cream sales increase when the temperature rises.

   I: _____

   D: _____

4. Food for the catered party costs $12.75 per person.

   I: _____

   D: _____

Identify the independent and dependent variables. Write a rule in function notation for each situation.

5. Carson charges $7 per hour for yard work.

   _____

   _____

   _____

6. Kay donates twice what Ed donates.

   _____

   _____

   _____

Evaluate each function for the given input values.

7. For $f(x) = 5x + 1$, find $f(x)$ when $x = 2$ and when $x = 3$. _____ _____

8. For $g(x) = -4x$, find $g(x)$ when $x = -6$ and when $x = 2$. _____ _____

9. For $h(x) = x - 3$, find $h(x)$ when $x = 3$ and when $x = 1$. _____ _____

Complete the following.

10. An aerobics class is being offered once a week for 6 weeks. The registration fee is $15 and the cost for each class attended is $10. Write a function rule to describe the total cost of the class. Find a reasonable domain and range for the function.

    _____

    _____

    _____

    _____

LESSON 4-4 Practice
Graphing Functions

Graph the function for the given domain.

1. $y = |x| - 1$; D: {–1, 0, 1, 2, 3}

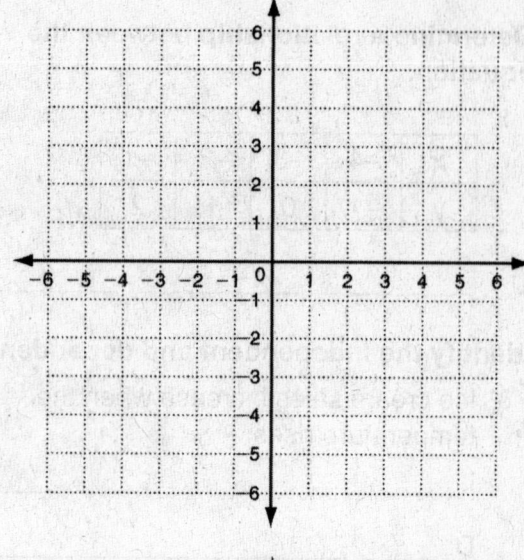

Graph the function.

2. $f(x) = x^2 - 3$

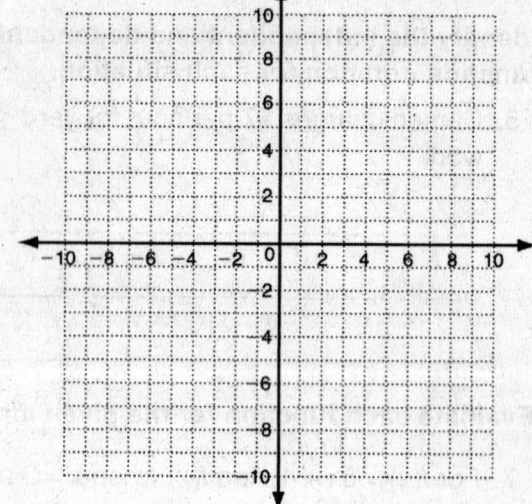

3. One of the slowest fish is the blenny fish. The function $y = 0.5x$ describes how many miles y the fish swims in x hours. Graph the function. Use the graph to estimate the number of miles the fish swims in 3.5 hours.

_____

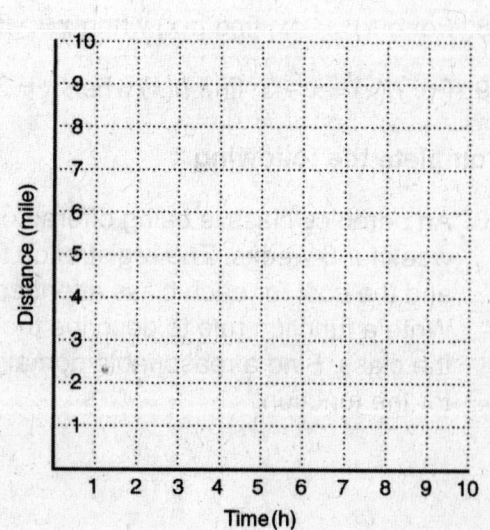

Name _____ Date _____ Class _____

LESSON 4-5 Practice
Scatter Plots and Trend Lines

Graph a scatter plot using the given data.

1. The table shows the percent of people ages 18–24 who reported they voted in the presidential elections. Graph a scatter plot using the given data.

Year	1988	1992	1996	2000	2004
% of 18-24 year olds	36	43	32	32	42

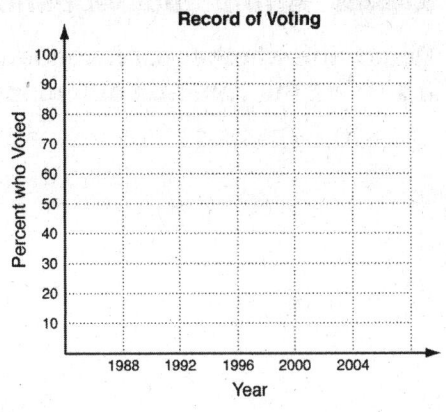

Write *positive*, *negative*, or *none* to describe the correlation illustrated by each scatter plot.

2.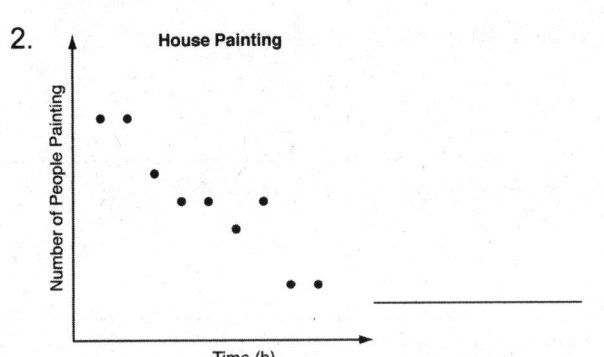

3.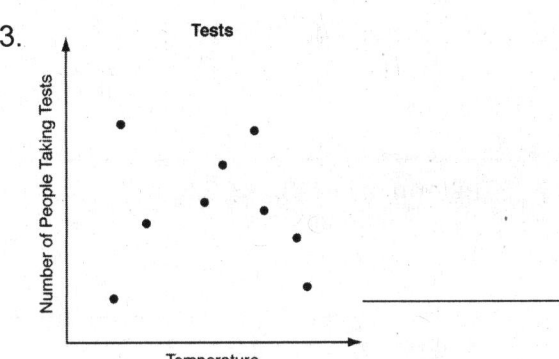

4. Identify the correlation you would expect to see between the number of pets a person has and the number of times they go to a pet store. Explain.

_____

_____

Neal kept track of the number of minutes it took him to assemble sandwiches at his restaurant. The information is in the table below.

Number of sandwiches	1	2	4	6	7
Minutes	3	4	5	6	7

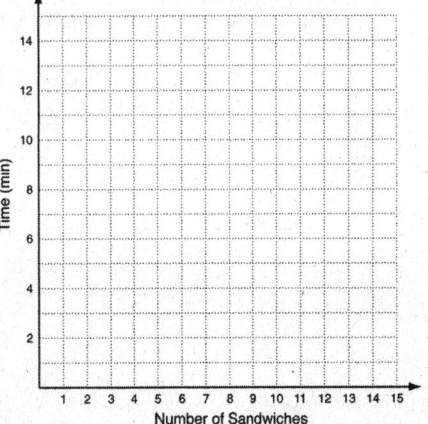

5. Graph a scatter plot of the data.
6. Draw a trend line.
7. Describe the correlation.

_____

8. Based on the trend line you drew, predict the amount of time it will take Neal to assemble 12 sandwiches.

_____

Original content Copyright © by Holt McDougal. Additions and changes to the original content are the responsibility of the instructor.

Holt McDougal Algebra 1

LESSON 4-6 Practice
Arithmetic Sequences

Determine whether each sequence is an arithmetic sequence. If so, find the common difference and the next three terms.

1. −10, −7, −4, −1, …

2. 0, 1.5, 3, 4.5, …

3. 5, 8, 12, 17, …

4. −20, −20.5, −21, −21.5, …

Find the indicated term of each arithmetic sequence.

5. 28th term: 0, −4, −8, −12, …

6. 15th term: 2, 3.5, 5, 6.5, …

7. 37th term: $a_1 = -3$; $d = 2.8$

8. 14th term: $a_1 = 4.2$; $d = -5$

9. 17th term; $a_1 = 2.3$; $d = -2.3$

10. 92nd term; $a_1 = 1$; $d = 0.8$

11. A movie rental club charges $4.95 for the first month's rentals. The club charges $18.95 for each additional month. How much is the total cost for one year?

12. A carnival game awards a prize if Kasey can shoot a basket. The charge is $5.00 for the first shot, then $2.00 for each additional shot. Kasey needed 11 shots to win a prize. What is the total amount Kasey spent to win a prize?

Name _____ Date _____ Class _____

LESSON 5-1 Practice
Identifying Linear Functions

Identify whether each graph represents a function. Explain. If the graph does represent a function, is the function linear?

1. 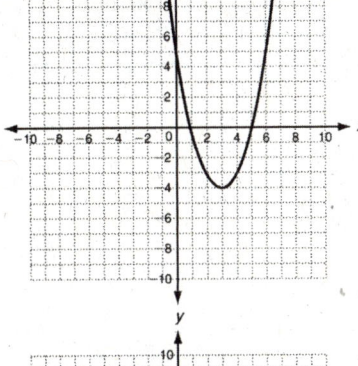 _____

_____

_____

2. 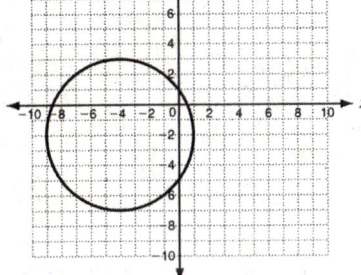 _____

_____

_____

3. Which set of ordered pairs satisfies a linear function? Explain.

Set A: {(5, 1), (4, 4), (3, 9), (2, 16), (1, 25)}   _____

Set B: {(1, −5), (2, −3), (3, −1), (4, 1), (5, 3)}   _____

4. Write $y = -2x$ in standard form. Then graph the function.

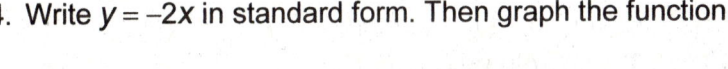

_____

5. In 2005, the Shabelle River in Somalia rose an estimated 5.25 inches every hour for 15 hours. The increase in water level is represented by the function $f(x) = 5.25x$, where x is the number of hours. Graph this function and give its domain and range.

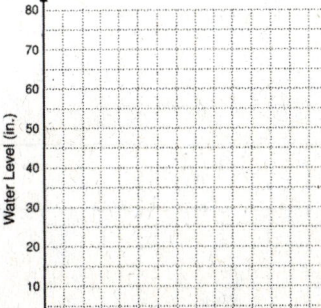

_____

Name _____ Date _____ Class _____

LESSON 5-2 Practice
Using Intercepts

Find the x- and y-intercepts.

1.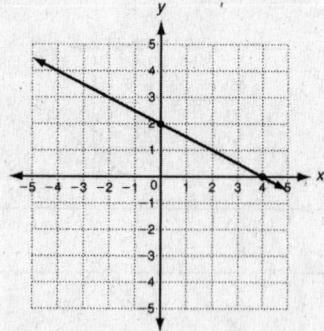

2.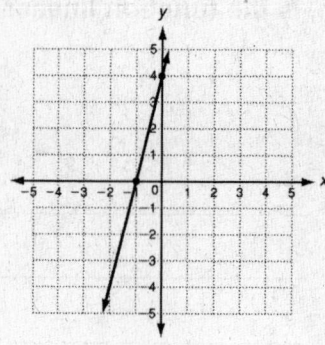

3.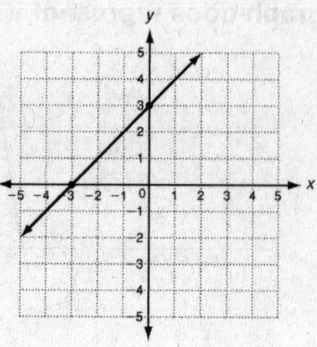

_____

_____

Use intercepts to graph the line described by each equation.

4. $3x + 2y = -6$

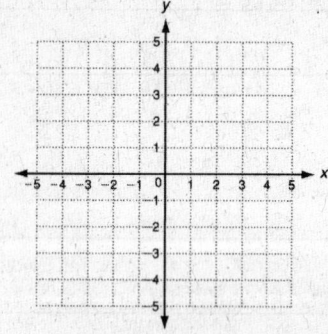

5. $x - 4y = 4$

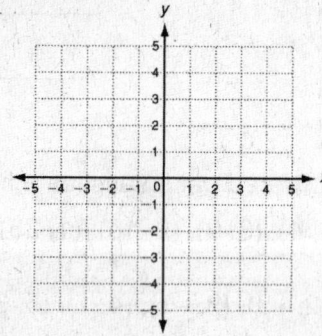

6. At a fair, hamburgers sell for $3.00 each and hot dogs sell for $1.50 each. The equation $3x + 1.5y = 30$ describes the number of hamburgers and hot dogs a family can buy with $30.

   a. Find the intercepts and graph the function.

   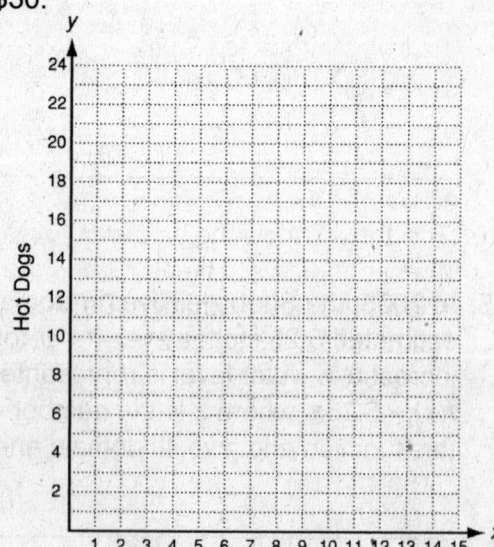

   b. What does each intercept represent?

   _____

   _____

   _____

Name _____ Date _____ Class _____

LESSON 5-3
Practice
Rate of Change and Slope

Find the rise and run between each set of points. Then, write the slope of the line.

1.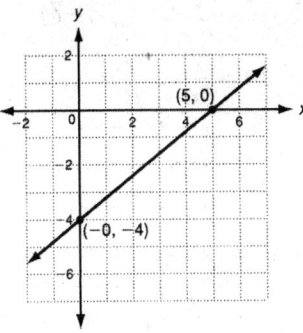

   rise = _____ run = _____

   slope = _____

2.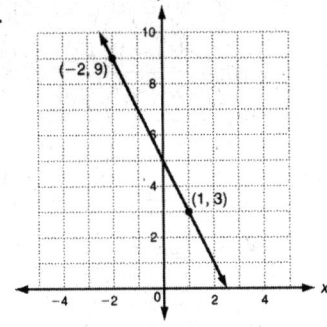

   rise = _____ run = _____

   slope = _____

3.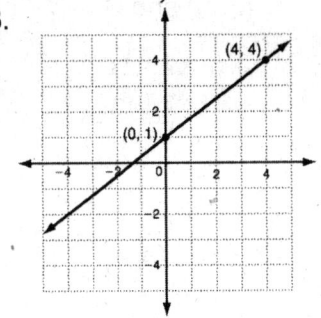

   rise = _____ run = _____

   slope = _____

4.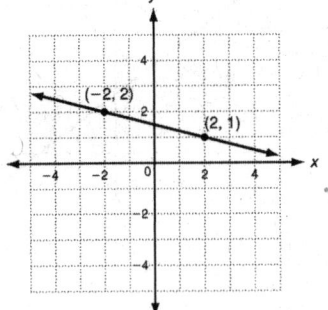

   rise = _____ run = _____

   slope = _____

5.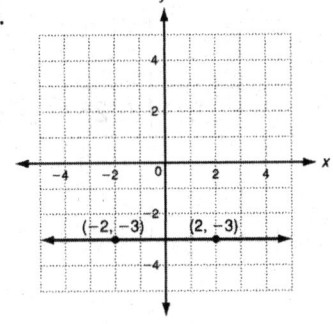

   rise = _____ run = _____

   slope = _____

6.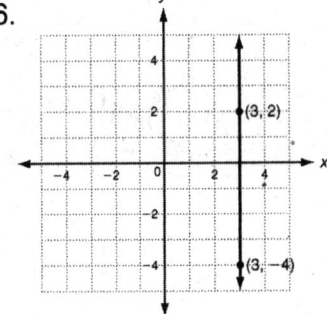

   rise = _____ run = _____

   slope = _____

Tell whether the slope of each line is positive, negative, zero, or undefined.

7.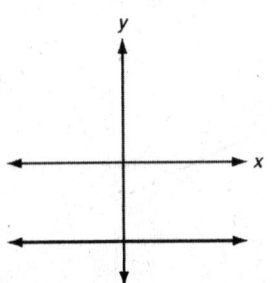

   _____

8.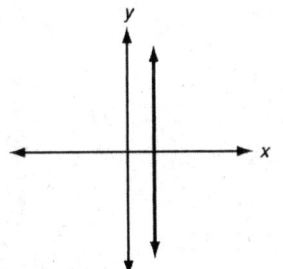

   _____

9.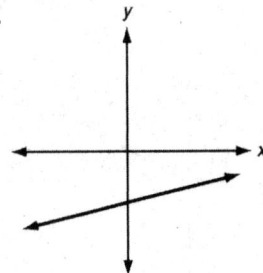

   _____

10. The table shows the amount of water in a pitcher at different times. Graph the data and show the rates of change. Between which two hours is the rate of change the greatest? _____

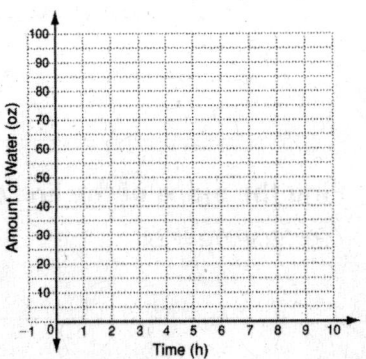

Time (h)	0	1	2	3	4	5	6	7
Amount (oz)	60	50	25	80	65	65	65	50

LESSON 5-4 Practice
The Slope Formula

Find the slope of the line that contains each pair of points.

1. (2, 8) and (1, −3)

$$m = \frac{y_2 - y_1}{x_2 - x_1}$$

$$= \frac{\boxed{} - \boxed{}}{\boxed{} - \boxed{}}$$

$$= \frac{\boxed{}}{\boxed{}} = \boxed{}$$

2. (−4, 0) and (−6, −2)

$$m = \frac{y_2 - y_1}{x_2 - x_1}$$

$$= \frac{\boxed{} - \boxed{}}{\boxed{} - \boxed{}}$$

$$= \frac{\boxed{}}{\boxed{}} = \boxed{}$$

3. (0, −2) and (4, −7)

$$m = \frac{y_2 - y_1}{x_2 - x_1}$$

$$= \frac{\boxed{} - \boxed{}}{\boxed{} - \boxed{}}$$

$$= \frac{\boxed{}}{\boxed{}}$$

Each graph or table shows a linear relationship. Find the slope.

4.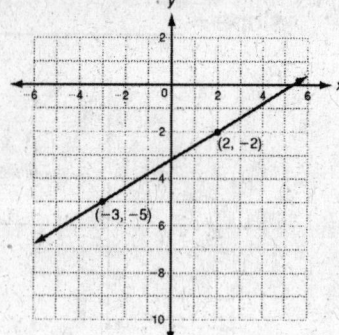

5.
x	y
1	3.75
2	5
3	6.25
4	7.50
5	8.75

6.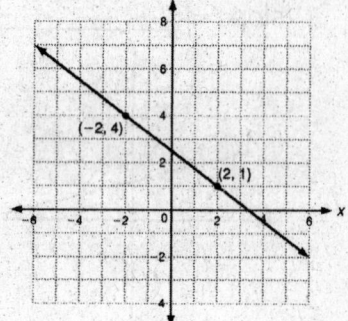

Find the slope of each line. Then tell what the slope represents.

7.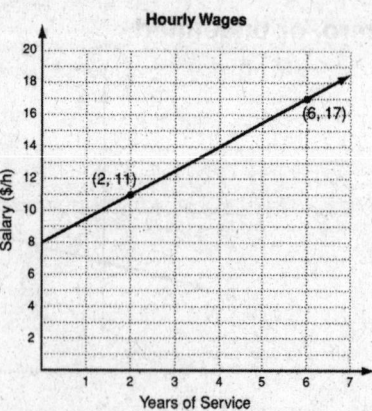

8.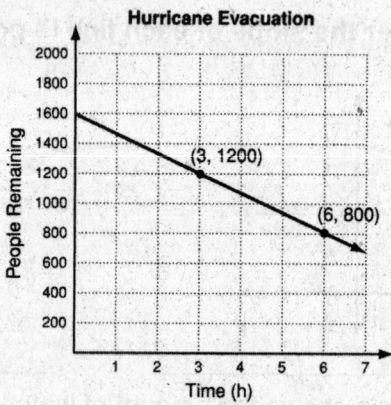

Find the slope of the line described by each equation.

9. $3x + 4y = 24$

10. $8x + 48 = 3y$

Name _____ Date _____ Class _____

LESSON 5-5 Practice
The Midpoint and Distance Formulas

Find the coordinates of the midpoint of each segment.

1. $\overline{AB}$ with endpoints $A(5, -4)$ and $B(9, 8)$ _____

2. $\overline{JK}$ with endpoints $J(-2, -1)$ and $K(8, 6)$ _____

3. $\overline{RS}$ with endpoints $R(-3, 2)$ and $S(-1, -6)$ _____

4. M is the midpoint of $\overline{AB}$. A has coordinates $(-2, 9)$, and M has coordinates $(2, 5)$.

   Find the coordinates of B. _____

5. T is the midpoint of $\overline{SY}$. Y has coordinates $(7, -3)$, and T has coordinates $(4, 4)$.

   Find the coordinates of S. _____

6. N is the midpoint of $\overline{PQ}$. P has coordinates $(-5, -6)$, and N has coordinates $\left(-\frac{1}{2}, -2\frac{1}{2}\right)$.

   Find the coordinates of Q. _____

Use the Distance Formula to find the distance, to the nearest tenth, between each pair of points.

7. $W(1, 14)$ and $Y(5, 6)$

8. $M(-3, 5)$ and $B(4, -2)$

9. $G(-4, -9)$ and $H(0, 8)$

10. $T(3, -2)$ and $X(12, -7)$

Each unit on the map of a neighborhood represents one mile.

11. Find the distance between the fire department and Fire 1, to the nearest tenth of a mile.

    _____

12. Find the distance between the fire department and Fire 2, to the nearest tenth of a mile.

    _____

13. Find the midpoint between the two fires.

    _____

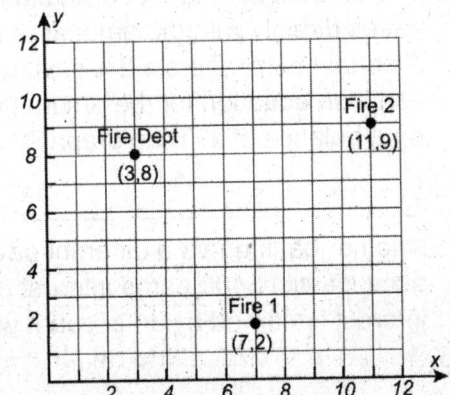

Name _____ Date _____ Class _____

LESSON 5-6 Practice
Direct Variation

Tell whether each equation is a direct variation. If so, identify the constant of variation.

1. $y = 3x$ _____

2. $y = 2x - 9$ _____

3. $2x + 3y = 0$ _____

4. $3y = 9x$ _____

Find the value of $\frac{y}{x}$ for each ordered pair. Then, tell whether each relationship is a direct variation.

5.
x	6	15	21
y	2	5	7
$\frac{y}{x}$			

_____

6.
x	6	10	25
y	24	40	100
$\frac{y}{x}$			

_____

7.
x	10	15	20
y	3	5	9
$\frac{y}{x}$			

_____

8. The value of y varies directly with x, and $y = -18$ when $x = 6$. Find y when $x = -8$.

   Find k: Use k to find y:
                   $y = kx$
                   $y = (\underline{\ \ })(\underline{\ \ })$
   ___ = k $y = $ _____

9. The value of y varies directly with x, and $y = \frac{1}{2}$ when $x = 5$. Find y when $x = 30$.

   Find k: Use k to find y:
                   $y = kx$
                   $y = (\underline{\ \ })(\underline{\ \ })$
   ___ = k $y = $ _____

10. The amount of interest earned in a savings account varies directly with the amount of money in the account. A certain bank offers a 2% savings rate. Write a direct variation equation for the amount of interest y earned on a balance of x. Then graph.

    _____

11. Another bank offers a different savings rate. If an account with $400 earns interest of $6, how much interest is earned by an account with $1800?

    _____

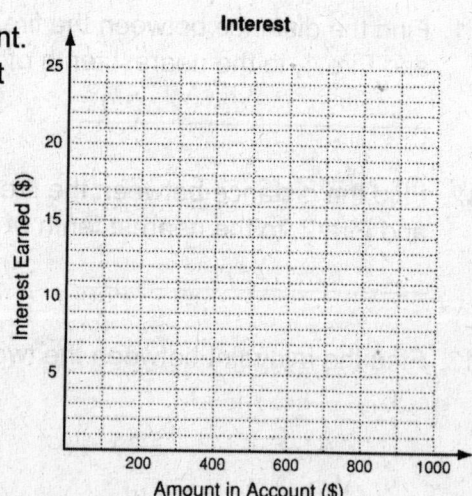

Name _____ Date _____ Class _____

LESSON 5-7 Practice
Slope-Intercept Form

Write the equation that describes each line in slope-intercept form.

1. slope = 4; y-intercept = –3

   y = _____

2. slope = –2; y-intercept = 0

   y = _____

3. slope = $-\dfrac{1}{3}$; y-intercept = 6

   y = _____

4. slope = $\dfrac{2}{5}$, (10, 3) is on the line.

   Find the y-intercept y = mx + b

   ____ = (____) ____ + b

   ____ = ____ + b

   ____ = b

   Write the equation: y = _____

Write each equation in slope-intercept form. Then graph the line described by the equation.

5. y + x = 3

6. y + 4 = $\dfrac{4}{3}$ x

7. 5x − 2y = 10

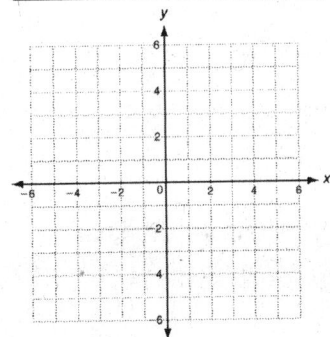
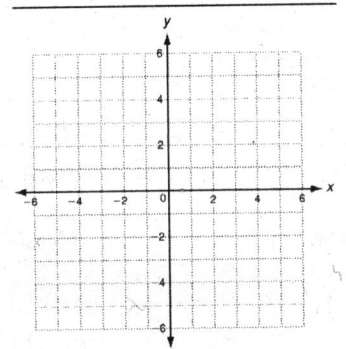
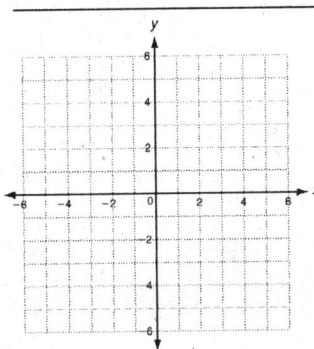

8. Daniel works as a volunteer in a homeless shelter. So far, he has worked 22 hours, and he plans to continue working 3 hours per week. His hours worked as a function of time is shown in the graph.

   a. Write an equation that represents the hours Daniel will work as a function of time. _____

   b. Identify the slope and y-intercept and describe their meanings. _____

   c. Find the number of hours worked after 16 weeks.
   _____

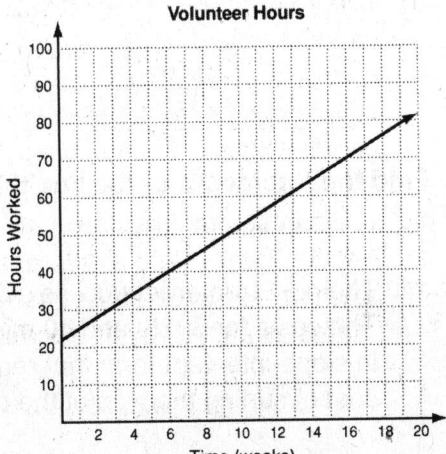

Original content Copyright © by Holt McDougal. Additions and changes to the original content are the responsibility of the instructor.

Holt McDougal Algebra 1

Name _____ Date _____ Class _____

LESSON 5-8 Practice
Point-Slope Form

Write an equation in point-slope form for the line with the given slope that contains the given point.

1. slope = 3; (–4, 2)

2. slope = –1; (6, –1)

_____   _____

Graph the line described by each equation.

3. $y + 2 = -\dfrac{2}{3}(x - 6)$

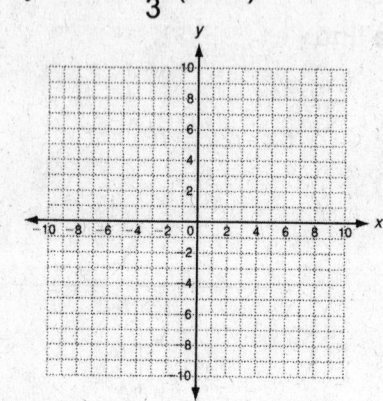

4. $y + 3 = -2(x - 4)$

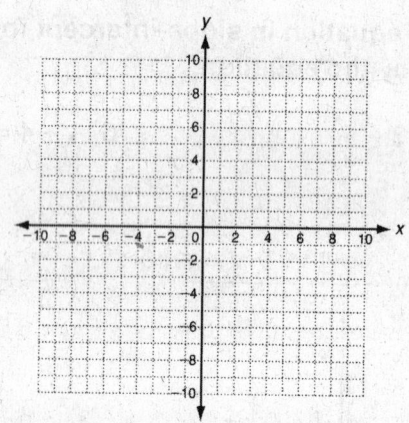

Write the equation that describes the line in slope-intercept form.

5. slope = –4; (1, –3) is on the line

6. slope = $\dfrac{1}{2}$; (–8, –5) is on the line

_____   _____

7. (2, 1) and (0, –7) are on the line

8. (–6, –6) and (2, –2) are on the line

_____   _____

Find the intercepts of the line that contains each pair of points.

9. (–1, –4) and (6, 10) _____

10. (3, 4) and (–6, 16) _____

11. The cost of internet access at a cafe is a function of time. The costs for 8, 25, and 40 minutes are shown. Write an equation in slope-intercept form that represents the function. Then find the cost of surfing the web at the cafe for one hour.

Time (min)	8	25	40
Cost ($)	4.36	7.25	9.80

_____

LESSON 5-9 Practice
Slopes of Parallel and Perpendicular Lines

Identify which lines are parallel.

1. $y = 3x + 4$; $y = 4$; $y + 3x$; $y = 3$

   _____

2. $y = \dfrac{1}{2}x + 4$; $x = \dfrac{1}{2}$; $2x + y = 1$; $y = \dfrac{1}{2}x + 1$

   _____

3. Find the slope of each segment.

   slope of $\overline{AB}$: _____

   slope of $\overline{AD}$: _____

   slope of $\overline{DC}$: _____

   slope of $\overline{BC}$: _____

   Explain why ABCD is a parallelogram.

   _____

   _____

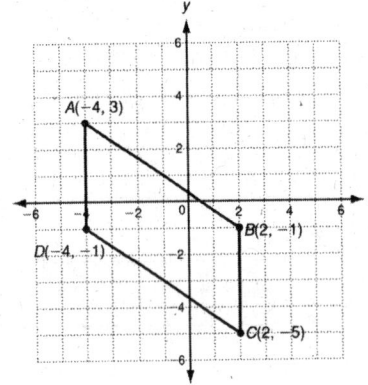

Identify which lines are perpendicular.

4. $y = 5$; $y = \dfrac{1}{8}x$; $x = 2$; $y = 8x - 5$

   _____

5. $y = -2$; $y = -\dfrac{1}{2}x - 4$; $y - 4 = 2(x + 3)$; $y = -2x$

   _____

6. Show that ABC is a right triangle.

   _____

   _____

   _____

   _____

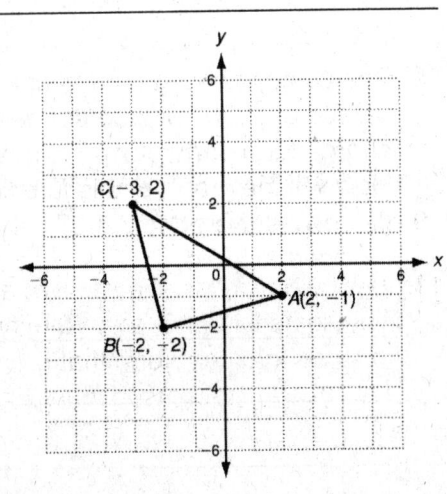

LESSON 5-10 Practice
Transforming Linear Functions

Graph $f(x)$ and $g(x)$. Then describe the transformation from the graph of $f(x)$ to the graph of $g(x)$.

1. $f(x) = x$; $g(x) = x + 3$

   _____

   _____

   _____

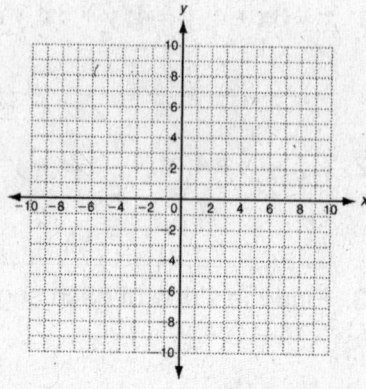

2. $f(x) = \frac{1}{3}x - 4$; $g(x) = \frac{1}{4}x - 4$

   _____

   _____

   _____

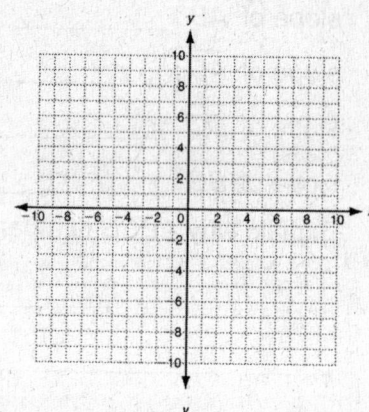

3. $f(x) = x$; $g(x) = 2x - 5$

   _____

   _____

   _____

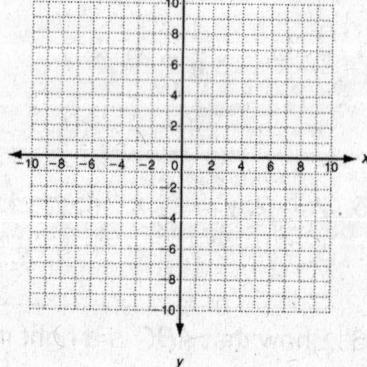

4. Graph $f(x) = -3x + 1$. Then reflect the graph of $f(x)$ across the y-axis. Write a function $g(x)$ to describe the new graph.

   _____

5. The cost of hosting a party at a horse farm is a flat fee of $250, plus $5 per person. The total charge for a party of x people is $f(x) = 5x + 250$. How will the graph of this function change if the flat fee is lowered to $200? if the per-person rate is raised to $8?

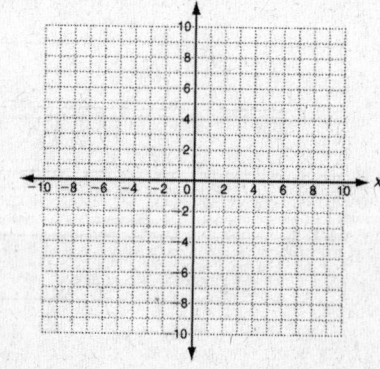

   _____

   _____

   _____

LESSON 6-1 Practice
Solving Systems by Graphing

Tell whether the ordered pair is a solution of the given system.

1. (3, 1); $\begin{cases} x + 3y = 6 \\ 4x - 5y = 7 \end{cases}$ _____

2. (6, –2); $\begin{cases} 3x - 2y = 14 \\ 5x - y = 32 \end{cases}$ _____

$x + 3y = 6$	$4x - 5y = 7$	$3x - 2y = 14$	$5x - y = 32$

Solve each system by graphing. Check your answer.

3. $\begin{cases} y = x + 4 \\ y = -2x + 1 \end{cases}$ Solution: _____

4. $\begin{cases} y = x + 6 \\ y = -3x + 6 \end{cases}$ Solution: _____

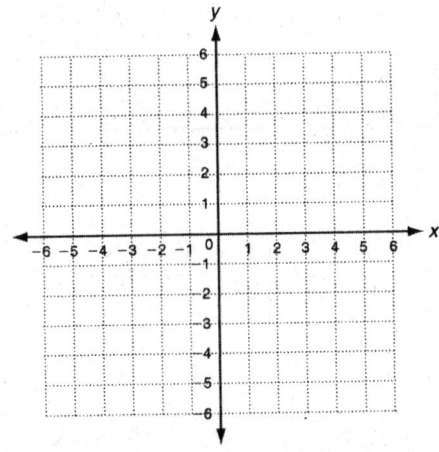

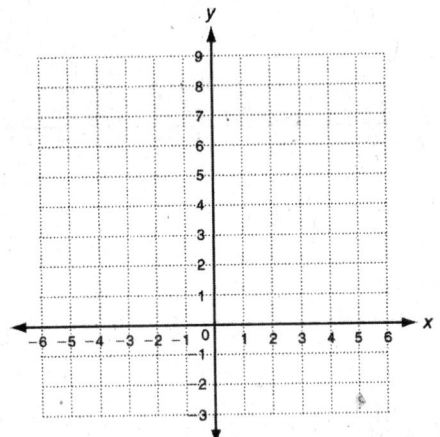

5. Maryann and Carlos are each saving for new scooters. So far, Maryann has $9 saved, and can earn $6 per hour babysitting. Carlos has $3 saved, and can earn $9 per hour working at his family's restaurant. After how many hours of work will Maryann and Carlos have saved the same amount? What will that amount be?

_____

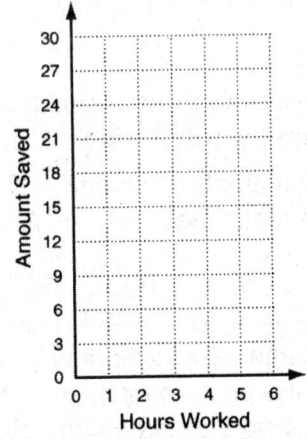

Name _____ Date _____ Class _____

LESSON 6-2 Practice
Solving Systems by Substitution

Solve each system by substitution. Check your answer.

1. $\begin{cases} y = x - 2 \\ y = 4x + 1 \end{cases}$

2. $\begin{cases} y = x - 4 \\ y = -x + 2 \end{cases}$

3. $\begin{cases} y = 3x + 1 \\ y = 5x - 3 \end{cases}$

_____   _____   _____

4. $\begin{cases} 2x - y = 6 \\ x + y = -3 \end{cases}$

5. $\begin{cases} 2x + y = 8 \\ y = x - 7 \end{cases}$

6. $\begin{cases} 2x + 3y = 0 \\ x + 2y = -1 \end{cases}$

_____   _____   _____

7. $\begin{cases} 3x - 2y = 7 \\ x + 3y = -5 \end{cases}$

8. $\begin{cases} -2x + y = 0 \\ 5x + 3y = -11 \end{cases}$

9. $\begin{cases} \dfrac{1}{2}x + \dfrac{1}{3}y = 5 \\ \dfrac{1}{4}x + y = 10 \end{cases}$

_____   _____   _____

Write a system of equations to represent the situation. Then, solve the system by substitution.

10. The length of a rectangle is 3 more than its width. The perimeter of the rectangle is 58 cm. What are the rectangle's dimensions?

_____

11. Carla and Benicio work in a men's clothing store. They earn commission from each suit and each pair of shoes they sell. For selling 3 suits and one pair of shoes, Carla has earned $47 in commission. For selling 7 suits and 2 pairs of shoes, Benicio has earned $107 in commission. How much do the salespeople earn for the sale of a suit? for the sale of a pair of shoes?

_____

LESSON 6-3

Practice
Solving Systems by Elimination

Follow the steps to solve each system by elimination.

1. $\begin{cases} 2x - 3y = 14 \\ 2x + y = -10 \end{cases}$

   Subtract the second equation:

   $2x - 3y = 14$
   $-(2x + y = -10)$
   _____

   _____

   Solve the resulting equation:

   $y = $ _____

   Use your answer to find the value of x:

   $x = $ _____

   Solution: (____ , ____)

2. $\begin{cases} 3x + y = 17 \\ 4x + 2y = 20 \end{cases}$

   Multiply the first equation by -2. Then, add the equations:

   ___ $x - $ ___ $y = $ ____
   $+ 4x + 2y = 20$
   _____

   Solve the resulting equation:

   $x = $ _____

   Use your answer to find the value of y:

   $y = $ _____

   Solution: (____ , ____)

Solve each system by elimination. Check your answer.

3. $\begin{cases} x + 3y = -7 \\ -x + 2y = -8 \end{cases}$

4. $\begin{cases} 3x + y = -26 \\ 2x - y = -19 \end{cases}$

5. $\begin{cases} x + 3y = -14 \\ 2x - 4y = 32 \end{cases}$

6. $\begin{cases} 4x - y = -5 \\ -2x + 3y = 10 \end{cases}$

7. $\begin{cases} y - 3x = 11 \\ 2y - x = 2 \end{cases}$

8. $\begin{cases} -10x + y = 0 \\ 5x + 3y = -7 \end{cases}$

Solve.

9. Brianna's family spent $134 on 2 adult tickets and 3 youth tickets at an amusement park. Max's family spent $146 on 3 adult tickets and 2 youth tickets. What is the price of a youth ticket? _____

10. Carl bought 19 apples of 2 different varieties to make a pie. The total cost of the apples was $5.10. Granny Smith apples cost $0.25 each and Gala apples cost $0.30 each. How many of each type of apple did Carl buy? _____

LESSON 6-4

Practice
Solving Special systems

Solve each system of linear equations.

1. $\begin{cases} y = 2x - 3 \\ y - 2x = -3 \end{cases}$

2. $\begin{cases} 3x + y = 4 \\ -3x = y - 7 \end{cases}$

3. $\begin{cases} y = -4x + 1 \\ 4x = -y - 6 \end{cases}$

4. $\begin{cases} y - x + 3 = 0 \\ x = y + 3 \end{cases}$

Classify each system. Give the number of solutions.

5. $\begin{cases} y = 3(x - 1) \\ -y + 3x = 3 \end{cases}$

6. $\begin{cases} y - 2x = 5 \\ x = y - 3 \end{cases}$

7. Sabina and Lou are reading the same book. Sabina reads 12 pages a day. She had read 36 pages when Lou started the book, and Lou reads at a pace of 15 pages per day. If their reading rates continue, will Sabina and Lou ever be reading the same page on the same day? Explain.

8. Brandon started jogging at 4 miles per hour. After he jogged 1 mile, his friend Anton started jogging along the same path at a pace of 4 miles per hour. If they continue to jog at the same rate, will Anton ever catch up with Brandon? Explain.

Name _____ Date _____ Class _____

LESSON 6-5 Practice
Solving Linear Inequalities

Tell whether the ordered pair is a solution of the given inequality.

1. $(1, 6)$; $y < x + 6$
2. $(-3, -12)$; $y \geq 2x - 5$
3. $(5, -3)$; $y \leq -x + 2$

_____   _____   _____

Graph the solutions of each linear inequality.

4. $y \leq x + 4$

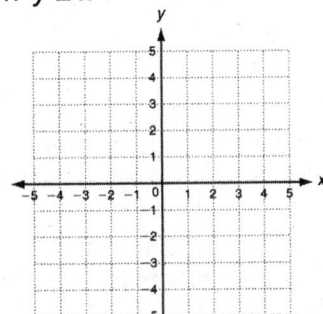

5. $2x + y > -2$

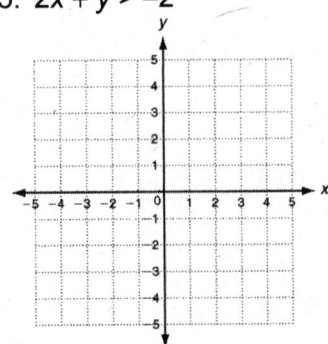

6. $x + y - 1 < 0$

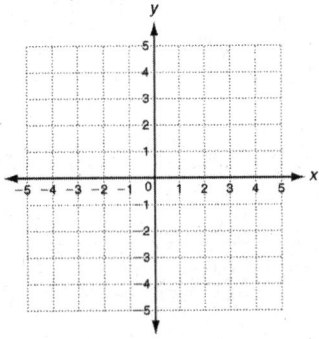

7. Clark is having a party at his house. His father has allowed him to spend at most $20 on snack food. He'd like to buy chips that cost $4 per bag, and pretzels that cost $2 per bag.

   a. Write an inequality to describe the situation.

   _____

   b. Graph the solutions.

   c. Give two possible combinations of bags of chips and pretzels that Clark can buy.

   _____

   _____

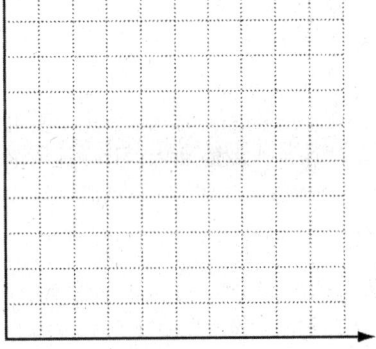

Write an inequality to represent each graph.

8.

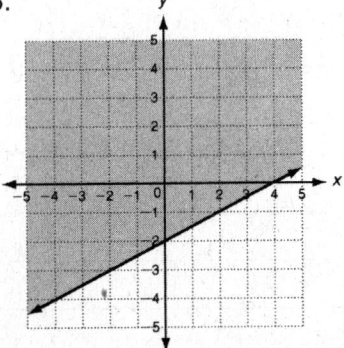

9.

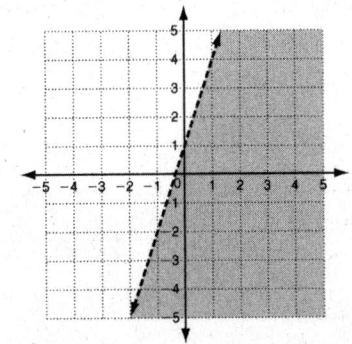

10.

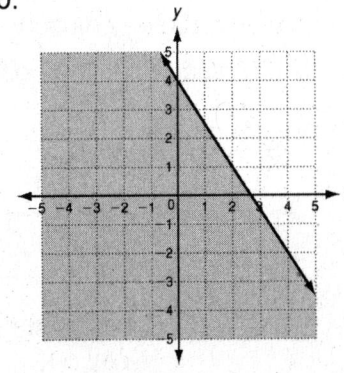

_____   _____   _____

Name _____ Date _____ Class _____

LESSON 6-6 Practice
Solving Systems of Linear Inequalities

Tell whether the ordered pair is a solution of the given system.

1. $(2, -2);\ \begin{cases} y < x - 3 \\ y > -x + 1 \end{cases}$
2. $(2, 5);\ \begin{cases} y > 2x \\ y \geq x + 2 \end{cases}$
3. $(1, 3);\ \begin{cases} y \leq x + 2 \\ y > 4x - 1 \end{cases}$

_____ _____ _____

Graph the system of linear inequalities. a. Give two ordered pairs that are solutions. b. Give two ordered pairs that are not solutions.

4. $\begin{cases} y \leq x + 4 \\ y \geq -2x \end{cases}$

5. $\begin{cases} y \leq \frac{1}{2}x + 1 \\ x + y < 3 \end{cases}$

6. $\begin{cases} y > x - 4 \\ y < x + 2 \end{cases}$

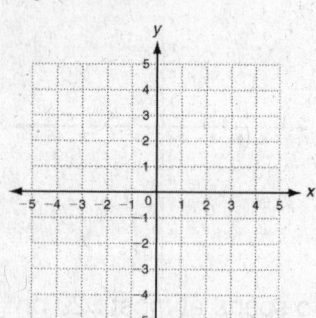 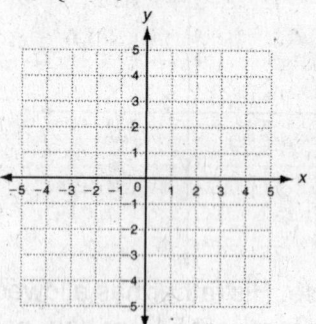 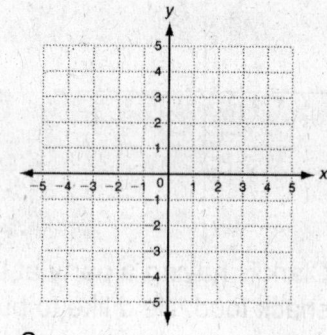

a. _____ a. _____ a. _____

b. _____ b. _____ b. _____

7. Charlene makes $10 per hour babysitting and $5 per hour gardening. She wants to make at least $80 a week, but can work no more than 12 hours a week.

   a. Write a system of linear equations.

   _____

   b. Graph the solutions of the system.

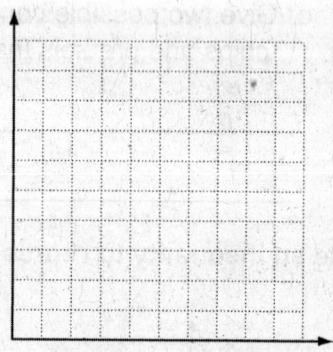

   c. Describe all the possible combinations of hours that Charlene could work at each job.

   _____

   _____

   d. List two possible combinations. _____

   _____

Name _____ Date _____ Class _____

LESSON 7-1 Practice
Integer Exponents

Simplify.

1. $5^{-3} = \dfrac{1}{\underline{}} = \dfrac{1}{\underline{}}$

2. $2^{-6} = \dfrac{1}{\underline{}} = \dfrac{1}{\underline{}}$

3. $(-5)^{-2}$ _____

4. $-(4)^{-3}$ _____

5. -6^0 _____

6. $(7)^{-2}$ _____

Evaluate each expression for the given value(s) of the variable(s).

7. d^{-3} for $d = -2$

8. $a^5 b^{-6}$ for $a = 3$ and $b = 2$

9. $(b-4)^{-2}$ for $b = 1$

10. $5z^{-x}$ for $z = -3$ and $x = 2$

11. $(5z)^{-x}$ for $z = -3$ and $x = 2$

12. $c^{-3}(16^{-2})$ for $c = 4$

Simplify.

13. t^{-4}

14. $3r^{-5}$

15. $\dfrac{s^{-3}}{t^{-5}}$

16. $\dfrac{h^0}{3}$

17. $\dfrac{2x^{-3}y^{-2}}{z^4}$

18. $\dfrac{4fg^{-5}}{5h^{-3}}$

19. $\dfrac{14a^{-4}}{20bc^{-1}}$

20. $\dfrac{a^4 c^2 e^0}{b^{-1}d^{-3}}$

21. $\dfrac{-3g^{-2}hk^{-2}}{-6h^0}$

22. A cooking website claims to contain 10^5 recipes. Evaluate this expression. _____

23. A ball bearing has diameter 2^{-3} inches. Evaluate this expression. _____

LESSON 7-2

Practice
Powers of 10 and Scientific Notation

Find the value of each power of 10.

1. 10^{-3} _____
2. 10^{5} _____
3. 10^{-4} _____
4. 10^{0} _____
5. 10^{7} _____
6. 10^{1} _____

Write each number as a power of 10.

7. 1,000,000 _____
8. 0.001 _____
9. 0.000001 _____
10. 0.00001 _____
11. 0.1 _____
12. 0.00000001 _____

Find the value of each expression.

13. 5.02×10^{3} _____
14. 603×10^{-4} _____
15. 52.8×10^{6} _____
16. 5.41×10^{-3} _____
17. 0.03×10^{-2} _____
18. 22.81×10^{-6} _____

Write each number in scientific notation.

19. 4500 _____
20. 6,560,000 _____
21. 0.00002 _____
22. 0.00203 _____

Order the list of numbers from least to greatest.

23. 3×10^{2}; 4.54×10^{-3}; 6.75×10^{2}; 8.2×10^{-4}; 9×10^{-1}; 6.18×10^{-4}

_____

24. 5.4×10^{-3}; 6.2×10^{-1}; 7.25×10^{3}; 6.87×10^{3}; 2.24×10^{-1}; 6.6×10^{-3}

_____

25. In 1970, the number of televisions sold in the United States was about 1.2×10^{7}. Write this number in standard form. _____

26. In 1950, about 3,880,000 households in the United States had televisions. Write this number in scientific notation. _____

27. Find the volume of the cube shown at right. Write the answer in both standard form and in scientific notation.

_____

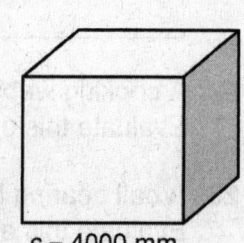

$s = 4000$ mm

Name _____ Date _____ Class _____

LESSON 7-3 Practice
Multiplication Properties of Exponents

Simplify.

1. $3^4 \cdot 3^2$

2. $2^5 \cdot 2^4$

3. $2^3 \cdot 2^5 \cdot 2^1$

4. $q^{-6} \cdot q^{-1}$

5. $r^{-3} \cdot r^4 \cdot s^{-4}$

6. $j^{-2} \cdot j^{-4} \cdot j^2$

7. $c^5 \cdot b^{-2} \cdot c^3$

8. $(h^2)^5$

9. $(g^4)^{-2}$

10. $(w^6)^0$

11. $(v^2)^5 \cdot v^4$

12. $(w^5)^{-2} \cdot w^{-3}$

13. $(f^6)^{-4} \cdot (f^{-2})^{-3}$

14. $(a^{-2})^{-3} \cdot (a^5)^2$

15. $(3b)^4$

16. $(-5k)^2$

17. $-(4m)^3$

18. $(-3p)^{-2}$

19. $(s^4 t)^3 \cdot (s^4 t^3)^2$

20. $(a^2 b^4)^2 \cdot (a^{-2} b^3)^{-1} \cdot a^4$

21. $(x^3 y^2)^{-4} \cdot (x^2 y^{-3})^{-2}$

22. The pitch of a sound is determined by the number of vibrations produced per second. The note "middle C" produces 2.62×10^2 vibrations per second. If a pianist plays middle C for 5×10^{-1} seconds, how many vibrations will occur?

Name _____ Date _____ Class _____

LESSON 7-4 Practice
Division Properties of Exponents

Simplify.

1. $\dfrac{6^7}{6^5} = 6^{7-5} = 6^{\Box} = $ _____

2. $\dfrac{t^{12}}{t^7} = t^{\Box - \Box} = $ _____

3. $\dfrac{w^9}{w^2}$

4. $\dfrac{j^2}{j^8}$

5. $\dfrac{20m^5}{4m^2}$

6. $\dfrac{c^3 d^2}{c^2 d^5}$

7. $\dfrac{(x^4)^2}{(x^3)^5}$

8. $\left(\dfrac{s^3 t}{st^4}\right)^2$

9. $\left(\dfrac{2}{3}\right)^{-3}$

10. $\left(\dfrac{3a}{2b}\right)^{-4}$

11. $-\left(\dfrac{-t}{3v}\right)^{-4}$

12. $\left(\dfrac{6}{7}\right)^{-2} \cdot \left(\dfrac{4s}{6t}\right)^{-2}$

13. $\left(\dfrac{3c}{-2}\right)^{-1} \left(\dfrac{d}{4}\right)^{-2}$

14. $\left(\left(\dfrac{3mn}{2}\right)^{-1}\right)^{-4}$

Simplify. Write the answer in scientific notation.

15. $(3.8 \times 10^5) \div (1.9 \times 10^{-6})$

16. $(2.5 \times 10^3) \div (5 \times 10^{-4})$

17. A textile factory produces 1.08×10^8 yards of fabric every year. If the factory is in operation 360 days a year, what is the average number of yards of fabric produced each day? Give your answer in standard form.

18. It takes 5 yards of fabric to manufacture a dress. If the textile factory turned their entire yearly production of 1.08×10^8 yards of fabric into dresses, how many could they make? Give your answer in scientific notation.

Original content Copyright © by Holt McDougal. Additions and changes to the original content are the responsibility of the instructor.

Holt McDougal Algebra 1

LESSON 7-5 Practice
Rational Exponents

Simplify each expression. All variables represent nonnegative numbers.

1. $27^{\frac{1}{3}}$

2. $121^{\frac{1}{2}}$

3. $0^{\frac{1}{3}}$

4. $64^{\frac{1}{2}} + 27^{\frac{1}{3}}$

5. $16^{\frac{1}{4}} + 8^{\frac{1}{3}}$

6. $100^{\frac{1}{2}} - 64^{\frac{1}{6}}$

7. $1^{\frac{1}{5}} + 49^{\frac{1}{2}}$

8. $25^{\frac{3}{2}}$

9. $32^{\frac{3}{5}}$

10. $16^{\frac{3}{4}}$

11. $1^{\frac{5}{6}}$

12. $121^{\frac{3}{2}}$

13. $\sqrt[5]{y^5}$

14. $\sqrt{x^4 y^{12}}$

15. $\sqrt[3]{a^6 b^3}$

16. $(x^{\frac{1}{2}})^4 \sqrt{x^6}$

17. $(x^{\frac{1}{3}} y)^3 \sqrt{x^2 y^2}$

18. $\dfrac{(x^{\frac{1}{4}})^8}{\sqrt[3]{x^3}}$

19. Given a cube with volume V, you can use the formula $P = 4V^{\frac{1}{3}}$ to find the perimeter of one of the cube's square faces. Find the perimeter of a face of a cube that has volume 125 m³.

LESSON 7-6 Practice
Polynomials

Find the degree and number of terms of each polynomial.

1. $14h^3 + 2h + 10$
2. $7y - 10y^2$
3. $2a^2 - 5a + 34 - 6a^4$

Write each polynomial in standard form. Then, give the leading coefficient.

4. $3x^2 - 2 + 4x^8 - x$
5. $7 - 50j + 3j^3 - 4j^2$
6. $6k + 5k^4 - 4k^3 + 3k^2$

Classify each polynomial by its degree and number of terms.

7. $-5t^2 + 10$
8. $8w - 32 + 9w^4$
9. $b - b^3 - 2b^2 + 5b^4$

Evaluate each polynomial for the given value.

10. $3m + 8 - 2m^3$ for $m = -1$
11. $4y^5 - 6y + 8y^2 - 1$ for $y = -1$
12. $2w + w^3 - \frac{1}{2}w^2$ for $w = 2$

13. An egg is thrown off the top of a building. Its height in meters above the ground can be approximated by the polynomial $300 + 2t - 4.9t^2$, where t is the time since it was thrown in seconds.

    a. How high is the egg above the ground after 5 seconds?

    b. How high is the egg above the ground after 6 seconds?

Practice
LESSON 7-7
Adding and Subtracting Polynomials

Add or subtract.

1. $3m^3 + 8m^3 - 3 + m^3 - 2m^2$ _____

2. $2pg - p^5 - 12pg + 5g - 6p^5$ _____

Add.

3. $3k^2 - 2k + 7$
   $\underline{+k - 2}$
   _____

4. $5x^2 - 2x + 3y$
   $\underline{+6x^2 + 5x + 6y}$
   _____

5. $11hz^3 + 3hz^2 + 8hz$
   $\underline{+9hz^3 + hz^2 - 3hz}$
   _____

6. $(ab^2 + 13b - 4a) + (3ab^2 + a + 7b)$ _____

7. $(4x^3 - x^2 + 4x) + (x^3 - x^2 - 4x)$ _____

Subtract.

8. $12d^2 + 3dx + x$
   $\underline{-(-4d^2 + 2dx - 8x)}$
   _____

9. $2v^5 - 3v^4 - 8$
   $\underline{-(3v^5 + 2v^4 - 8)}$
   _____

10. $-y^4 + 6ay^2 - y + a$
    $\underline{-(-6y^4 - 2ay^2 + y)}$
    _____

11. $(-r^2 + 8pr - p) - (-12r^2 - 2pr + 8p)$ _____

12. $(un - n^2 + 2un^3) - (3un^3 + n^2 + 4un)$ _____

13. Antoine is making a banner in the shape of a triangle. He wants to line the banner with a decorative border. How long will the border be?

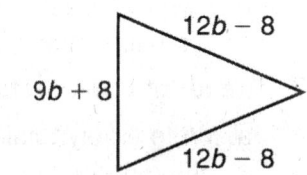

14. Darnell and Stephanie have competing refreshment stand businesses. Darnell's profit can be modeled with the polynomial $c2 + 8c - 100$, where c is the number of items sold. Stephanie's profit can be modeled with the polynomial $2c^2 - 7c - 200$.

    a. Write a polynomial that represents the difference between Stephanie's profit and Darnell's profit.

    _____

    b. Write a polynomial to show how much they can expect to earn if they decided to combine their businesses.

    _____

Practice
LESSON 7-8
Multiplying Polynomials

Multiply.

1. $(6m^4)(8m^2)$

2. $(5x^3)(4xy^2)$

3. $(10s^5t)(7st^4)$

4. $4(x^2 + 5x + 6)$

5. $2x(3x - 4)$

6. $7xy(3x^2 + 4y + 2)$

7. $(x + 3)(x + 4)$

8. $(x - 6)(x - 6)$

9. $(x - 2)(x - 5)$

10. $(2x + 5)(x + 6)$

11. $(m^3 + 3)(5m + n)$

12. $(a^2 + b^2)(a + b)$

13. $(x + 4)(x^2 + 3x + 5)$

14. $(3m + 4)(m^2 - 3m + 5)$

15. $(2x - 5)(4x^2 - 3x + 1)$

16. **The length of a rectangle is 3 inches greater than the width.**

    a. Write a polynomial that represents the area of the rectangle. _____

    b. Find the area of the rectangle when the width is 4 inches. _____

17. **The length of a rectangle is 8 centimeters less than 3 times the width.**

    a. Write a polynomial that represents the area of the rectangle. _____

    b. Find the area of the rectangle when the width is 10 centimeters. _____

18. Write a polynomial to represent the volume of the rectangular prism.

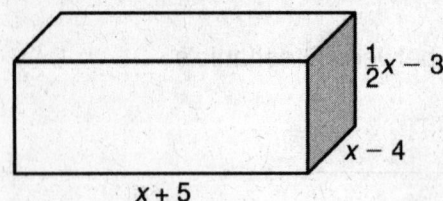

$\frac{1}{2}x - 3$

$x - 4$

$x + 5$

Name _____ Date _____ Class _____

LESSON 7-9 Practice
Special Products of Binomials

Multiply.

1. $(x + 2)^2$

2. $(m + 4)^2$

3. $(3 + a)^2$

4. $(2x + 5)^2$

5. $(3a + 2)^2$

6. $(6 + 5b)^2$

7. $(b - 3)^2$

8. $(8 - y)^2$

9. $(a - 10)^2$

10. $(3x - 7)^2$

11. $(4m - 9)^2$

12. $(6 - 3n)^2$

13. $(x + 3)(x - 3)$

14. $(8 + y)(8 - y)$

15. $(x + 6)(x - 6)$

16. $(5x + 2)(5x - 2)$

17. $(10x + 7y)(10x - 7y)$

18. $(x^2 + 3y)(x^2 - 3y)$

19. Write a simplified expression that represents the...

   a. area of the large rectangle.

   _____

   b. area of the small rectangle.

   _____

   c. area of the shaded area.

   _____

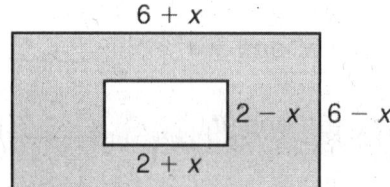

20. The small rectangle is made larger by adding 2 units to the length and 2 units to the width.

   a. What is the new area of the smaller rectangle?

   _____

   b. What is the area of the new shaded area?

   _____

LESSON 8-1 Practice
Factors and Greatest Common Factors

Write the prime factorization of each number.

1. 18 _____
2. 120 _____
3. 56 _____

4. 390 _____
5. 144 _____
6. 153 _____

Find the GCF of each pair of numbers.

7. 16 and 20 _____
8. 9 and 36 _____

9. 15 and 28 _____
10. 35 and 42 _____

11. 33 and 66 _____
12. 100 and 120 _____

13. 78 and 30 _____
14. 84 and 42 _____

Find the GCF of each pair of monomials.

15. $15x^4$ and $35x^2$ _____
16. $12p^2$ and $30q^5$ _____

17. $-6t^3$ and $9t$ _____
18. $27y^3z$ and $45x^2y$ _____

19. $12ab$ and 12 _____
20. $-8d^3$ and $14d^4$ _____

21. $-m^8n^4$ and $3m^6n$ _____
22. $10gh^2$ and $5h$ _____

23. Kirstin is decorating her bedroom wall with photographs. She has 36 photographs of family and 28 photographs of friends. She wants to arrange the photographs in rows so that each row has the same number of photographs, and photographs of family and photographs of friends do not appear in the same row.

   a. How many rows will there be if Kirstin puts the greatest possible number of photographs in each row?

   _____

   b. How many photographs will be in each row? _____

Name _____ Date _____ Class _____

LESSON 8-2 Practice
Factoring by GCF

Factor each polynomial. Check your answer.

1. $8c^2 + 7c$

2. $3n^3 + 12n^2$

3. $15x^5 - 18x$

4. $-8s^4 + 20t^3 - 28$

5. $6n^6 + 18n^4 - 24n$

6. $-5m^4 - 5m^3 + 5m^2$

7. A ball is hit vertically into the air using a paddle at a speed of 32 ft/sec. The expression $-16t^2 + 32t$ gives the ball's height after t seconds. Factor this expression.

8. The area of Margo's laptop computer screen is $12x^2 + 3x$ in^2. Factor this polynomial to find expressions for the dimensions of her computer screen.

Factor each expression.

9. $3m(m + 5) + 4(m + 5)$

10. $16b(b - 3) + (b - 3)$

Factor each polynomial by grouping.

11. $2x^3 + 8x^2 + 3x + 12$

12. $4n^3 + 3n^2 + 4n + 3$

13. $10d^2 - 6d + 35d - 21$

14. $12n^3 - 15n^2 - 8n + 10$

15. $5b^4 - 15b^3 + 3 - b$

16. $t^3 - 5t^2 + 10 - 2t$

Original content Copyright © by Holt McDougal. Additions and changes to the original content are the responsibility of the instructor.

Holt McDougal Algebra 1

LESSON 8-3

Practice
Factoring $x^2 + bx + c$

Factor each trinomial.

1. $x^2 + 7x + 10$

2. $x^2 + 9x + 8$

3. $x^2 + 13x + 36$

4. $x^2 + 9x + 14$

5. $x^2 + 7x + 12$

6. $x^2 + 9x + 18$

7. $x^2 - 9x + 18$

8. $x^2 - 5x + 4$

9. $x^2 - 9x + 20$

10. $x^2 - 12x + 20$

11. $x^2 - 11x + 18$

12. $x^2 - 12x + 32$

13. $x^2 + 7x - 18$

14. $x^2 + 10x - 24$

15. $x^2 + 2x - 3$

16. $x^2 + 2x - 15$

17. $x^2 + 5x - 6$

18. $x^2 + 5x - 24$

19. $x^2 - 5x - 6$

20. $x^2 - 2x - 35$

21. $x^2 - 7x - 30$

22. $x^2 - x - 56$

23. $x^2 - 2x - 8$

24. $x^2 - x - 20$

25. Factor $n^2 + 5n - 24$. Show that the original polynomial and the factored form describe the same sequence of numbers for $n = 0, 1, 2, 3,$ and 4.

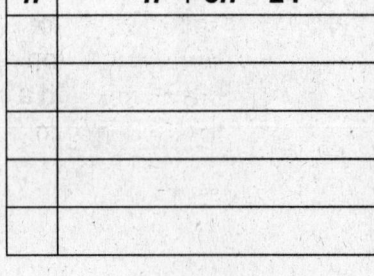

n	$n^2 + 5n - 24$

n	

LESSON 8-4 Practice
Factoring $ax^2 + bx + c$

Factor each trinomial.

1. $2x^2 + 13x + 15$

2. $3x^2 + 10x + 8$

3. $4x^2 + 24x + 27$

_____   _____   _____

4. $5x^2 + 21x + 4$

5. $4x^2 + 11x + 7$

6. $6x^2 - 23x + 20$

_____   _____   _____

7. $7x^2 - 59x + 24$

8. $3x^2 - 14x + 15$

9. $8x^2 - 73x + 9$

_____   _____   _____

10. $2x^2 + 11x - 13$

11. $3x^2 + 2x - 16$

12. $2x^2 + 17x - 30$

_____   _____   _____

13. $8x^2 + 29x - 12$

14. $11x^2 + 25x - 24$

15. $9x^2 - 3x - 2$

_____   _____   _____

16. $12x^2 - 7x - 12$

17. $9x^2 - 49x - 30$

18. $6x^2 + x - 40$

_____   _____   _____

19. $-12x^2 - 35x - 18$

20. $-20x^2 + 29x - 6$

21. $-2x^2 + 5x + 42$

_____   _____   _____

22. The area of a rectangle is $20x^2 - 27x - 8$.
    The length is $4x + 1$. What is the width?   _____

LESSON 8-5

Practice
Factoring Special Products

Determine whether each trinomial is a perfect square. If so, factor it. If not, explain why.

1. $x^2 + 6x + 9$

2. $4x^2 + 20x + 25$

3. $36x^2 - 24x + 16$

4. $9x^2 - 12x + 4$

5. A rectangular fountain in the center of a shopping mall has an area of $(4x^2 + 12x + 9)$ ft². The dimensions of the fountain are of the form $cx + d$, where c and d are whole numbers. Find an expression for the perimeter of the fountain. Find the perimeter when $x = 2$ ft.

Determine whether each binomial is the difference of two squares. If so, factor it. If not, explain why.

6. $x^2 - 16$

7. $9b^4 - 200$

8. $1 - m^6$

9. $36s^2 - 4t^2$

10. $x^2y^2 + 196$

LESSON 8-6 Practice
Choosing a Factoring Method

Tell whether each polynomial is completely factored. If not, factor it.

1. $6(t^2 + 12)$

2. $5(m^2 + 9m)$

3. $2p(p^4 - 9)$

4. $(x - 8)(2x + 3)$

5. $3k^3(5k^2 + 19)$

6. $7(14g^4 - 4g + 10)$

Factor each polynomial completely.

7. $24x + 40$

8. $5r^3 - 10r$

9. $3x^3y + x^2y^2$

10. $-3a^2b + 12ab - 12b$

11. $5t^3 - 45t + 3t^2 - 27$

12. $2y^2 - 6y - 56$

13. $6a^3 + 39a^2 + 45a$

14. $x^3 - 9x$

15. $12n^3 - 48$

16. $3c^4 + 24c^3 + 48c^2$

17. $3d^3 + 4d - 2$

18. $10w^6 - 160w^2$

Name _____ Date _____ Class _____

LESSON 9-1 Practice
Identifying Quadratic Functions

Tell whether each function is quadratic. Explain.

1. (0, 6), (1, 12), (2, 20), (3, 30)

   _____

   _____

2. $3x + 2y = 8$

   _____

   _____

Use a table of values to graph each quadratic function.

3. $y = -\dfrac{1}{2}x^2$

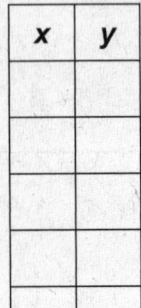
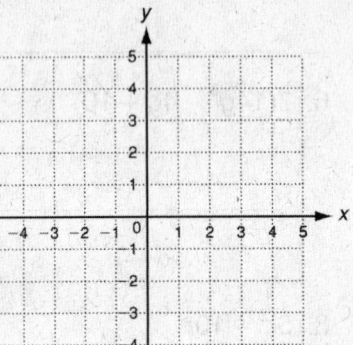

4. $y = 2x^2 - 3$

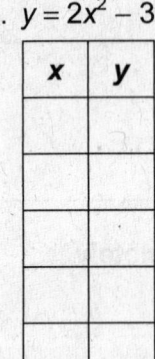
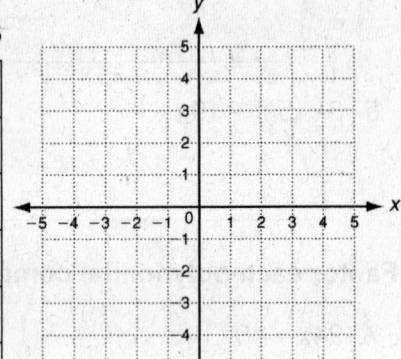

Tell whether the graph of each quadratic function opens upward or downward. Explain.

5. $y = -3x^2 + 5$

   _____

6. $-x^2 + y = 8$

   _____

For each parabola, a) identify the vertex; b) give the minimum or maximum value of the function; c) find the domain and range.

7.

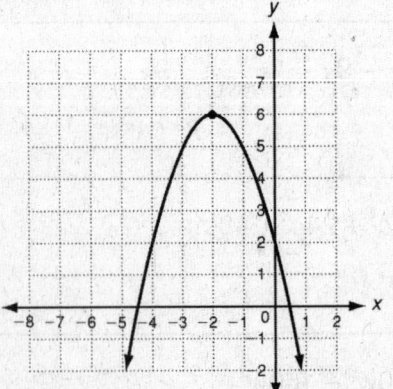

8.

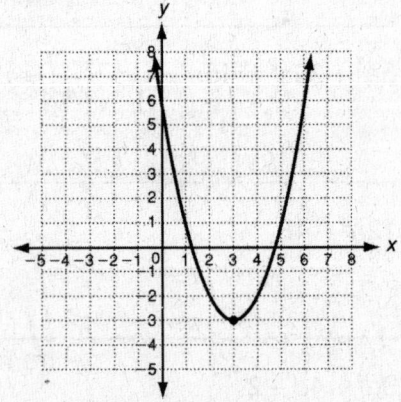

a. _____

b. _____

c. _____

a. _____

b. _____

c. _____

Name _____ Date _____ Class _____

LESSON 9-2

Practice
Characteristics of Quadratic Functions

Find the zeros of each quadratic function from its graph.

1.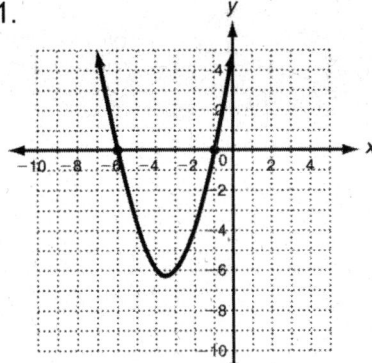

2.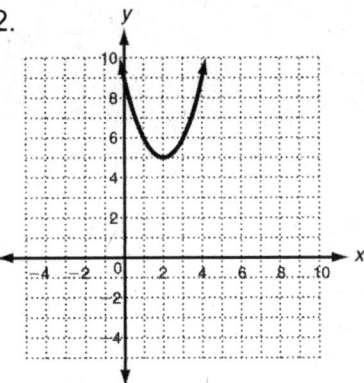

3.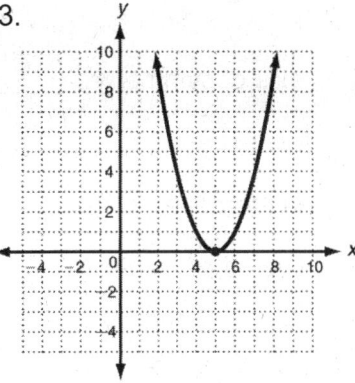

_____ _____ _____

Find the axis of symmetry of each parabola.

4.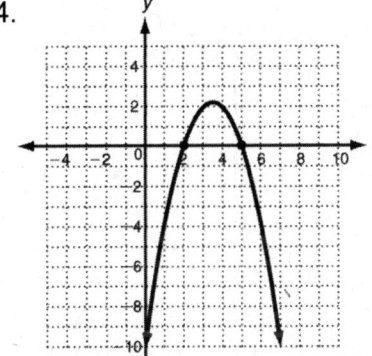

5.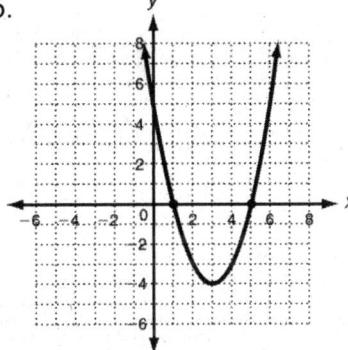

6.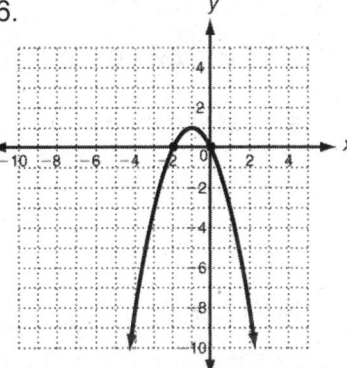

_____ _____ _____

For each quadratic function, find the axis of symmetry of its graph.

7. $y = 3x^2 - 6x + 4$

8. $y = -x^2 + 4x$

9. $y = 4x^2 + \dfrac{1}{2}x + 3$

_____ _____ _____

Find the vertex of each parabola.

10. $y = 3x^2 - 6x - 2$

11. $y = 3x^2 + 12x - 10$

12. $y = x^2 + 2x - 35$

_____ _____ _____

Name _____ Date _____ Class _____

LESSON 9-3

Practice
Graphing Quadratic Functions

Graph each quadratic function.

1. $y = x^2 + 4x - 4$

   axis of symmetry: _____

   vertex: _____

   y-intercept: _____

   two other points: _____

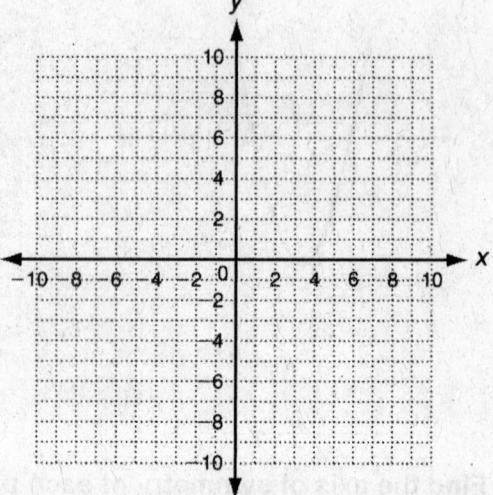

2. $y + 2x^2 - 4x - 6 = 0$

   axis of symmetry: _____

   vertex: _____

   y-intercept: _____

   two other points: _____

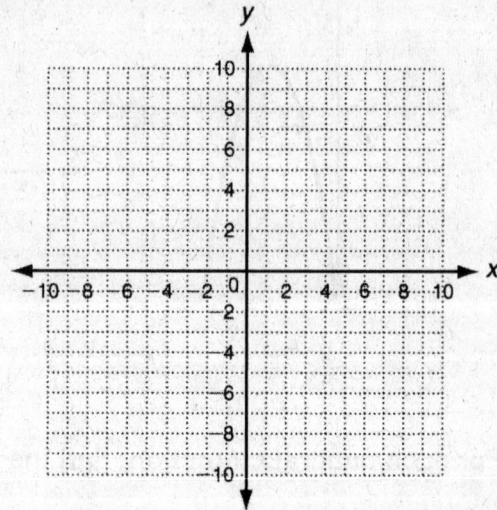

3. The height in feet of a soccer ball that is kicked can be modeled by the function $f(x) = -8x^2 + 24x$, where x is the time in seconds after it is kicked. Find the soccer ball's maximum height and the time it takes the ball to reach this height. Then find how long the soccer ball is in the air.

   maximum height: _____

   time to reach maximum height: _____

   time in the air: _____

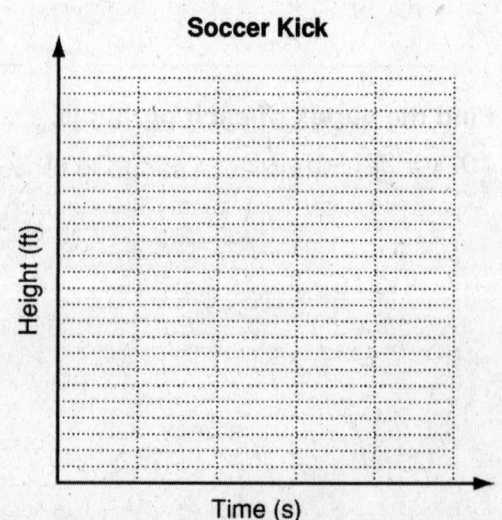

Soccer Kick

Practice

LESSON 9-4: Transforming Quadratic Functions

Order the functions from narrowest graph to widest.

1. $f(x) = 3x^2;\ g(x) = -2x^2$

2. $f(x) = \dfrac{1}{2}x^2;\ g(x) = 5x^2;\ h(x) = x^2$

3. $f(x) = 4x^2;\ g(x) = -3x^2;\ h(x) = \dfrac{1}{4}x^2$

4. $f(x) = 0.5x^2;\ g(x) = \dfrac{1}{4}x^2;\ h(x) = \dfrac{1}{3}x^2$

Compare the graph of each function with the graph of $f(x) = x^2$.

5. $g(x) = 5x^2 + 10$ _____

6. $g(x) = \dfrac{1}{8}x^2 - 3$ _____

7. $g(x) = -3x^2 + 8$ _____

8. $g(x) = -\dfrac{3}{4}x^2 + \dfrac{1}{4}$ _____

9. Two sandbags are dropped from a hot air balloon, one from a height of 400 feet and the other from a height of 1600 feet.

   a. Write the two height functions.

   $h_1(t) = $ _____ $h_2(t) = $ _____

   b. Sketch and compare their graphs.

   _____

   c. Tell when each sandbag reaches the ground.

   _____

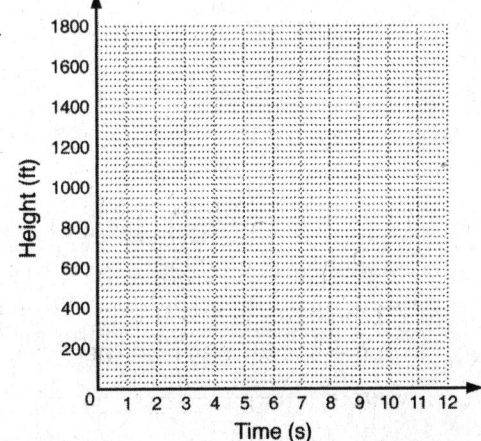

Sandbag Drop

Height (ft) vs Time (s)

Holt McDougal Algebra 1

LESSON 9-5

Practice
Solving Quadratic Equations by Graphing

Solve each equation by graphing the related function.

1. $x^2 - 6x + 9 = 0$

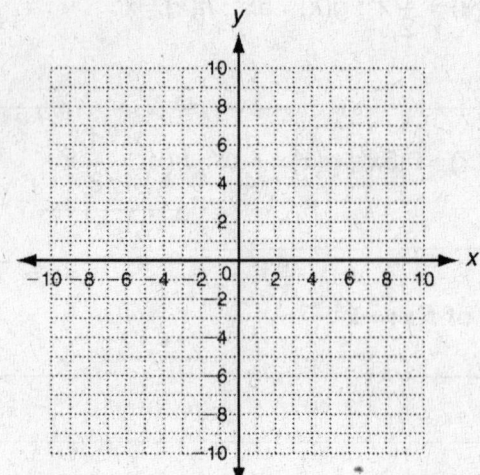

2. $x^2 = 4$

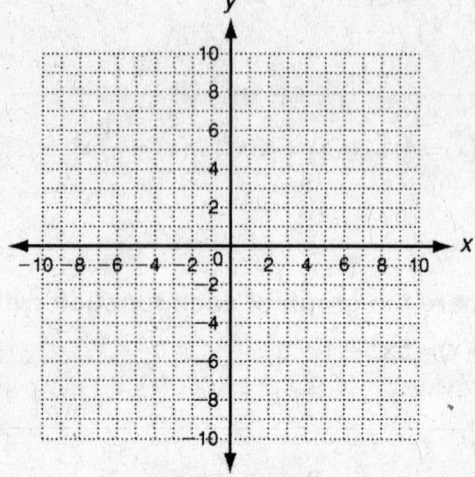

3. $2x^2 + 4x = 6$

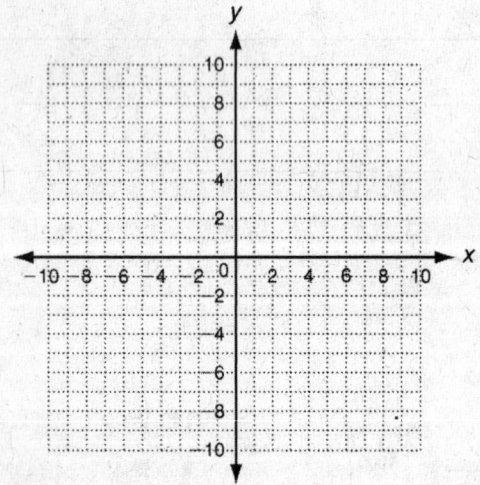

4. $x^2 = 5x - 10$

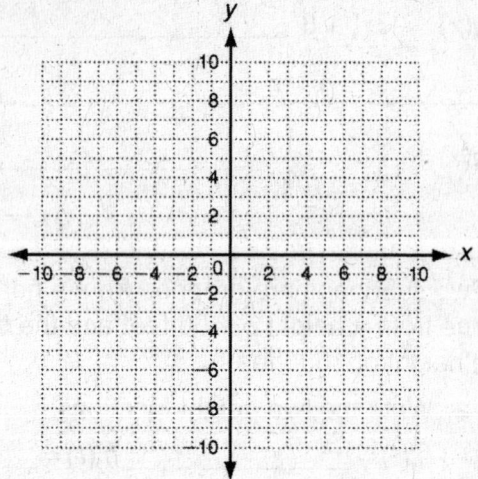

5. Water is shot straight up out of a water soaker toy. The quadratic function $y = -16x^2 + 32x$ models the height in feet of a water droplet after x seconds. How long is the water droplet in the air?

_____

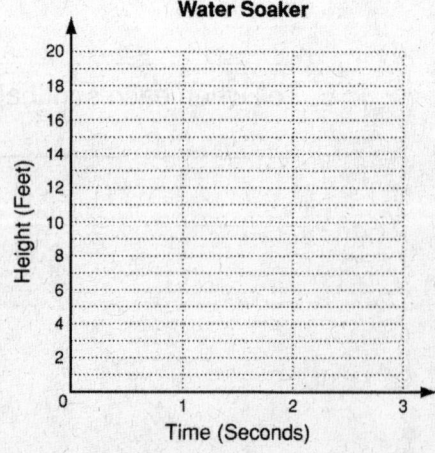

LESSON 9-6

Practice
Solving Quadratic Equations by Factoring

Use the Zero Product Property to solve each equation. Check your answers.

1. $(x-1)(x-5) = 0$

   $x - 1 = 0$ or $x - 5 = 0$

   $x = $ _____   or $x = $ _____

2. $(x-2)(x-9) = 0$

   $x - 2 = 0$ or $x - 9 = 0$

   $x = $ _____   or $x = $ _____

3. $(x-2)(x+4) = 0$

4. $(2x+1)(x-6) = 0$

Solve each quadratic equation by factoring.

5. $x^2 - 3x = 0$

6. $x^2 + 4x + 3 = 0$

7. $x^2 + 5x - 6 = 0$

8. $x^2 + 11x + 24 = 0$

9. $x^2 - 12x + 11 = 0$

10. $x^2 + 18x - 65 = 0$

11. $x^2 - 4x - 12 = 0$

12. $x^2 + 11x + 10 = 0$

13. $x^2 + 12x + 35 = 0$

14. $2x^2 - 3x - 5 = 0$

15. $3x^2 - 5x - 2 = 0$

16. $x^2 = 3x + 40$

17. $x^2 - 14 = 5x$

18. $2x - 1 = -8x^2$

19. $x = 10x^2 - 2$

20. $2x^2 = 13x + 7$

21. $6x^2 + x = 5$

22. $x^2 = 5x$

23. The height of a flare fired from the deck of a ship in distress can be modeled by $h = -16t^2 + 104t + 56$, where h is the height of the flare above water and t is the time in seconds. Find the time it takes the flare to hit the water.

Name _____ Date _____ Class _____

LESSON 9-7 Practice
Solving Quadratic Equations by Using Square Roots

Solve using square roots. Check your answer.

1. $x^2 = 81$

   $x = \pm\sqrt{81}$

   $x = \pm$ _____

   The solutions are _____ and _____.

2. $x^2 = 100$

   $x = \pm\sqrt{\rule{1cm}{0.15mm}}$

   $x = \pm$ _____

   The solutions are _____ and _____.

3. $x^2 = 225$

   $x = \pm\sqrt{\rule{1cm}{0.15mm}}$

   $x =$ _____

4. $441 = x^2$

   $\pm\sqrt{\rule{1cm}{0.15mm}} = x$

   _____ $= x$

5. $x^2 = -400$

   _____

6. $3x^2 = 108$

   _____

7. $100 = 4x^2$

   _____

8. $x^2 + 7 = 71$

   _____

9. $49x^2 - 64 = 0$

   _____

10. $-2x^2 = -162$

    _____

11. $9x^2 + 100 = 0$

    _____

12. $0 = 81x^2 - 121$

    _____

13. $100x^2 = 25$

    _____

14. $100x^2 = 121$

    _____

Solve. Round to the nearest hundredth.

15. $8x^2 = 56$

16. $5 - x^2 = 20$

17. $x^2 + 35 = 105$

18. The height of a skydiver jumping out of an airplane is given by $h = -16t^2 + 3200$. How long will it take the skydiver to reach the ground? Round to the nearest tenth of a second. _____

19. The height of a triangle is twice the length of its base. The area of the triangle is 50 m². Find the height and base to the nearest tenth of a meter. _____

20. The height of an acorn falling out of a tree is given by $h = -16t^2 + b$. If an acorn takes 1 second to fall to the ground. What is the value of b? _____

LESSON 9-8

Practice
Completing the Square

Complete the square to form a perfect square trinomial.

1. $x^2 + 4x +$ ☐
2. $x^2 - 16x +$ ☐
3. $x^2 + 7x +$ ☐

Solve each equation by completing the square.

4. $x^2 + 6x = -8$
5. $x^2 + 4x = 12$
6. $x^2 - 2x = 15$

_____   _____   _____

7. $x^2 - 8x + 13 = 0$
8. $x^2 + 6x + 34 = 0$
9. $x^2 - 2x - 35 = 0$

_____   _____   _____

10. $2x^2 + 16x + 42 = 10$
11. $4x^2 - 7x - 2 = 0$
12. $2x^2 + 9x + 4 = 0$

_____   _____   _____

13. A rectangular pool has an area of 880 ft². The length is 10 feet longer than the width. Find the dimensions of the pool. Solve by completing the square. Round answers to the nearest tenth of a foot.

_____

14. A small painting has an area of 400 cm². The length is 4 more than 2 times the width. Find the dimensions of the painting. Solve by completing the square. Round answers to the nearest tenth of a centimeter.

_____

Holt McDougal Algebra 1

LESSON 9-9

Practice
The Quadratic Formula and the Discriminant

Solve using the quadratic formula.

1. $x^2 + x = 12$

2. $4x^2 - 17x - 15 = 0$

3. $2x^2 - 5x = 3$

4. $3x^2 + 14x - 5 = 0$

Find the number of real solutions of each equation using the discriminant.

5. $x^2 + 25 = 0$

6. $x^2 - 11x + 28 = 0$

7. $x^2 + 8x + 16 = 0$

Solve using any method.

8. $x^2 + 8x + 15 = 0$

9. $x^2 - 49 = 0$

10. $6x^2 + x - 1 = 0$

11. $x^2 + 8x - 20 = 0$

12. In the past, professional baseball was played at the Astrodome in Houston, Texas. The Astrodome has a maximum height of 63.4 m. The height of a baseball t seconds after it is hit straight up in the air with a velocity of 45 ft/s is given by $h = -9.8t^2 + 45t + 1$. Will a baseball hit straight up with this velocity hit the roof of the Astrodome? Use the discriminant to explain your answer.

Name _____ Date _____ Class _____

LESSON 10-1 Practice
Organizing and Describing Data

Look at the double bar graph.

1. Which was the first year that the Barnes rented more DVDs than VHS tapes?

   _____

2. About how many videos did the Barnes family rent in all in 2003?

   _____

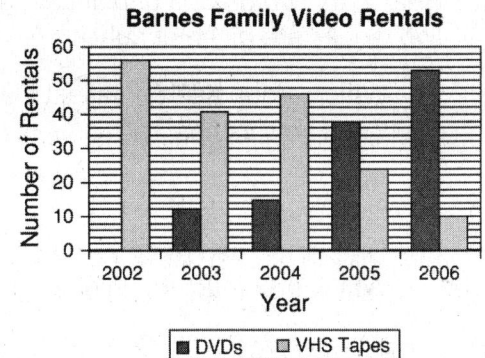

Look at the line graph.

3. During which time interval did the car's speed increase the least?

   _____

4. Describe how the speed changed over time.

   _____

   _____

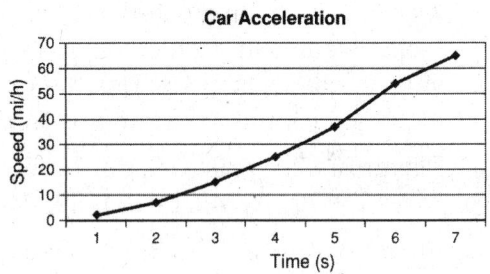

Look at the circle graph.

5. There were 5 times the number of orders for _____ as there were for strawberry.

6. What percent of the orders for ice cream were for mint chip or vanilla? _____

7. The table shows the number of customers who pumped 4 types of fuel at a gas station in a given time period. Use the given data to make a graph. Explain why you chose that type of graph.

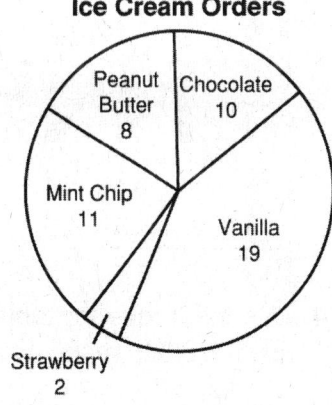

87 Octane	89 Octane	93 Octane	Diesel
12	1	5	2

Original content Copyright © by Holt McDougal. Additions and changes to the original content are the responsibility of the instructor.

Practice

LESSON 10-2
Frequency and Histograms

1. Heights of two groups of plants after two weeks are given at right.

Group A		Group B
	1	2
	2	3 4
9 7 3 3	3	5 5 8
8 1	4	1
0	5	

    Key: |2|3 means 2.3
    1|4| means 1.4

    a. Which group had the tallest plant? What was its height?

    _____

    b. One group had twice as much sunlight as the other. Which group do you think it was? Explain.

    _____

2. The receiving yards completed by two wide receivers on different professional football teams in each of the 16 regular season games is given. Use the data to make a back-to-back stem-and-leaf plot.

    Player A: 32, 17, 94, 79, 68, 73, 63, 84, 72, 73, 45, 69, 94, 89, 84, 34

    Player B: 79, 12, 97, 73, 54, 82, 21, 32, 28, 67, 74, 88, 41, 38, 78, 67

3. The number of calls per day received by a traveling Vet Van service for three weeks is given below. Use the data to make a frequency table with intervals.

Number of Calls						
18	22	13	15	16	21	22
26	17	14	12	13	18	14
16	22	23	20	21	18	22

Vet Van	
Number of Calls	Frequency

4. Use the frequency table in Exercise 3 to make a histogram.

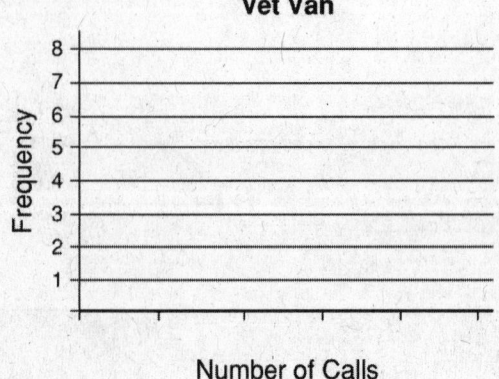

Vet Van

5. Complete the "third column" for the table in Exercise 3 to make it a cumulative frequency table.

Cumulative Frequency

LESSON 10-3

Practice
Data Distributions

Find the mean, median, mode, and range of each data set.

1. 22, 45, 30, 18, 22

2. 8, 10, 8, 14, 8, 15

3. 1.25, 0.5, 3.25, 0.75, 1.75

4. 95, 92, 96, 93, 94, 95, 93

Identify the outlier in each data set, and determine how the outlier affects the mean, median, mode, and range of the data.

5. 31, 35, 41, 40, 40, 98

6. 82, 24, 100, 96, 79, 93, 86

7. The amounts of Cathy's last six clothing purchases were $109, $72, $99, $15, $99, and $89. For each question, choose the mean, median, or mode, and give its value.

   a. Which value describes the average of Cathy's purchases? _____

   b. Which value would Cathy tell her parents to convince them that she is not spending too much money on clothes? Explain.

   c. Which value would Cathy tell her parents to convince them that she needs an increase in her allowance? Explain.

Use the data to make a box-and-whisker plot.

8. 71, 79, 56, 24, 35, 37, 81, 63, 75

9. 210, 195, 350, 250, 260, 300

The finishing times of two runners for several one-mile races, in minutes, are shown in the box-and-whisker plots.

10. Who has the faster median time? _____

11. Who has the slowest time? _____

12. Overall, who is the faster runner? Explain.

Name _____ Date _____ Class _____

LESSON 10-4
Practice
Misleading Graphs and Statistics

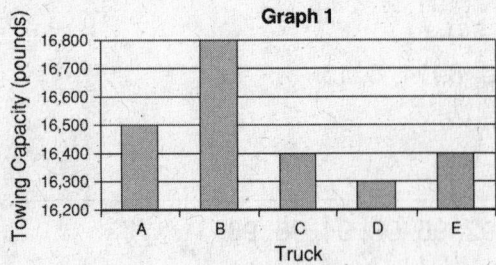
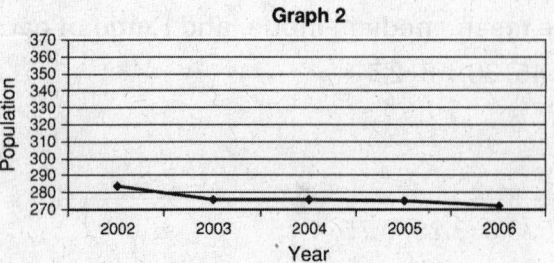

Graph 1 shows the maximum towing capacity of five full-size pickup trucks.

1. Explain why the graph is misleading. _____

_____

2. What might someone believe because of the graph? _____

_____

3. The manufacturer of which truck would be most upset with this graph? _____

Graph 2 shows the change in population of a certain animal species in a wooded area.

4. Explain why the graph is misleading. _____

_____

5. What might someone believe because of the graph? _____

_____

6. Who might want to use this graph? _____

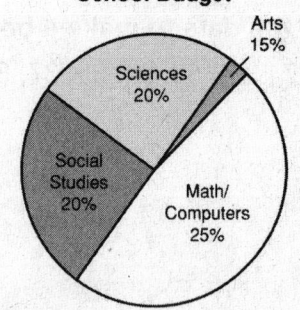

The circle graph shows how a school distributed money.

7. Explain why the graph is misleading.

_____

8. What might someone believe because of the graph?

_____

_____

9. Who might want to use this graph? _____

10. Sue surveyed people at a baseball stadium about their leisure activities. Explain why her statement is misleading: "85% of this town prefers sports over music."

_____

LESSON 10-5 Practice
Experimental Probability

Identify the sample space and the outcome shown for each experiment.

1. spinning a spinner

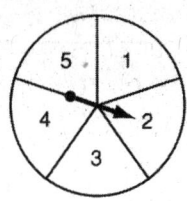

_____

_____

2. tossing two coins

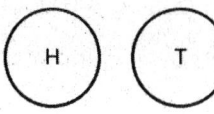

_____

_____

Write *impossible, unlikely, as likely as not, likely,* **or** *certain* **to describe each event.**

3. The mail was delivered before noon on 4 of the last 5 days. The mail will be delivered before noon today.   _____

4. Sean rolls a number cube and gets an even number.   _____

5. The pages of a book are numbered 1 – 350. Amelia begins reading on page 400.   _____

An experiment consists of rolling a standard number cube. Use the results in the table to find the experimental probability of each event.

Outcome	Frequency
1	6
2	7
3	4
4	10
5	8
6	5

6. rolling a 1   _____

7. rolling a 5   _____

8. not rolling a 3   _____

9. not rolling a number less than 5   _____

10. A tire manufacturer checks 80 tires and finds 6 of them to be defective.

    a. What is the experimental probability that a tire chosen at random will be defective?   _____

    b. The factory makes 200 tires. Predict the number of tires that are likely to be defective.   _____

11. A safety commission tested 1500 electric scooters and found that 15 of them had defective handles.

    a. What is the experimental probability that a scooter will have a defective handle?   _____

    b. The factory makes 40,000 scooters. Predict the number of scooters that are likely to have defective handles.   _____

LESSON 10-6 Practice
Theoretical Probability

Find the theoretical probability of each outcome.

1. rolling a number less than 4 on a standard number cube _____

2. randomly choosing a day of the week and it is a weekend _____

3. spinning red on a spinner with equal sections of red, blue, and green _____

4. randomly choosing the letter N from the letters in NUMBER _____

5. The probability it will snow is 60%. What is the probability it will not snow? _____

6. The probability of tossing two coins and having them land heads up is $\frac{1}{4}$. What is the probability the coins will not land heads up? _____

7. A spinner has red, green, blue, and yellow. The probability of spinning a red is 0.4, the probability of spinning a blue is 0.05 and the probability of spinning a yellow is 0.25. What is the probability of spinning a green? _____

8. Miguel entered a contest offering prizes to the top 3 finishers. The probability of winning 1st is 12%, the probability of winning 2nd is 18% and probability of winning 3rd is 20%. What is the probability that Miguel will not win any prize? _____

9. The odds of winning a contest are 1:50. What is the probability of winning the contest? _____

10. The odds against a spinner landing on yellow are 3:1. What is the probability the spinner will not land on yellow? _____

11. The probability of a thunderstorm is 80%. What are the odds that there will be a thunderstorm? _____

12. The odds of selecting a red card from a box of cards are 2:5. What is the probability of not selecting a red card from a box? _____

The table shows how many of each letter are in a bag. Use the table for 13–16. Find the following.

13. P(A)

14. P(B)

_____   _____

15. odds in favor of C

16. odds against E

_____   _____

Letter	How Many in Bag
A	5
B	4
C	6
D	2
E	8

Practice

LESSON 10-7: Independent and Dependent Events

Tell whether each set of events is independent or dependent. Explain your answer.

1. You roll a die and flip a coin. _____

   _____

2. You select one marble, do not replace it, then select another marble. _____

   _____

3. A number cube is rolled three times. What is the probability of rolling a 2 each time? _____

4. The numbers 1 – 40 are written on pieces of paper and put in a box. Two pieces of paper are randomly selected. What is the probability both numbers will be multiples of 4? _____

5. A coin is tossed 4 times. What is the probability of getting 4 tails? _____

6. **A bag contains 2 yellow, 12 red, and 6 green marbles.**

   a. What is the probability of selecting a red marble, replacing it, then selecting another red marble? _____

   b. What is the probability of selecting a red marble, not replacing it, then selecting another red marble? _____

   c. What is the probability of selecting 1 yellow marble, not replacing it, then selecting a green marble? _____

7. **There are 7 girls and 3 boys in a class. Two students are to be randomly chosen for a special project.**

   a. What is the probability both students will be girls? _____

   b. What is the probability both students will be boys? _____

   c. What is the probability of selecting a boy and a girl? _____

A music class consists of 9th and 10th graders as shown in the table. Two students will be selected at the same time.

Music Class	9th	10th
male	9	8
female	12	11

8. What is the probability both students are male? _____

9. What is the probability both students are 9th graders? _____

10. What is the probability one student is female and the second student is male? _____

Practice
Lesson 10-8: Combinations and Permutations

1. A code consists of 3 letters and then 3 digits. Any of the letters and numbers can be repeated. How many different codes are there? _____

2. A restaurant is having a breakfast special. The choices are shown in the table. How many different breakfasts with one of each item are possible?

Eggs	Meat	Bread	Juice
fried	bacon	biscuits	apple
scrambled	sausage	toast	orange
	ham		

   _____

3. A movie on DVD comes with different viewing options as shown in the table. How many different ways can the movie be watched?

Audio	Commentary	Language
on	on	English
off	off	Spanish
		French

   _____

Write C for combinations or P for permutations. Then answer the question.

4. A coach must pick 5 players out of 30 to go on a trip. How many ways can the 5 players be chosen? _____

5. Jenn has 5 types of flowers in her garden. How many ways can she make a bouquet consisting of 2 types of flowers? _____

6. How many different ways can the letters in MUSIC be arranged? _____

7. A grocery store carries 15 different types of cereals. Only 4 of the cereals can be displayed on the middle shelf. How many different ways can the 4 cereals be displayed? _____

Answer each question.

8. A science fair awards prizes to the first, second and third place winners. There are 48 people entered in the science fair. How many ways can the winners be selected? _____

9. A 3-digit computer password consists only of odd numbers that cannot be repeated. How many different 3-digit passwords are possible? _____

10. In a lottery, 6 different numbers are selected from a set of 50 numbers. A winner can have the numbers in any order. How many sets of winning numbers are there? _____

11. A band competition awards prizes to the top 3 schools. If 12 schools are entered, how many ways can 3 schools be chosen? _____

LESSON 11-1 Practice
Geometric Sequences

Find the next three terms in each geometric sequence.

1. −5, −10, −20, −40, …

2. 7, 56, 448, 3584…

3. −10, 40, −160, 640, …

4. 40, 10, $\dfrac{5}{2}$, $\dfrac{5}{8}$, …

5. The first term of a geometric sequence is 6 and the common ratio is −8. Find the 7th term.

6. The first term of a geometric sequence is −3 and the common ratio is $\dfrac{1}{2}$. Find the 6th term.

7. The first term of a geometric sequence is −0.25 and the common ratio is −3. Find the 10th term.

8. What is the 12th term of the geometric sequence −4, −12, −36, …?

9. What is the 10th term of the geometric sequence 2, −6, 18, …?

10. What is the 6th term of the geometric sequence 50, 10, 2, …?

11. A shoe store is discounting shoes each month. A pair of shoes cost $80. The table shows the discount prices for several months. Find the cost of the shoes after 8 months. Round your answer to the nearest cent.

Month	Price
1	$80.00
2	$72.00
3	$64.80

LESSON 11-2 Practice
Exponential Functions

1. If a basketball is bounced from a height of 15 feet, the function $f(x) = 15(0.75)^x$ gives the height of the ball in feet of each bounce, where x is the bounce number. What will be the height of the 5th bounce? Round to the nearest tenth of a foot.

_____

Tell whether each set of ordered pairs satisfies an exponential function. Explain your answer.

2. $\{(2, 4), (4, 8), (6, 16), (8, 32)\}$ _____

_____

3. $\{(-2, 5), (-1, 10), (0, 15), (1, 20)\}$ _____

_____

4. $\{(1, 750), (2, 150), (3, 30), (4, 6)\}$ _____

_____

5. $\left\{\left(-5, \dfrac{1}{3}\right), (0, 1), (5, 3), (10, 9)\right\}$ _____

_____

Graph each exponential function.

6. $y = 5(2)^x$

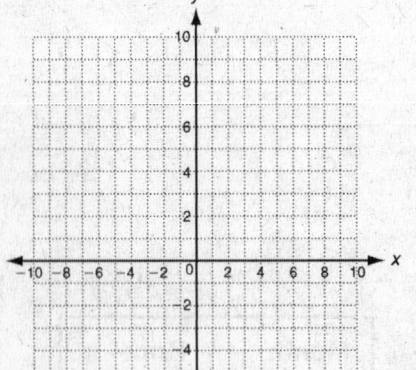

7. $y = -2(3)^x$

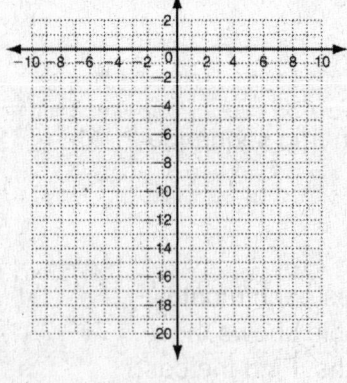

8. $y = 3\left(\dfrac{1}{2}\right)^x$

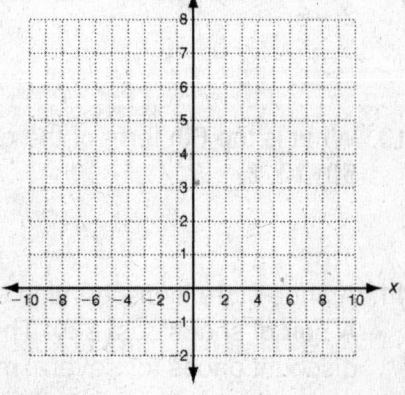

In the year 2000, the population of Virginia was about 7,400,000. Between the years 2000 and 2004, the population in Virginia grew at a rate of 5.4%. At this growth rate, the function $f(x) = 7,400,000(1.054)^x$ gives the population x years after 2000.

9. In what year will the population reach 15,000,000? _____

10. In what year will the population reach 20,000,000? _____

Name _____ Date _____ Class _____

LESSON 11-3

Practice
Exponential Growth and Decay

Write an exponential growth function to model each situation. Then find the value of the function after the given amount of time.

1. Annual sales for a fast food restaurant are $650,000 and are increasing at a rate of 4% per year; 5 years   _____

2. The population of a school is 800 students and is increasing at a rate of 2% per year; 6 years   _____

3. During a certain period of time, about 70 northern sea otters had an annual growth rate of 18%; 4 years   _____

Write a compound interest function to model each situation. Then find the balance after the given number of years.

4. $50,000 invested at a rate of 3% compounded monthly; 6 years   _____

5. $43,000 invested at a rate of 5% compounded annually; 3 years   _____

6. $65,000 invested at a rate of 6% compounded quarterly; 12 years   _____

Write an exponential decay function to model each situation. Then find the value of the function after the given amount of time.

7. The population of a town is 2500 and is decreasing at a rate of 3% per year; 5 years   _____

8. The value of a company's equipment is $25,000 and decreases at a rate of 15% per year; 8 years   _____

9. The half-life of Iodine-131 is approximately 8 days. Find the amount of Iodine-131 left from a 35 gram sample after 32 days.   _____

LESSON 11-4 Practice
Linear, Quadratic, and Exponential Models

Graph each data set. Which kind of model best describes the data?

1. {(−2, 0), (−1, −3), (0, −4), (1, −3), (2, 0)}

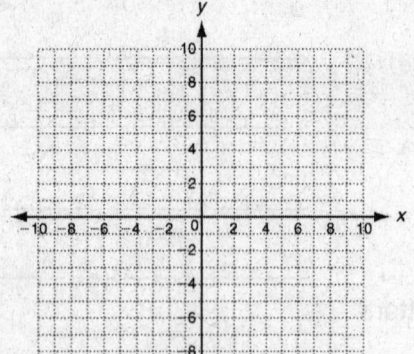

2. {(0, 3), (1, 6), (2, 12), (3, 24), (4, 48)}

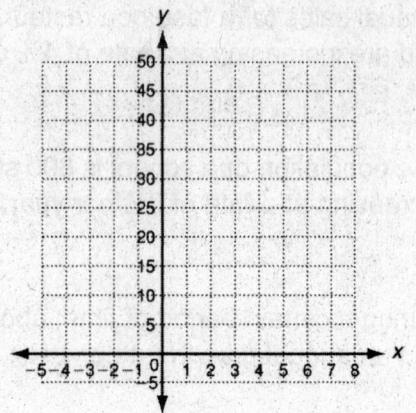

_____   _____

Look for a pattern in each data set to determine which kind of model best describes the data.

3. {(−5, 9), (−4, 0), (−3, −7), (−2, −12)}   _____

4. {(−2, 9), (−1, 13), (0, 17), (1, 21)}   _____

5. {(1, 4), (2, 6), (3, 9), (4, 13.5)}   _____

6. {(0, 4), (2, 12), (4, 36), (6, 76)}   _____

7. $\left\{(1, 17), \left(3, 8\frac{1}{2}\right), \left(5, 4\frac{1}{4}\right), \left(7, 2\frac{1}{8}\right)\right\}$ _____

8. Use the data in the table to describe how the restaurant's sales are changing. Then write a function that models the data. Use your function to predict the amount of sales after 8 years.

Restaurant				
Year	0	1	2	3
Sales ($)	20,000	19,000	18,050	17,147.50

_____

9. Use the data in the table to describe how the clothing store's sales are changing. Then write a function that models the data. Use your function to predict the amount of sales after 10 years.

Clothing Store				
Year	0	1	2	3
Sales ($)	15,000	15,750	16,500	17,250

_____

Practice

11-5 Square-Root Functions

1. An apartment manager needs to order wallpaper border for the remodeled bathrooms. The function $y = 640\sqrt{x}$ gives the amount of border needed, in feet, if x is the square footage of each bathroom. Find the amount of border needed if each bathroom is 100 ft². _____

2. The current I, in amps, flowing through a household appliance is given by $I = \sqrt{\dfrac{P}{R}}$, where P is the power required in watts and R is the resistance in ohms. What is the current in an electric skillet when the power required is 1500 watts and the resistance is 75 ohms? Round your answer to the nearest tenth. _____

Find the domain of each square-root function.

3. $y = \sqrt{x+6}$

    $x \geq$ _____

4. $y = \sqrt{-3x}$

    _____

5. $y = \sqrt{2x+8}$

    _____

6. $y = \sqrt{\dfrac{2}{3}x - 6}$

    _____

7. $y = -2\sqrt{10-5x}$

    _____

8. $y = \sqrt{7(x-3)}$

    _____

Complete each function table. Then graph each square-root function.

9. $f(x) = \sqrt{4x}$

x	f(x)
0	
$\dfrac{1}{4}$	
1	
4	
9	

10. $f(x) = \sqrt{-x} + 3$

x	f(x)
0	
−1	
−4	
−9	
−16	

11. $f(x) = \dfrac{1}{2}\sqrt{x} - 2$

x	f(x)

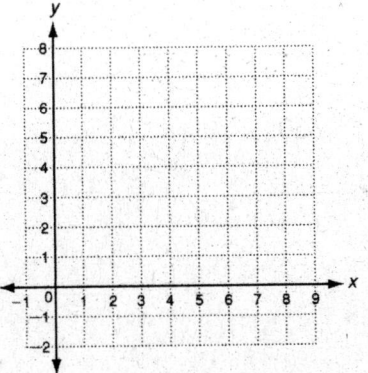
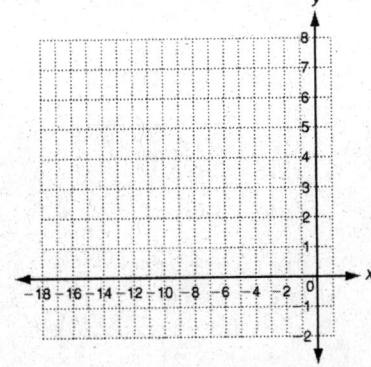
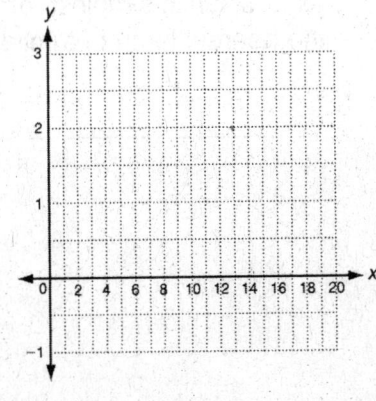

Name _____ Date _____ Class _____

LESSON 11-6

Practice
Radical Expressions

Simplify each expression.

1. $\sqrt{225} =$ _____

2. $\sqrt{\dfrac{75}{3}} = \sqrt{\Box} =$ _____

3. $\sqrt{7^2 + 24^2} =$ _____

4. $\sqrt{(x+8)^2} = |\text{_____}|$

5. $\sqrt{\dfrac{4}{100}} =$ _____

6. $\sqrt{x^2 + 8x + 16} =$ _____

Simplify. All variables represent nonnegative numbers.

7. $\sqrt{32}$

8. $\sqrt{28}$

9. $\sqrt{x^4 y^3}$

10. $\sqrt{147}$

11. $\sqrt{45}$

12. $\sqrt{36x^4 y^5}$

13. $\sqrt{\dfrac{7}{25}}$

14. $\sqrt{\dfrac{3b^2}{27b^4}}$

15. $\sqrt{\dfrac{m^3}{121n^4}}$

16. $\sqrt{\dfrac{10b^4}{2b^3}}$

17. $\sqrt{\dfrac{9y^6}{36y^2}}$

18. $\sqrt{\dfrac{40m^3}{10n^4}}$

19. $\sqrt{\dfrac{128}{25}}$

20. $\sqrt{\dfrac{4}{81x^8}}$

21. $\sqrt{\dfrac{250q^{10}}{5q^4}}$

22. Two hikers leave a ranger station at noon. Tom heads due south at 5 mi/h and Kyle heads due east at 3 mi/h. How far apart are the hikers at 4 PM? Give your answer as a radical expression in simplest form. Then estimate the distance to the nearest tenth of a mile.

_____

Name _____ Date _____ Class _____

LESSON 11-7 Practice
Adding and Subtracting Radical Expressions

Add or subtract.

1. $9\sqrt{7} + 4\sqrt{7} = $ ___ $\sqrt{7}$

2. $-10\sqrt{5} + 2\sqrt{5} = $ ___ $\sqrt{5}$

3. $4\sqrt{y} + 6\sqrt{y} = $ _____

4. $-2\sqrt{3b} + 10\sqrt{3b} = $ _____

5. $6\sqrt{15} - \sqrt{15} + \sqrt{15} = $ _____

6. $5\sqrt{2} - 3\sqrt{2x} - 4\sqrt{2} = $ _____

Simplify each expression.

7. $\sqrt{108} + \sqrt{75}$

8. $\sqrt{63} + \sqrt{175} + \sqrt{112}$

9. $\sqrt{28x} + \sqrt{63x}$

10. $\sqrt{45} + \sqrt{180}$

11. $\sqrt{52} - \sqrt{1300}$

12. $5\sqrt{98} - 3\sqrt{32}$

13. $\sqrt{32} + \sqrt{128}$

14. $\sqrt{147} + 6\sqrt{3}$

15. $\sqrt{168} + \sqrt{42}$

16. $5\sqrt{17} + 17\sqrt{5}$

17. $6\sqrt{3} + \sqrt{300}$

18. $-2\sqrt{3b} + \sqrt{27b}$

19. $4\sqrt{2m} + 6\sqrt{3m} - 4\sqrt{2m}$

20. $\sqrt{50m} + \sqrt{72m}$

21. $\sqrt{16z} + 2\sqrt{8z} - 3\sqrt{z}$

22. $\sqrt{216t} + \sqrt{96t}$

23. $4\sqrt{52x} + \sqrt{117x} - 2\sqrt{13}$

24. $3\sqrt{96k} + 2\sqrt{180}$

25. Write the numbers $3\sqrt{8}$, $4\sqrt{2}$ and $\sqrt{50}$ in order from least to greatest.

26. The map at right shows the path traveled by a delivery person on his afternoon route. Write the total distance traveled as a simplified radical expression.

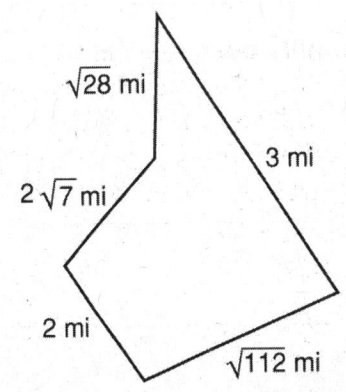

Name _____ Date _____ Class _____

LESSON 11-8 Practice
Multiplying and Dividing Radical Expressions

Multiply. Write each product in simplest form.

1. $\sqrt{15} \cdot \sqrt{6}$
   $\sqrt{15 \cdot 6}$
   _____

2. $(3\sqrt{6})^2$
   $3\sqrt{6} \cdot 3\sqrt{6}$
   _____

3. $4\sqrt{7x} \cdot \sqrt{20x}$
   $4 \cdot \sqrt{(7x)(20x)}$
   _____

4. $\sqrt{12} \cdot \sqrt{5}$
   _____

5. $(2\sqrt{7})^2$
   _____

6. $-2\sqrt{5b} \cdot \sqrt{10b}$
   _____

7. $3\sqrt{10y}\sqrt{6y}$
   _____

8. $\sqrt{8}(\sqrt{12} - \sqrt{2})$
   _____

9. $\sqrt{2x}(\sqrt{5} + \sqrt{2x})$
   _____

10. $\sqrt{2}(\sqrt{7} - 5)$
    _____

11. $\sqrt{10}(\sqrt{5m} - \sqrt{4})$
    _____

12. $(4 + \sqrt{3})(2 - \sqrt{3})$
    _____

13. $\sqrt{3}(\sqrt{8} - 6)$
    _____

14. $\sqrt{5}(\sqrt{2} + \sqrt{8})$
    _____

15. $(5 + \sqrt{2})(6 - \sqrt{2})$
    _____

16. $\sqrt{5}(\sqrt{2} - \sqrt{6})$
    _____

17. $(3 - \sqrt{2})(5 + \sqrt{2})$
    _____

18. $(7 + \sqrt{3})(7 - \sqrt{3})$
    _____

Simplify each quotient.

19. $\dfrac{\sqrt{2}}{\sqrt{6}}$

20. $\dfrac{\sqrt{10}}{\sqrt{11}}$

21. $\dfrac{\sqrt{13}}{\sqrt{50t}}$

22. $\dfrac{\sqrt{7}}{\sqrt{15}}$

23. $\dfrac{\sqrt{2}}{\sqrt{17}}$

24. $\dfrac{\sqrt{32}}{\sqrt{48z}}$

25. $\dfrac{\sqrt{3}}{\sqrt{3a}}$

26. $\dfrac{\sqrt{8x}}{\sqrt{5}}$

27. $-\dfrac{\sqrt{75k}}{10\sqrt{2k}}$

LESSON 11-9

Practice
Solving Radical Equations

Solve each equation. Check your answer.

1. $\sqrt{x} = 11$
   $(\sqrt{x})^2 = (11)^2$
   $x = \underline{\quad}$

2. $\dfrac{\sqrt{x}}{3} = 5$
   $\sqrt{x} = 15$
   $x = \underline{\quad}$

3. $\sqrt{3x+5} = 11$
   $\sqrt{3x} = \underline{\quad}$
   $3x = \underline{\quad}$
   $x = \underline{\quad}$

4. $2\sqrt{x} = 16$

5. $\dfrac{\sqrt{4x}}{2} = 4$

6. $\dfrac{3\sqrt{20x+4}}{4} = 6$

7. $\sqrt{x+5} = 9$

8. $\dfrac{\sqrt{x}}{4} = 1$

9. $\dfrac{3\sqrt{2x}}{4} = 12$

10. $\dfrac{\sqrt{2x}}{4} = 2$

11. $\dfrac{\sqrt{x+5}}{3} = 4$

12. $3\sqrt{6-x} = 6$

13. $\sqrt{10-x} = \sqrt{x-2}$

14. $\sqrt{x+2} = \sqrt{2x-1}$

15. $\sqrt{2x+10} - \sqrt{x+13} = 0$

16. $\sqrt{-x} = \sqrt{x+128}$

17. $\sqrt{4+x} = 5\sqrt{x-20}$

18. $4 + x = \sqrt{x+4}$

19. $-3\sqrt{x} = 8$

20. $x = \sqrt{2x+15}$

21. According to Heron's formula, the area of a triangle is given by $A = \sqrt{s(s-a)(s-b)(s-c)}$, where s is equal to one half its perimeter, and a, b, and c are the lengths of its sides. If a triangle has area 20 m², $s = 10$ m, $a = 5$ m and $b = 2$ m, what is c? _____

LESSON 12-1 Practice
Inverse Variation

Tell whether each relationship is an inverse relation. Explain.

1.
x	y
2	12
3	8
4	6

_____

2.
x	y
1	4
2	8
3	12

_____

3. $x = \dfrac{y}{5}$

_____

4. $xy = 8$

_____

5. Write and graph the inverse variation in which $y = 3$ when $x = 2$.

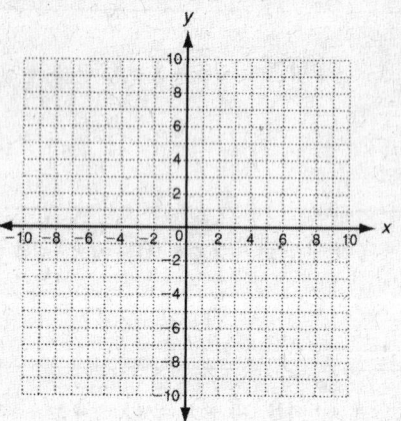

_____

6. Write and graph the inverse variation in which $y = 1$ when $x = -3$.

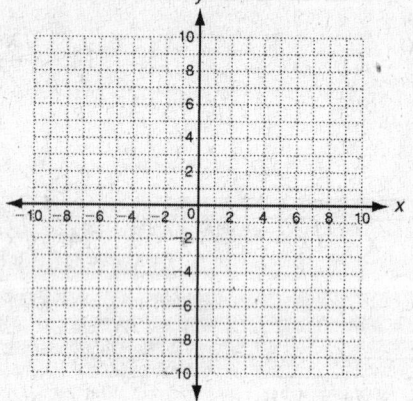

_____

7. Let $x_1 = 4$, $y_1 = 12$, and $x_2 = 3$. Let y vary inversely as x. Find y_2. _____

8. Let $x_1 = 3$, $y_1 = 10$, and $y_2 = 15$. Let y vary inversely as x. Find x_2. _____

9. While traveling in a car, the speed of the car is inversely proportional to the time it takes to travel a certain distance. At 25 mi/h, it takes 15 minutes to travel to work. How many minutes would it take traveling 30 mi/h?

_____

10. The amount of pizza that Kirby can buy varies inversely as the price of the pizza increases. Kirby can afford to buy 3 pizzas that cost $15.00 each. How many pizzas that cost $9.00 each can Kirby buy?

_____

Name _____ Date _____ Class _____

LESSON 12-2 Practice
Rational Functions

Identify the excluded value for each rational function.

1. $y = \dfrac{-6}{x}$

2. $y = \dfrac{8}{x+3}$

3. $y = \dfrac{5}{3x-6}$

_____   _____   _____

Identify the asymptotes.

4. $y = \dfrac{5}{2x-5}$

5. $y = \dfrac{2}{x+3} - 4$

6. $y = \dfrac{4}{x-6} + 3$

_____   _____   _____

Graph each function.

7. $y = \dfrac{12}{x+3}$

   a. Vertical asymptote: _____

   b. Horizontal asymptote: _____

   c. Graph.

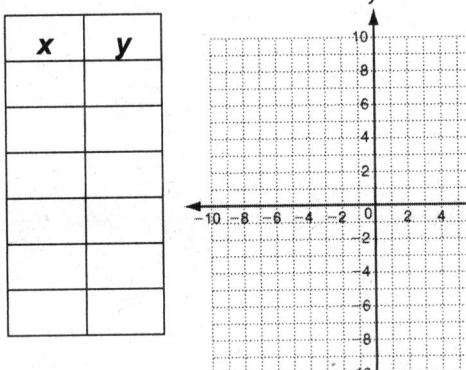

8. $y = \dfrac{6}{x-1} - 3$

   a. Vertical asymptote: _____

   b. Horizontal asymptote: _____

   c. Graph.

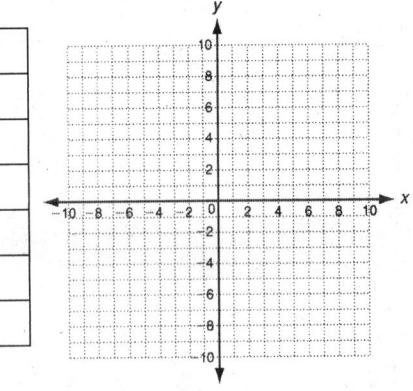

9. A music website is offering 5 free songs when you download any songs from their website. Catrina has $25 to spend on songs. The number of songs y that she can buy is given by $y = \dfrac{25}{x} + 5$, where x is the price per song.

   a. Describe the reasonable domain and range values.

   _____

   _____

   b. Graph the function.

Original content Copyright © by Holt McDougal. Additions and changes to the original content are the responsibility of the instructor.

Holt McDougal Algebra 1

LESSON 12-3 Practice
Simplifying Rational Expressions

Find any excluded values for each rational expression.

1. $\dfrac{6}{3+x}$

2. $\dfrac{5}{x^2-4x}$

3. $\dfrac{x+6}{x^2+3x-4}$

Simplify each rational expression, if possible. Identify any excluded values.

4. $\dfrac{7}{x-3}$

5. $\dfrac{5x^2+10x}{5x}$

6. $\dfrac{2x}{4x^2+6x}$

Simplify each rational expression, if possible.

7. $\dfrac{x+3}{x^2-2x-15}$

8. $\dfrac{3x+6}{x^2+3x+2}$

9. $\dfrac{x-6}{x^2-7x+6}$

10. $\dfrac{x^2-49}{x^2+8x+7}$

11. $\dfrac{x^2+4x-5}{x^2-4x+3}$

12. $\dfrac{x^2-2x}{x^2+2x-8}$

13. $\dfrac{x^2-x-12}{4-x}$

14. $\dfrac{5-5x}{x^2-1}$

15. $\dfrac{3-x}{x^2-6x+9}$

16. When packaging food, a company wants a package that uses the least amount of material to hold the greatest volume of product. Some containers with mixed nuts are in the shape of a right circular cylinder.

   a. Find the surface-area-to-volume ratio of a right circular cylinder. (Hint: For a right circular cylinder, $S = 2\pi rh + 2\pi r^2$ and $V = \pi r^2 h$.)

   b. Container A has a radius of 2 in. and a height of 5 in. Container B has a radius of 4 in. and a height of 8 in. Which container should the company choose? Explain.

Name _____ Date _____ Class _____

LESSON 12-4
Practice
Multiplying and Dividing Rational Expressions

Multiply. Simplify your answer.

1. $\dfrac{8a^2b^5}{a^3} \cdot \dfrac{3a^2}{4b^9}$

2. $\dfrac{4x+8}{3} \cdot \dfrac{6x}{x+2}$

_____ _____

3. $\dfrac{7}{2t-6} \cdot (t^2 + t - 12)$

4. $\dfrac{3x^2 + xy^3}{y^3} \cdot \dfrac{2xy + 8y}{4x + x^2}$

_____ _____

Divide. Simplify your answer.

5. $\dfrac{5j^2k^2}{3jk^5} \div \dfrac{10j^2k}{9j^3}$

6. $\dfrac{3c^2 + 24c}{c^2 - 2c + 1} \div \dfrac{c^2 + 9c + 8}{9c - 9}$

_____ _____

7. Ramon is playing a game in which he must pull two blocks out of a bag containing red and yellow blocks. He cannot look, and he cannot replace the block. The bag has 4 more red blocks than yellow blocks.

   a. Write and simplify an expression that represents Ramon's probability of picking a red block, then a yellow block. _____

   b. What is the probability that Ramon pulls a red block then a yellow block if there are 6 yellow blocks in the bag before his first pick? _____

   c. What is the probability that Ramon pulls two yellow blocks if there are 6 yellow blocks in the bag before his first pick? _____

LESSON 12-5

Practice
Adding and Subtracting Rational Expressions

Add or subtract. Simplify your answer.

1. $\dfrac{3m}{8m^3} + \dfrac{m}{8m^3}$

2. $\dfrac{x^2 - 6x}{x+3} + \dfrac{4x-15}{x+3}$

3. $\dfrac{c^2 + c}{c^2 - 25} - \dfrac{c^2 + 5}{c^2 - 25}$

4. $\dfrac{6a-1}{a^2 + 7a + 10} - \dfrac{2a-9}{a^2 + 7a + 10}$

Find the LCM of the given expressions.

5. $4a^2 b$, $6a$, $10b^3$

6. $x^2 + 5x + 6$, $(x+3)(x-1)$

Add or subtract. Simplify your answer.

7. $\dfrac{5}{3n} - \dfrac{2}{2n}$

8. $\dfrac{y^2 + 4y}{y^2 + 6y + 8} + \dfrac{3}{y+2}$

9. $\dfrac{x+2}{x^2 - 9} - \dfrac{1}{9 - x^2}$

10. $\dfrac{1}{6y^2 + 24y} - \dfrac{3}{y^2 - y - 20}$

11. Kendrick walked 1 mile, and then jogged 5 miles. His jogging speed was 4 times his walking speed w in mi/h.

   a. Write and simplify an expression that represents Kendrick's total exercise time.

   b. How many minutes did Kendrick exercise if his walking speed was 3 mi/h?

Name _____ Date _____ Class _____

LESSON 12-6
Practice
Dividing Polynomials

Divide.

1. $(15c^3 + 3c^2) \div 3c$

2. $(20b^4 - 12b + 4) \div 4b$

3. $(27q^6 - 3q^3 + 18) \div 9q^5$

4. $(15t^4 - 30t^2 + 6) \div 15t^3$

5. $(d^2 - 4d - 77) \div (d - 11)$

6. $(x^2 - 12x + 27) \div (x - 3)$

7. $(9p^2 + 6p + 1) \div (3p + 1)$

8. $(4b^2 + b - 3) \div (b + 1)$

Divide using long division.

9. $\dfrac{m^2 + 4m - 12}{m + 6}$

10. $(12y^2 + 31y + 14) \div (y + 2)$

11. $(t^2 + t - 6) \div (t - 1)$

12. $(3p^3 + 4p - 6) \div (p + 2)$

Original content Copyright © by Holt McDougal. Additions and changes to the original content are the responsibility of the instructor.

Name _____ Date _____ Class _____

LESSON 12-7
Practice
Solving Rational Equations

Solve. Check your answer.

1. $\dfrac{6}{t+3} = \dfrac{4}{t}$

2. $\dfrac{3}{m} = \dfrac{4}{m-2}$

3. $\dfrac{a}{4} + \dfrac{1}{2} = \dfrac{2}{3}$

4. $\dfrac{3}{2x} - \dfrac{3}{x-2} = \dfrac{1}{2x}$

5. $\dfrac{3}{2x} + \dfrac{5}{x} = \dfrac{13}{x+4}$

6. $\dfrac{3}{x} + \dfrac{3x+1}{x^2} = \dfrac{13}{x^2}$

Solve. Identify any extraneous solutions.

7. $\dfrac{8}{x-2} = \dfrac{x+3}{x-2}$

8. $\dfrac{-2}{x-1} = \dfrac{x-8}{x+1}$

9. Caroline can paint a fence in 6 hours. Her sister Lily can paint the same fence in 4 hours. How long will it take them to paint the fence if they work together?

10. Jalon bicycled against the wind for 10 miles in the same time he bicycled with the wind for 25 miles. The wind speed was 4 mi/h. What was Jalon's average bicycling speed?

    (*Hint*: Use $t = \dfrac{d}{r}$.)

11. There are two positive numbers. The second number is 6 less than the first number. When the reciprocal of the second number is subtracted from the reciprocal of the first, the difference is $-\dfrac{3}{8}$. Find the first number.

Name _____ Date _____ Class _____

LESSON 1-1

Problem Solving
Variables and Expressions

Write the correct answer.

1. For her book club, Sharon reads for 45 minutes each day. Write an expression for the number of hours she reads in d days.

2. The minimum wage in 2003 was $5.15. This was w more than the minimum wage in 1996. Write an expression for the minimum wage in 1996.

3. According to the 2000 census, the number of people per square mile in Florida was about 216 more than the number of people per square mile in Texas. Write an expression for the number of people per square mile in Florida if there were t people per square mile in Texas.

4. The cost of a party is $550. The price per person depends on how many people attend the party. Write an expression for the price per person if p people attend the party. Then find the price per person if 25, 50, and 55 people attend the party.

Use the table below to answer questions 5–6, which shows the years five states entered the Union. Select the best answer.

5. North Carolina entered the Union x years after Pennsylvania. Which expression shows the year North Carolina entered the Union?

   A $1845 + x$ C $1787 + x$
   B $1845 - x$ D $1787 - x$

6. The expression $f - 26$ represents the year Alabama entered the Union, where f is the year Florida entered. In which year did Alabama enter the Union?

   F 1819   H 1837
   G 1826   J 1871

State	Year Entered into Union
Florida	1845
Indiana	1816
Pennsylvania	1787
Texas	1845
West Virginia	1863

7. The number of states that entered the Union in 1889 was half the number of states s that entered in 1788. Which expression shows the number of states that entered the Union in 1889?

   A $2s$ C $s + 2$
   B $s \div 2$ D $2 - s$

LESSON 1-2

Problem Solving
Adding and Subtracting Real Numbers

Write the correct answer.

1. The Pacific Ocean has an average depth of 12,925 feet, while the Atlantic Ocean has an average depth of 11,730 feet. Find the difference in average depths.

2. A kite flies 74 feet above the ground. The person flying the kite is 5 feet 6 inches tall. How far above the person is the kite?

3. Stock in ABC Company fell 12.67 points on Monday and 31.51 points on Tuesday. Determine the total change in the stock for the two days.

4. Muriel scored 30 points lower on her first practice SAT test than she did on her PSAT. She scored 20 points better on her second practice SAT test than she did on her first practice SAT test. How does her second practice SAT test score compare with her PSAT test score?

Use the table below to answer questions 5–7, which shows some of the world's most extreme elevations. A negative number means the location is *below* sea level. Select the best answer.

5. Find the difference in elevation between the Puerto Rico Trench and the Java Trench.

    A 4856 ft   C 51,608 ft
    B 7608 ft   D 59,216 ft

6. Find the difference in elevation between the highest and lowest locations.

    F 64,868 ft   H 6812 ft
    G 52,404 ft   J 5652 ft

7. Denver is called the "Mile High City" because it is approximately 5280 feet above sea level. How much higher in elevation is Denver than the Mariana Trench?

    A 30,560 ft   C 35,840 ft
    B 34,308 ft   D 41,120 ft

Location	Elevation (ft)
Mount Everest	29,028
Aconcagua	22,834
Mount McKinley	20,320
Mariana Trench	−35,840
Puerto Rico Trench	−28,232
Java Trench	−23,376

Name _____ Date _____ Class _____

LESSON 1-3

Problem Solving
Multiplying and Dividing Real Numbers

Write the correct answer.

1. Jane's grade point average changed by −0.16 points each term. How much did her grade point average change after 4 terms?

2. Isari's recipe for strawberry smoothies requires $\frac{1}{2}$ cup of sliced strawberries per smoothie. How many smoothies can she make using 8 cups of strawberries?

3. The value of an investor's stock changed by $-1\frac{3}{4}$ points last week. This week, the value changed by 3 times as much. How much did the value of the investor's stock change this week?

4. Jogging on pavement burns 13 calories per minute. Jogging on grass burns 1.07 times as many calories per minute. How many calories would you burn by jogging on grass for 5 minutes? (Round your answer to the nearest tenth.)

Use the table below for exercises 5–7, which shows the cost of three different types of season tickets during the Dallas Cowboys 2005 season. Select the best answer.

5. How much money was spent on Upper Level Sideline season tickets in 2005 if 2500 fans bought Upper Level Sideline season tickets?

   A $1,315,000   C $1,757,500
   B $1,550,000   D $1,825,000

6. Tom and his two brothers gave their father two Upper Level Far Corner season tickets as a gift. If the brothers shared the cost equally, how much did each one pay towards the gift?

   F $163   H $327
   G $245   J $980

7. If sales of Upper Level Corner season tickets totaled $1,116,000, how many Upper Level Corner season ticket holders were there?

   A 1529   C 2278
   B 1800   D 6919

2005 Season Tickets	
Seat Location	Cost
Upper Level Sideline	$730
Upper Level Corner	$620
Upper Level Far Corner	$490

8. Four friends bought a pair of Upper Level Sideline season tickets. If they shared the cost equally, how much did each pay?

   F $122.50   H $310
   G $182.50   J $365

Name _____ Date _____ Class _____

LESSON 1-4 Problem Solving
Powers and Exponents

Write the correct answer.

1. The population of a certain bacteria doubles in size every 3 hours. If a population begins with one bacterium, how many will there be after one day?

2. The top of Julie's nightstand has the shape of a circle with diameter 14 inches. Find the area of the top of Julie's nightstand. (Recall that the area of a circle can be approximated by squaring the length of its radius and then multiplying by 3.14.)

3. The population of Bridgeville triples every decade. If its population in 2000 was 25,000, how many people will be living in Bridgeville in 2030?

4. The number of subscribers to a popular new magazine quadruples every month. If there were initially 500 subscribers, how many subscribers will there be after six months?

A square photograph measuring 8 inches by 8 inches is positioned within a 1-inch wide picture frame as shown below. Select the best answer.

5. What is the area of the photograph alone?
   - A 16 in^2
   - B 32 in^2
   - C 49 in^2
   - D 64 in^2

6. What is the combined area of the photograph and frame?
   - F 64 in^2
   - G 81 in^2
   - H 100 in^2
   - J 144 in^2

7. What is the area of the frame alone?
   - A 8 in^2
   - B 17 in^2
   - C 36 in^2
   - D 49 in^2

8. If the 1-inch wide frame is replaced with a 2-inch wide frame, how much more wall space will be needed to hang the framed photograph?
   - F 19 in^2
   - G 44 in^2
   - H 102 in^2
   - J 144 in^2

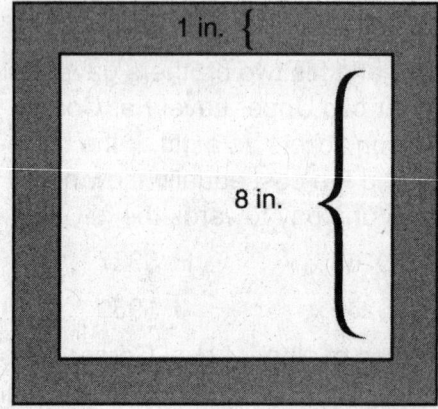

Problem Solving
1-5 Square Roots and Real Numbers

1. Jack is building a square pen for his dog. If he wants the area of the pen to be 121 square feet, how long should he make each side of the pen?

   _____

2. Danny needs a square-shaped picture to cover a hole in his wall. It has to cover at least 441 square inches of wall space. What is the smallest side length the picture can have?

   _____

3. The Statue of Liberty, which sits on Liberty Island in New York Harbor, is $151\frac{1}{12}$ feet high, from base to torch. Write all classifications that apply to $151\frac{1}{12}$: natural, whole, integer, rational, terminating decimal, repeating decimal, and irrational.

   _____

4. A square note card has an area of 5 in². Estimate the length of the side to the nearest tenth. Then write all classifications that apply to the actual side length: natural, whole, integer, rational, terminating decimal, repeating decimal, and irrational.

   _____

Use the table below to answer questions 5–7, which shows the area of four sizes of square-shaped pizzas sold at Town Pizza. Complete the table by finding the length of each side of the four pizzas. Round to the nearest tenth if needed. Select the best answer.

5. What is the length of each side of an extra large pizza?

   A 24 in. 　　C 26 in.
   B 25 in. 　　D 36 in.

6. Which of the following classifications applies to the length of each side of a large pizza?

   F natural 　　H integer
   G whole 　　J rational

7. Which of the following is NOT a classification for the length of each side of a small pizza?

   A whole 　　C rational
   B irrational 　　D integer

Pizza Size	Area (in²)	Side length (in.)
Small	100	
Medium	200	
Large	420.25	
Extra Large	576	

Name _____ Date _____ Class _____

LESSON 1-6
Problem Solving
Order of Operations

Write the correct answer.

1. A can of soup is in the shape of a cylinder with radius 3.8 cm and height 11 cm. What is the surface area of the can to the nearest tenth? Use 3.14 for π. (Hint: The expression $2\pi r^2 + 2\pi rh$ represents the surface area of a cylinder, where r is the radius and h is the height.)

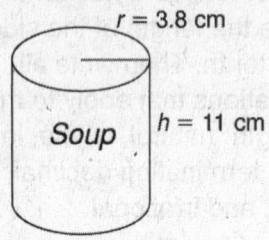

_____

2. One Boston household used the following amounts of electricity to run its heating system during the winter.

Month	Kilowatt-Hours Used
December	1500
January	1463
February	2260

Write an expression that can be used to find the average number of kilowatt hours used. Then simplify the expression.

_____

3. In a polygon with n sides, the sum of the measures of the interior angles is $180(n-2)°$. What is the sum of the measures of the interior angles of a hexagon?

_____

4. In a regular polygon with n sides, the measure of each interior angle is $\dfrac{180(n-2)°}{n}$. What is the measure of an interior angle of an octagon?

_____

Select the best answer.

5. Anthony had 10 packages of markers. Each package contained 8 markers. He gave his 3 best friends 2 packages each. Which expression shows how many markers he kept for himself?
   A $10 \cdot 8 - 10 \cdot 3 \cdot 2$
   B $8(10 - 3 \cdot 2)$
   C $10 \cdot 8 - 3 \cdot 2$
   D $8(10 + 3 \cdot 2)$

7. Each month, Mrs. Li pays her phone company $28 for phone service, and $0.07 per minute for long distance calls. Which expression represents her bill for a month in which long distance calls totaled 4 hours?
   A $4[28 + 60(0.07)]$
   B $28 + 4(60)(0.07)$
   C $28 + 0.07 + 4$
   D $28 + 0.07(4)$

6. The area of the wall hanging below can be approximated by simplifying
$$14^2 + \dfrac{1}{2} \cdot 14 \cdot 8 + \dfrac{1}{2}(3.14)(7^2).$$

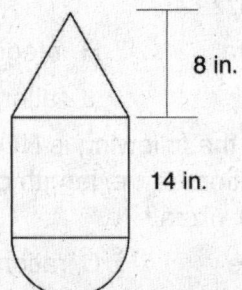

Which is closest to the area of the wall hanging?
   F 160.93 sq in.   H 328.93 sq in.
   G 273.98 sq in.   J 372.78 sq in.

Problem Solving
LESSON 1-7: Simplifying Expressions

Write the correct answer.

1. An English teacher gives students 1 point for reading a magazine article, 5 points for reading a chapter of a book, and 20 points for completing an entire book. If Sue reads 4 magazine articles, 7 chapters, and completes 2 books this term, how many points will she earn?

2. A recipe for chocolate chip cookies calls for $2\frac{1}{2}$ cups of flour, 1 cup of butter, $\frac{1}{2}$ cup of brown sugar, $\frac{3}{4}$ cup of sugar, and 1 cup of chocolate chips. Find the total number of cups of ingredients.

3. A rectangular desktop has a length of $3(x + 2)$ units and a width of $x - 7$ units. Write an expression, in simplified form, for the perimeter of the desktop.

4. Lucy is k years old. She has a sister who is three years younger than she is and another sister who is five years less than twice Lucy's age. Write an expression, in simplified form, for the sum of the three girls' ages.

Use the table below for questions 5–7, which shows expected flight times to and from New York City and five other cities. The legs of each trip vary in time due to the wind. Select the best answer.

Expected Flight Times

City	Inbound (h)	Outbound (h)
Mexico City	5.5	4.5
Paris	7.25	8.0
San Diego	5.4	4.75
Atlanta	2.3	2
Rome	7.75	8.5

5. Find the sum of the expected outbound flight times.
   A 23 h
   B 26 h
   C 27.75 h
   D 28.25 h

6. If Marty plans to travel from New York to Paris and back in February, and then from New York to Rome and back in April, what will be his total flight time for both trips?
   F 15.25 h
   G 16.25 h
   H 31.0 h
   J 31.5 h

7. Juan's flight time to San Diego was x hours longer than expected. His flight back was y hours less than expected. Which expression shows Juan's total flight time?
   A 10.15xy
   B $5.4x - 4.75y$
   C $10.15 + x - y$
   D $5.4x(4.75y)$

8. Last month, Heather flew from New York to Atlanta and back twice a week for 3 weeks. What was her total flight time if there were no delays?
   F 12.9 h
   G 13.8 h
   H 19.8 h
   J 25.8 h

Name _____ Date _____ Class _____

LESSON 1-8
Problem Solving
Introduction to Functions

Write the correct answer.

1. The number of teachers at a university is $\frac{1}{15}$ the number of students. Write a rule for the number of teachers at the university.

2. Use the rule in problem 1 to write ordered pairs for the number of teachers when there are 1230, 1500, 3045, and 4515 students.

3. The starting salary for a new teacher in a certain school district is $29,000 plus $2100 for each year of previous teaching experience. Write a rule for the starting salary of a teacher in this school district.

4. Use the rule in problem 3 to write ordered pairs for the starting salaries of teachers with 0, 3, 5, and 10 years of teaching experience.

A class officer will buy picture frames as favors for the prom. To ensure she has enough frames, she plans to buy frames for the 18 teacher chaperones plus 1.2 times the number of students who buy tickets to the prom.
Select the best answer.

5. Which rule represents the number of frames the class officer will buy?

    A $y = 19.2 + x$
    B $y = 19.2x$
    C $y = 18x + 1.2$
    D $y = 18 + 1.2x$

6. How many picture frames will the class officer buy if 225 students buy tickets to the prom?

    F 244   H 270
    G 252   J 288

7. Since both the number of students who buy tickets and the number of frames the class officer will buy cannot be negative, which quadrant will the ordered pairs that satisfy the rule in problem 5 lie in?

    A Quadrant I   C Quadrant III
    B Quadrant II   D Quadrant IV

8. If the class officer generates and graphs ordered pairs for the rule in problem 5, which statement would be true?

    F The points would form a line.
    G The points would form a U-shape.
    H The points would form a V-shape.
    J There will be no pattern.

Problem Solving

Lesson 2-1: Solving Equations by Adding or Subtracting

Write the correct answer.

1. Michelle withdrew $120 from her bank account. She now has $3345 in her account. Write and solve an equation to find how much money m was in her account before she made the withdrawal.

   _____

2. Max lost 23 pounds while on a diet. He now weighs 184 pounds. Write and solve an equation to find his initial weight w.

   _____

3. Earth takes 365 days to orbit the Sun. Mars takes 687 days. Write and solve an equation to find how many more days d Mars takes than Earth to orbit the Sun.

   _____

4. In 1990, 53.4% of commuters took public transportation in New York City, which was 19.9% greater than the percentage in San Francisco. Write and solve an equation to find what percentage of commuters p took public transportation in San Francisco.

   _____

Use the circle graph below to answer questions 5–7. Select the best answer. The circle graph shows the colors for SUVs as percents of the total number of SUVs manufactured in 2000 in North America.

5. The percent of silver SUVs increased by 7.9% between 1998 and 2000. If $x\%$ of SUVs were silver in 1998, which equation represents this relationship?

   A $x + 7.9 = 14.1$ C $7.9x = 14.1$
   B $x - 7.9 = 14.1$ D $7.9 - x = 14.1$

6. Solve the equation from problem 5. What is the value of x?

   F 1.8   H 7.1
   G 6.2   J 22

7. The sum of the percents of dark red SUVs and white SUVs was 26.3%. What was the percent of dark red SUVs?

   A 2.3%   C 12.2%
   B 3.2%   D 18%

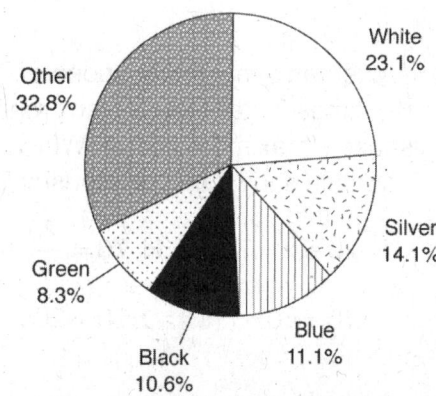

Percent of SUVs by Color

Name _____ Date _____ Class _____

LESSON 2-2

Problem Solving
Solving Equations by Multiplying or Dividing

Write the correct answer.

1. John threw a surprise birthday party for his friend. Food, drinks, and a DJ cost $480 for a group of 32 people. Write and solve an equation to find the cost c per person.

   _____

2. One serving of soybeans contains 10 grams of protein, which is 4 times the amount in one serving of kale. Write and solve an equation to find the amount of protein x in one serving of kale.

   _____

3. Maria earned $10.50 per hour working at an ice cream shop. She earned $147 each week before taxes. Write and solve an equation to find the number of hours h she worked each week.

   _____

4. Ben is saving $\frac{1}{5}$ of his weekly pay to buy a car. Write and solve an equation to find what weekly pay w results in savings of $61.50.

   _____

Use the table below to answer questions 5–7. Select the best answer.
The table shows the maximum speed in miles per hour for various animals.

5. The speed of a snail is how many times that of a cat?

   A $\frac{1}{1000}$ C 100

   B $\frac{1}{100}$ D 1000

Animal	mi/h
Falcon	200
Zebra	40
Cat (domestic)	30
Black Mamba Snake	20
Snail	0.03

6. A cheetah's maximum speed of 70 mi/h is x times faster than a black mamba snake's maximum speed. Which equation shows this relationship?

   F $20 + x = 70$ H $70 = \frac{20}{x}$

   G $20 = 70x$ J $70 = 20x$

7. Use your equation in problem 6 to find how many times faster a cheetah is than a black mamba snake if they are both traveling at their maximum speed.

   A 0.3 times   C 10 times

   B 3.5 times   D 50 times

Original content Copyright © by Holt McDougal. Additions and changes to the original content are the responsibility of the instructor.

Problem Solving
LESSON 2-3 Solving Two-Step and Multi-Step Equations

Write the correct answer.

1. Stephen belongs to a movie club in which he pays an annual fee of $39.95 and then rents DVDs for $0.99 each. In one year, Stephen spent $55.79. Write and solve an equation to find how many DVDs d he rented.

2. In 2003, the population of Zimbabwe was about 12.6 million, which was 1 million more than 4 times the population in 1950. Write and solve an equation to find the population p of Zimbabwe in 1950.

3. Maggie's brother is three years younger than twice her age. The sum of their ages is 24. How old is Maggie?

4. Kate is saving to take an SAT prep course that costs $350. So far, she has saved $180, and she adds $17 to her savings each week. How many more weeks must she save to be able to afford the course?

Use the graph below to answer questions 5–7. Select the best answer. The graph shows the population density (number of people per square mile) of various states given in the 2000 census.

5. One seventeenth of Rhode Island's population density minus 17 equals the population density of Colorado. What is Rhode Island's population density?

   A 425   C 714
   B 697   D 1003

6. One more than sixteen times the population density of New Mexico equals the population density of Texas. To the nearest whole number, what is New Mexico's population density?

   F 5   H 13
   G 8   J 63

7. Three times the population density of Missouri minus 26 equals the population density of California. What is Missouri's population density?

   A 64   C 98
   B 81   D 729

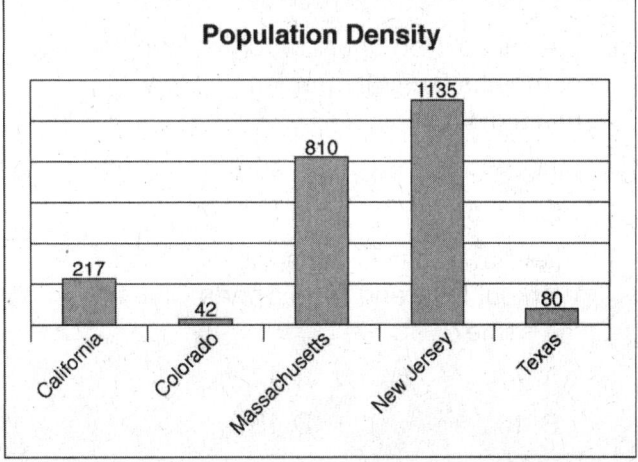

Problem Solving
Solving Equations with Variables on Both Sides

LESSON 2-4

Write the correct answer.

1. Claire purchased just enough fencing to border either a rectangular or triangular garden, as shown, whose perimeters are the same.

   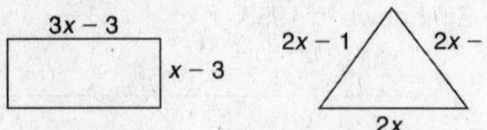

   How many feet of fencing did she buy?

2. Celia and Ryan are starting a nutrition program. Celia currently consumes 1200 calories a day and will increase that number by 100 calories each day. Ryan currently consumes 3230 calories a day and will decrease that number by 190 each day. They will continue this pattern until they are both consuming the same number of calories per day. In how many days will that be?

3. A moving company charges $800 plus $16 per hour. Another moving company charges $720 plus $21 per hour. How long is a job that costs the same no matter which company is used?

4. Aaron needs to take out a loan to purchase a motorcycle. At one bank, he would pay $2500 initially and $150 each month for the loan. At another bank, he would pay $3000 initially and $125 each month. After how many months will the two loan payments be the same?

Use the table below to answer questions 5–7. Select the best answer.
The table shows the membership fees of three different gyms.

5. After how many months will the fees for Workout Now and Community Gym be the same?

   A 2.5   C 25
   B 15   D 30

6. Sal joined Workout Now for the number of months found in problem 5. How much did he pay?

   F $695   H $1325
   G $875   J $1550

7. After how many months will the fees for Workout Now and Ultra Sports Club be the same?

   A 7   C 12
   B 10   D 15

Gym	Fees
Workout Now	$200 plus $45 per month
Community Gym	$50 plus $55 per month
Ultra Sports Club	$20 plus $60 per month

LESSON 2-5 Problem Solving
Solving for a Variable

Use the table below, which shows some track and field gold medal winners, to answer questions 1–4. Round all answers to the nearest tenth.

1. Solve the formula $d = rt$ for r.

   _____

2. Find Johnson's average speed in meters per second.

   _____

3. Find Garcia's average speed in meters per second.

   _____

2000 Summer Olympics		
Gold Medal Winner	Race	Time (s)
M. Greene, USA	100 m	9.87
K. Kenteris, Greece	200 m	20.09
M. Johnson, USA	400 m	43.84
A. Garcia, Cuba	110 m hurdles	13.00

4. The world record of 19.32 seconds in the 200-meter race was set by Michael Johnson in 1996. Find the difference between Johnson's average speed and Kenteris' average speed.

   _____

Select the best answer.

5. The cost to mail a letter in the United States in 2008 was $0.41 for the first ounce and $0.26 for each additional ounce. Solve $C = 0.41 + 0.26(z - 1)$ for z.

   A $z = \dfrac{C - 0.41}{0.26}$

   B $z = \dfrac{C - 0.41}{0.26} + 1$

   C $z = \dfrac{C + 0.15}{0.26}$

   D $z = C - 0.67$

6. The formula $V = \dfrac{Bh}{3}$ shows how to find the volume of a pyramid. Solve for B.

   F $B = \dfrac{3V}{h}$ H $B = 3Vh$

   G $B = 3V - h$ I $B = 3V + h$

7. Degrees Celsius and degrees Fahrenheit are related by the equation $C = \dfrac{5}{9}(F - 32)$. Solve for F.

   A $F = 9C + 27$ C $F = \dfrac{5}{9}C + 32$

   B $F = \dfrac{9}{5}C$ D $F = \dfrac{9}{5}C + 32$

8. The cost of operating an electrical device is given by the formula $C = \dfrac{Wtc}{1000}$ where W is the power in watts, t is the time in hours, and c is the cost in cents per kilowatt-hour. Solve for W.

   F $W = 1000C - tc$

   G $W = \dfrac{Ctc}{1000}$

   H $W = 1000C + tc$

   I $W = \dfrac{1000C}{tc}$

Lesson 2-6: Problem Solving — Solving Absolute-Value Equations

Write the correct answer.

1. A machine manufactures wheels with a diameter of 70 cm. It is acceptable for the diameter of a wheel to be within 0.02 cm of this value. Write and solve an absolute-value equation to find the minimum and maximum acceptable diameters.

2. A pedestrian bridge is 53 meters long. Due to changes in temperature, the bridge may expand or contract by as much as 21 millimeters. Write and solve an absolute-value equation to find the minimum and maximum lengths of the bridge.

3. Two numbers on a number line are represented by the absolute-value equation $|n - 5| = 6$. What are the two numbers?

4. A jewelry maker cuts pieces of wire to shape into earrings. The equation $|x - 12.2| = 0.3$ gives the minimum and maximum acceptable lengths of the wires in centimeters. What is the minimum acceptable length of a wire?

The table shows the recommended daily intake of several minerals for adult women. Use the table for questions 5–7. Select the best answer.

5. Which absolute-value equation gives the minimum and maximum recommended intakes for zinc?

   A $|x - 8| = 32$ C $|x - 16| = 24$

   B $|x - 24| = 16$ D $|x - 40| = 32$

6. For which mineral are the minimum and maximum recommended intakes given by the absolute-value equation $|x - 31.5| = 13.5$?

   F Fluoride   H Zinc
   G Iron   I None of these

7. Jason writes an equation for the minimum and maximum intakes of fluoride. He writes it in the form $|x - b| = c$. What is the value of b?

   A 3   C 6.5
   B 3.5   D 7

Mineral	Daily Minimum (mg)	Daily Maximum (mg)
Fluoride	3	10
Iron	18	45
Zinc	8	40

Source: http://www.supplementquality.com/news/multi_mineral_chart.html

Name _____ Date _____ Class _____

LESSON 2-7 Problem Solving
Rates, Ratios, and Proportions

Write the correct answer.

1. A donut shop bakes 4 dozen donuts every 18 minutes. Find the unit rate to the nearest hundredth.

   _____

2. At one time, the ratio of in-state to out-of-state tuition at Texas A & M University in College Station, Texas was about 3:11. About how much was the out-of-state tuition if the in-state tuition at that time was about $2400?

   _____

3. The birth rate in Namibia is 35 babies to every 1000 people. In 2001, the country had a population of about 1,800,000 people. How many babies were there?

   _____

4. A boat travels 160 miles in 5 hours. What is its speed in miles per minute?

   _____

Use the table below to answer questions 5–7. Select the best answer.
The table shows the ratio of female to male students at various institutions in 2002.

5. If there are 209 women at the US Naval Academy, how many men are there?
   - A 11
   - B 190
   - C 3971
   - D 4180

6. If there are 7282 male students at the Georgia Institute of Technology, how many females are there?
   - F 2427
   - G 2974
   - H 8282
   - J 17,828

7. If there are 4959 male students at Baylor University, which proportion can be used to find the number of female students?

   - A $\dfrac{21}{4959} = \dfrac{x}{21}$
   - B $\dfrac{21}{4959} = \dfrac{x}{29}$
   - C $\dfrac{21}{29} = \dfrac{x}{4959}$
   - D $\dfrac{29}{21} = \dfrac{x}{4959}$

Institution	female:male
Massachusetts Institute of Technology	41:59
Tulane University	53:47
US Naval Academy	1:19
Georgia Institute of Technology	29:71
University of Massachusetts at Amherst	51:49
Baylor University	29:21

8. For which institution is the ratio of female to male students the greatest?
   - F Baylor University
   - G Tulane University
   - H University of Massachusetts at Amherst
   - J US Naval Academy

LESSON 2-8
Problem Solving
Applications of Proportions

Write the correct answer.

1. A 4 by 5 inch photo is enlarged by multiplying every dimension by 2 to form a similar 8 by 10 inch photo. What is the ratio of the perimeter of the smaller rectangle to that of the larger? What is the ratio of the two areas?

   _____

2. Pamela wants to buy a suitcase whose dimensions are $1\frac{1}{2}$ times those of her $28 \times 16 \times 8$ inch suitcase. How is the ratio of the volumes related to the ratio of corresponding dimensions? What is the ratio of the volumes?

   _____

3. The Taylor's plan to expand their 80 square foot garage by tripling the dimensions. What will be the area of the new garage?

   _____

4. A tent has a volume of 26.25 in^3. Every dimension is multiplied by a scale factor so that the new tent has a volume of 1680 in^3. What was the scale factor?

   _____

Complete the table below and use it to answer questions 5–8. Select the best answer. Assume the shadow lengths were measured at the same time of day.

5. The flagpole casts an 8 foot shadow, as shown in the table. At the same time, the oak tree casts a 12 foot shadow. How tall is the oak tree?

   A 4.8 ft   C 30 ft
   B 24 ft   D 32 ft

6. How tall is the goal post?

   F 7.2 ft   H 38 ft
   G 30 ft   J 45 ft

Object	Length of Shadow (ft)	Height (ft)
Flagpole	8	20
Oak tree	12	
Goal post	18	
Telephone pole		17.5
Fence		6.5

7. What is the length of the telephone pole's shadow?

   A 5.5 ft   C 25.5 ft
   B 7 ft   D 43.8 ft

8. What is the length of the fence's shadow?

   F 1.5 ft   H 16.25 ft
   G 2.6 ft   J 21.5 ft

Name _____ Date _____ Class _____

LESSON 2-9
Problem Solving
Percents

Use the table below, which shows the recommended daily allowance of food components for a 2000-calorie diet, to answer questions 1–8. Round your answers to the nearest tenth.

Component	Recommended Daily Allowance
Total fat	65 g
Saturated fat	20 g
Cholesterol	300 mg
Sodium	2400 mg
Total Carbohydrates	300 g
Fiber	25 g

1. One serving of oatmeal contains 16% of the recommended daily allowance of fiber. How many grams of fiber are in one serving?

   _____

2. A certain can of soup contains 30% of the recommended daily allowance of sodium. How many milligrams of sodium are in one can?

   _____

3. One serving of pure Vermont maple syrup contains 53 grams of total carbohydrates. What percent of the recommended daily allowance is this?

   _____

4. One serving of pumpkin pie contains 12 total grams of fat. What percent of the recommended daily allowance is this?

   _____

Select the best answer.

5. A certain nutrition bar contains 15% of the recommended daily allowance of saturated fat. How many grams of saturated fat are in the bar?
   A 2.5 g   C 4 g
   B 3 g   D 5 g

6. One serving of plain yogurt contains 6 mg of cholesterol. What percent of the recommended daily allowance is this?
   F 2%   H 20%
   G 5%   J 50%

7. A cereal contains 90 mg of potassium, and this is 3% of the recommended daily allowance. What is the recommended daily allowance of potassium?
   A 27 mg   C 300 mg
   B 270 mg   D 3000 mg

8. A slice of whole grain bread contains 7 grams of fiber. What percent of the recommended daily allowance is this?
   F 18%   H 28%
   G 25%   J 30%

LESSON 2-10

Problem Solving
Applications of Percents

Write the correct answer.

1. Use the formula $I = PRT$ to find the simple interest paid annually for 3 years on a $1260 loan at 13% per year.

2. A snack food distributor earns $400 a week plus a 4% commission on sales. What is her total pay for a week in which her sales are $1080?

3. After 8 months, the simple interest earned annually on an investment of $4500 is $165. What is the interest rate?

4. Estimate the tax on a digital camera that costs $399 with a 6.25% sales tax.

Vira recorded her weekend expenses to start budgeting her money. Use Vira's weekend spending list to answer questions 5–8. Select the best answer.

5. What is the tip on Saturday's dinner?
   A $3.62   C $10.86
   B $7.24   D $14.48

6. Estimate the tax on Vira's new shoes.
   F $4.50   H $6.30
   G $5.40   J $7.20

7. What is the tip on Sunday's breakfast?
   A $0.26   C $1.28
   B $0.64   D $2.55

8. What is the tip on Vira's manicure?
   F $0.13   H $1.30
   G $0.26   J $2.60

9. At what percent rate did Vira tip the taxi driver?
   A about 5%   C about 15%
   B about 10%   D about 20%

Weekend Spending

Saturday:
Dinner
   $72.40 + 15% tip
Taxi
   $22 + $2 tip

Sunday:
Breakfast
   $12.75 + 20% tip
Manicure
   $13 + 10% tip
New shoes
   $89 + 6.25% sales tax

Problem Solving
Percent Increase and Decrease

LESSON 2-11

Write the correct answer.

1. The entrance fee at an art museum is $22. Senior citizens receive a 15% discount. How much do seniors pay?

2. Kylie paid $38.62 to fill the gas tank of her Jeep. Two weeks ago, she paid $34.18 to fill the tank. Find the percent increase.

3. In 2001, the population of Barbados was approximately 275,000. In 2002, the population increased by 0.5%. What was the approximate population of Barbados in 2002?

4. A shoe salesman marked up a pair of sandals in the spring by 75% and advertised them for $42.00. In the fall, he put them on sale at a 30% discount. What was the original price of the sandals, before the markup? How much were they selling for after the fall discount?

Use the table below to answer questions 5–8. The table shows the U.S. population by region as given in the 1990 and 2000 Census. Select the best answer.

5. By what percent did the population of the South increase from 1990 to 2000?
   A 14.8%
   B 17.3%
   C 18.6%
   D 19.8%

6. By what percent did the population of the West increase from 1990 to 2000?
   F 16.5%
   G 18.1%
   H 19.7%
   J 21.1%

Region	Population (1990)	Population (2000)
Northeast	50,809,229	53,594,378
Midwest	59,668,632	64,392,776
South	85,445,930	100,236,820
West	52,786,082	63,197,932

7. Which statement is NOT true?

   A The percent increase in the West was twice that of the Northeast.

   B The Northeast had the smallest percent change.

   C The South had the greatest increase in population.

   D All regions had a percent increase.

Name _____ Date _____ Class _____

LESSON 3-1
Problem Solving
Graphing and Writing Inequalities

Write the correct answer.

1. A citizen must be at least 35 years old in order to run for the Presidency of the United States. Define a variable and write an inequality for this situation.

   _____

2. A certain elevator can hold no more than 2500 pounds. Define a variable and write an inequality for this situation.

   _____

3. Approximately 30% of the land on Earth is forested, but this percent is decreasing due to construction. Write and graph an inequality for this situation.

   _____

   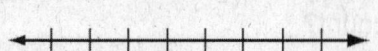

4. Khalil weighed 125 pounds before he started to gain weight to play football. Write and graph an inequality for this situation.

   _____

   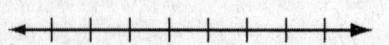

The Sanchez family is visiting an amusement park. When they enter the park, they receive a brochure which lists several requirements and restrictions. Select the best answer.

5. You must be at least 50 inches tall to ride The Wild Tornado roller coaster. Which of the following inequalities fits this situation?

   A $h \leq 50$ C $h \geq 50$
   B $h < 50$ D $h > 50$

6. Children less than 12 years old must be accompanied by an adult inside The Haunted House. Which of the following inequalities shows the ages of children who require an adult inside the house?

   F $y \leq 12$ H $y \geq 12$
   G $y < 12$ J $y > 12$

7. Totland is an area of the amusement park set aside for children who are 6 years old or younger. Which of the following inequalities represents the ages of children who are allowed in Totland?

   A $a \leq 6$ C $a \geq 6$
   B $a < 6$ D $a > 6$

8. The Bumpy Cars will not be turned on if there are 5 or more empty cars. Which of the following inequalities shows the possible numbers of empty cars if the ride is going to start?

   F $c \leq 5$ H $c \geq 5$
   G $c < 5$ J $c > 5$

LESSON 3-2 Problem Solving
Solving Inequalities by Adding or Subtracting

Write the correct answer.

1. Sumiko is allowed to watch no more than 10 hours of television each week. She has watched 4 hours of television already. Write and solve an inequality to show how many more hours of television Sumiko can watch.

2. A satellite will be released into an orbit of more than 400 miles above the Earth. The rocket carrying it is currently 255 miles above Earth. Write and solve an inequality to show how much higher the rocket must climb before it releases the satellite.

3. Wayne's homework is to solve at least 20 questions from his textbook. So far, he has completed 9 of them. Write, solve, and graph an inequality to show how many more problems Wayne must complete.

4. Felix wants to get at least one hour of exercise each day. Today, he has run for 40 minutes. Write, solve, and graph an inequality that shows how much longer Felix needs to exercise to reach his goal.

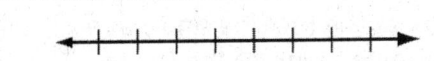
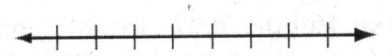

The high school has been raising money for charity and the class that raises the most will be awarded a party at the end of the year. The table below shows how much money each class has raised so far. Use this information to answer questions 5–7.

5. The school has a goal of raising at least $3000. Which inequality shows how much more money *m* they need to raise to reach their goal?

   A $m \geq 215$ C $m \leq 215$
   B $m < 215$ D $m > 2785$

Class	Amount Raised ($)
Seniors	870
Juniors	650
Sophomores	675
First-Years	590

6. The juniors would like to raise more money than the seniors. The seniors have completed their fundraising for the year. Which expression shows how much more money *j* the juniors must raise to overtake the seniors?

   F $j \leq 220$ H $j \geq 220$
   G $j < 220$ J $j > 220$

7. A local business has agreed to donate no more than half as much as the senior class raises. Which inequality shows how much money *b* the business will contribute?

   A $\frac{1}{2}(870) \leq b$ C $\frac{1}{2}(870) \geq b$
   B $870 \leq \frac{1}{2}b$ D $870 \geq \frac{1}{2}b$

Problem Solving
LESSON 3-3
Solving Inequalities by Multiplying or Dividing

Write and solve an inequality for each situation.

1. Karin has $3 to spend in the arcade. The game she likes costs 50¢ per play. What are the possible numbers of times that she can play?

    _____

2. Tyrone has $21 and wants to buy juice drinks for his soccer team. There are 15 players on his team. How much can each drink cost so that Tyrone can buy one drink for each person?

    _____

3. A swimming pool is 7 feet deep and is being filled at the rate of 2.5 feet per hour. How long can the pool be left unattended without the water overflowing?

    _____

4. Megan is making quilts that require 11 feet of cloth each. She has 50 feet of cloth. What are the possible numbers of quilts that she can make?

    _____

Alyssa, Reggie, and Cassie are meeting some friends at the movies and have stopped at the refreshment stand. The table below shows some of the items for sale and their prices. Use this information to answer questions 5–7.

5. Alyssa has $7 and would like to buy fruit snacks for as many of her friends as possible. Which inequality below can be solved to find the number of fruit snacks f she can buy?

    A $2f \leq 7$ C $7f \leq 2$
    B $2f < 7$ D $7f < 2$

Menu Item	Price($)
Popcorn	3.50
Drink	3.00
Hot Dog	2.50
Nachos	2.50
Fruit Snack	2.00

6. Reggie brought $13 and is going to buy popcorn for the group. Which answer below shows the possible numbers of popcorns p Reggie can buy for his friends?

    F 0, 1, or 2   H 0, 1, 2, 3, or 4
    G 0, 1, 2, or 3   J 0, 1, 2, 3, 4, or 5

7. The movie theater donates 12% of its sales to charity. From Cassie's purchases, the theater will donate at least $2.15. Which inequality below shows the amount of money m that Cassie spent at the refreshment stand?

    A $m \geq 17.92$ C $m \geq 25.80$
    B $m \leq 17.92$ D $m \leq 25.80$

Problem Solving
3-4 Solving Two-Step and Multi-Step Inequalities

Write and solve an inequality for each situation.

1. Jillene is playing in a basketball tournament and scored 24 points in her first game. If she averages over 20 points for both games, she will receive a trophy. How many points can Jillene score in the second game and receive a trophy?

2. Marcus has accepted a job selling cell phones. He will be paid $1500 plus 15% of his sales each month. He needs to earn at least $2430 to pay his bills. For what amount of sales will Marcus be able to pay his bills?

3. A 15-foot-tall cedar tree is growing at a rate of 2 feet per year beneath power lines that are 58 feet above the ground. The power company will have to prune or remove the tree before it reaches the lines. How many years can the power company wait before taking action?

4. Binh brought $23 with her to the county fair. She purchased a $5 T-shirt and now wants to buy some locally grown plants for $2.50 each. What are the numbers of plants that she can purchase with her remaining money?

Benedict, Ricardo, and Charlie are considering opportunities for summer work. The table below shows the jobs open to them and the pay for each. Use this information to answer questions 5–7.

5. Benedict has saved $91 from last year and would like to baby-sit to earn enough to buy a mountain bike. A good quality bike costs at least $300. What numbers of hours h can Benedict baby-sit to reach his goal?

   A $h \geq 14$ C $h \geq 38$
   B $h \geq 23$ D $h \geq 71$

6. Ricardo has agreed to tutor for the school. He owes his older brother $59 and would like to end the summer with at least $400 in savings. How many sessions s can Ricardo tutor to meet his goal?

   F $s \geq 31$ H $s \geq 51$
   G $s \geq 38$ J $s \geq 83$

Job	Pay
Mowing Lawns	$15 per lawn
Baby-Sitting	$5.50 per hour
Tutoring	$9 per session

7. Charlie has agreed to mow his neighbor's lawn each week and will also baby-sit some hours. If he makes $100 or more each week, his parents will charge him rent. How many hours h should Charlie agree to baby-sit each week to avoid paying rent?

   A $h \leq 15$ C $h \leq 21$
   B $h \geq 15$ D $h \geq 21$

Name _____ Date _____ Class _____

LESSON 3-5
Problem Solving
Solving Inequalities With Variables on Both Sides

Write and solve an inequality for each situation.

1. Rosa has decided to sell pet rocks at an art fair for $5 each. She has paid $50 to rent a table at the fair and it costs her $2 to package each rock with a set of instructions. For what numbers of sales will Rosa make a profit?

   _____

   _____

2. Jamie has a job paying $25,000 and expects to receive a $1000 raise each year. Wei has a job paying $19,000 a year and expects a $1500 raise each year. For what span of time is Jamie making more money than Wei?

   _____

   _____

3. Sophia types 75 words per minute and is just starting to write a term paper. Patton already has 510 words written and types at a speed of 60 words per minute. For what numbers of minutes will Sophia have more words typed than Patton?

   _____

   _____

4. Keith is racing his little sister Pattie and has given her a 15 foot head start. She runs 5 ft/sec and he is chasing at 8 ft/sec. For how long can Pattie stay ahead of Keith?

   _____

   _____

The table below shows the population of four cities in 2004 and the amount of population change from 2003. Use this table to answer questions 5–6.

5. If the trends in this table continue, after how many years y will the population of Manchester, NH, be more than the population of Vallejo, CA? Round your answer to the nearest tenth of a year.

   A $y > 0.2$ C $y > 34.6$
   B $y > 6.4$ D $y > 78.6$

6. If the trends in this table continue, for how long x will the population of Carrollton, TX be less than the population of Lakewood, CO? Round your answer to the nearest tenth of a year.

   F $x < 11.7$ H $x < 20.1$
   G $x < 14.6$ J $x < 28.3$

City	Population (2004)	Population Change (from 2003)
Lakewood, CO	141,301	−830
Vallejo, CA	118,349	−1155
Carrollton, TX	117,823	+1170
Manchester, NH	109,310	+261

Problem Solving

3-6 Solving Compound Inequalities

Write and solve an inequality for each situation.

1. The Mexican Tetra is a tropical fish that requires a water temperature between 68 and 77 degrees Fahrenheit, inclusive. An aquarium is heated 8 degrees so that a Tetra can live in it. What temperatures could the water have been before the heating?

   _____

   _____

2. Nerissa's car can travel between 380 and 410 miles on a full tank of gas. She filled her gas tank and drove 45 miles. How many more miles can she drive without running out of gas?

   _____

   _____

3. A local company is hiring trainees with less than 1 year of experience and managers with 5 or more years of experience. Graph the solutions.

   _____

   _____

   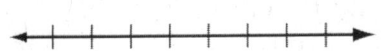

4. Marty's allowance is doubled and is now between $10 and $15, inclusive. What amounts could his allowance have been before the increase? Graph the solutions.

   _____

   _____

   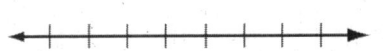

The elliptical orbits of planets bring them closer to and farther from the Sun at different times. The closest (perihelion) and furthest (aphelion) points are given for three planets below. Use this data to answer questions 5–7.

5. Which inequality represents the distances d from the sun to Neptune?

   A $d \leq 4444.5$

   B $d \leq 4545.7$

   C $4444.5 \leq d \leq 4545.7$

   D $d = 4444.5$ OR $d \geq 4545.7$

Planet	Perihelion (in 10^6 km)	Aphelion (in 10^6 km)
Uranus	2741.3	3003.6
Neptune	4444.5	4545.7
Pluto	4435.0	7304.3

6. A NASA probe is traveling between Uranus and Neptune. It is currently between their orbits. Which inequality shows the possible distance p from the probe to the Sun?

   F $1542.1 < p < 1703.2$

   G $2741.3 < p < 4545.7$

   H $3003.6 < p < 4444.5$

   J $7185.8 < p < 7549.3$

7. At what distances o do the orbits of Neptune and Pluto overlap?

   A $4435.0 \leq o \leq 4444.5$

   B $4435.0 \leq o \leq 4545.7$

   C $4444.5 \leq o \leq 7304.3$

   D $4545.7 \leq o \leq 7304.3$

Problem Solving
Solving Absolute-Value Inequalities

Write the correct answer.

1. A carpenter cuts boards that are 2 meters long. It is acceptable for the length to differ from this value by at most 0.05 meters. Write and solve an absolute-value inequality to find the range of acceptable lengths.

2. During a workout, Vince tries to keep his heart rate at 134 beats per minute. His actual heart rate varies from this value by as much as 8 beats per minute. Write and solve an absolute-value inequality to find Vince's range of heart rates.

3. Mai thinks of a secret number. She says that her secret number is more than 11 units away from 50. Write an absolute-value inequality that gives the possible values of Mai's number.

4. Boxes of cereal are supposed to weigh 15.3 ounces each. A quality-control manager finds that the boxes are no more than 0.4 ounces away from this weight. Write an absolute-value inequality that gives the range of possible weights of the boxes.

The table gives the typical lifespan for several mammals. Use the table for questions 5–7. **Select the best answer.**

5. Which absolute-value inequality gives the number of years a goat may live?
   A $|x-6| \leq 11$ C $|x-24| \leq 6$
   B $|x-15| \leq 9$ D $|x-30| \leq 9$

6. Which mammal has a lifespan that can be represented by the absolute-value inequality $|x - 12.5| \leq 2.5$?
   F Antelope   H Otter
   G Koala   I Wolf

7. The inequality $|x - 17| \leq c$ gives the number of years a panda may live. What is the value of c?
   A 3   C 14
   B 6   D 20

Mammal	Lifespan (years)	Mammal	Lifespan (years)
Antelope	10 to 25	Otter	15 to 20
Goat	6 to 24	Panda	14 to 20
Koala	10 to 15	Wolf	13 to 15

Source: http://www.sandiegozoo.org/animalbytes/a-mammal.html

Name _____ Date _____ Class _____

LESSON 4-1 Problem Solving
Graphing Relationships

Sketch a graph for the given situation. Tell whether the graph is discrete or continuous.

1. A giraffe is born 6 feet tall and continues to grow at a steady rate until it is fully grown.

   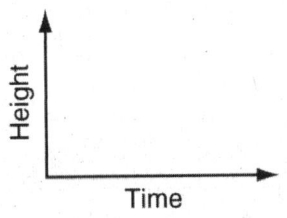

2. The price of a used car is discounted $200 each week.

   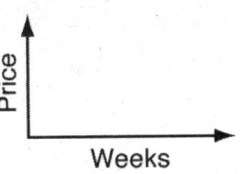

3. A city planner buys more buses as the population of her city grows.

   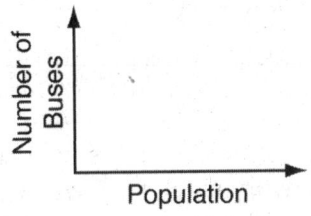

4. Joseph is sky-diving. At first, he is free-falling rapidly and then he releases his parachute to slow his descent until he reaches the ground.

   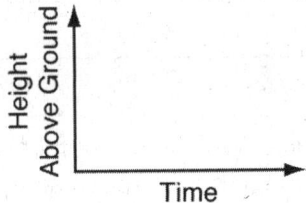

Choose the graph that best represents the situation.

5. Rebekah turns on the oven and sets it to 300 °F. She bakes a tray of cookies and then turns the oven off.
   - A Graph 1
   - B Graph 2
   - C Graph 3
   - D Graph 4

6. Leon puts ice cubes in his soup to cool it down before eating it.
   - F Graph 1
   - G Graph 2
   - H Graph 3
   - J Graph 4

7. Barlee has the flu and her temperature rises slowly until it reaches 101 °F.
   - A Graph 1
   - B Graph 2
   - C Graph 3
   - D Graph 4

8. On a hot day, Karin walks into and out of an air-conditioned building.
   - F Graph 1
   - G Graph 2
   - H Graph 3
   - J Graph 4

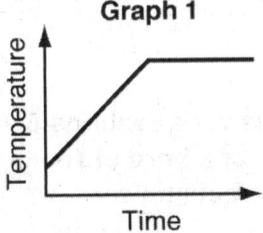
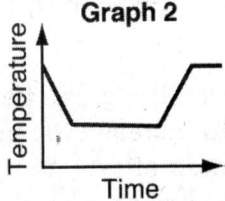
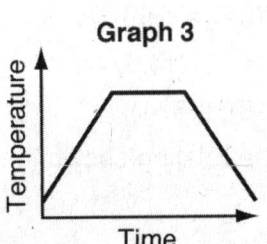
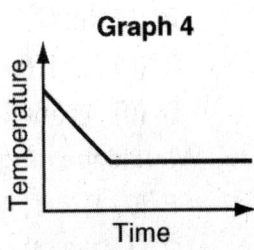

Name _____ Date _____ Class _____

LESSON 4-2

Problem Solving
Relations and Functions

Give the domain and range of each relation and tell whether it is a function.

1. The mapping diagram shows the ages x and grade level y of four children.

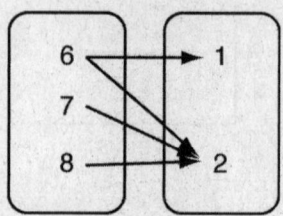

_____
_____

2.

Age x	Shoe Size y
6	8
9	10
12	10
15	10.5
18	11

_____
_____

3. The list represents the number of cars sold and the bonus received by the salespeople of a car dealership.
{(1, 50), (2, 50), (3, 100), (4, 150)}

_____
_____

4. A 2-inch-tall plant grows at a rate of 2.5 inches every week for 5 weeks. Let x represent the number of weeks and y represent the height of the plant.

_____
_____

Use the graph below to answer questions 5–6. A conservation group has been working to increase the population of a herd of Asian elephants. The graph shows the results of their efforts. Select the correct answer.

5. Which relation represents the information in the graph?

   A {(1, 4.5), (2, 6), (3, 10), (4, 14.5)}

   B {(1, 5), (2, 6), (3, 10), (4, 15)}

   C {(4.5, 1), (6, 2), (10, 3), (14.5, 4)}

   D {(5, 1), (6, 2), (10, 3), (15, 4)}

6. What is the range of the relation shown in the graph?

   F {0, 1, 2, 3, 4, 5}

   G {1, 2, 3, 4}

   H {4.5, 6, 10, 14.5}

   J {5, 6, 10, 15}

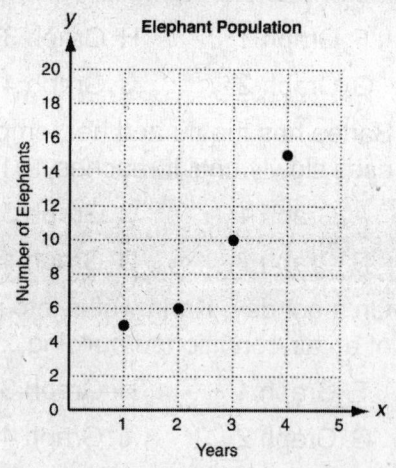

Name _____ Date _____ Class _____

LESSON 4-3 Problem Solving
Writing Functions

Identify the independent and dependent variables. Write a rule in function notation for each situation.

1. Each state receives electoral votes based on the number of representatives it has in the House of Representatives.

Representatives	2	4	6	8
Electoral Votes	4	6	8	10

   _____
   _____
   _____

2. Terry has 30 pieces of gum and gives 2 pieces to each of his friends.

   _____
   _____
   _____

3. Ronaldo is buying bacon that costs $4.29 per pound.

   _____
   _____
   _____

4. A personal trainer charges $50 for the first session and $40 for every session thereafter.

   _____
   _____
   _____

International travel and business require the conversion of American dollars into foreign currency. During part of 2005, one American dollar was worth 6 Croatian Kuna. Select the best answer.

5. An American bank wishes to convert d dollars into kuna. Which function rule describes the situation?

   A $f(d) = \dfrac{d}{6}$ C $f(d) = \dfrac{6}{d}$

   B $f(d) = 6d$ D $f(d) = d + 6$

6. A Croatian company already has $100,000 and is going to convert k kuna into dollars. Which function rule can be used to determine the total amount of American dollars this company will have?

   F $f(x) = 100{,}000 + 6k$

   G $f(x) = 100{,}000 + \dfrac{k}{6}$

   H $f(x) = 100{,}000k + 6$

   J $f(x) = 100{,}000 + \dfrac{6}{k}$

7. Macon has $100 and is thinking about converting some of it into kuna. What is a reasonable range for this situation?

   A $0 \le y \le 6$ C $0 \le y \le 100$

   B $0 \le y \le 16.7$ D $0 \le y \le 600$

8. Robin converts x dollars into y kuna. Which expression is the independent variable in this situation?

   F x H $6x$

   G y J $6y$

9. Jakov converts n kuna into c dollars. Which expression is the dependent variable in this situation?

   A n C $\dfrac{n}{6}$

   B c D $\dfrac{c}{6}$

Name _____ Date _____ Class _____

LESSON 4-4 Problem Solving
Graphing Functions

In 1998, Hurricane Bonnie approached the United States at a speed of 8 miles per hour. The function $y = 8x$ describes how many miles y Hurricane Bonnie traveled in x hours.

1. Complete the table by generating ordered pairs.

x	y = 8x	(x, y)
0		
1		
2		
3		
4		

2. Graph the function $y = 8x$.

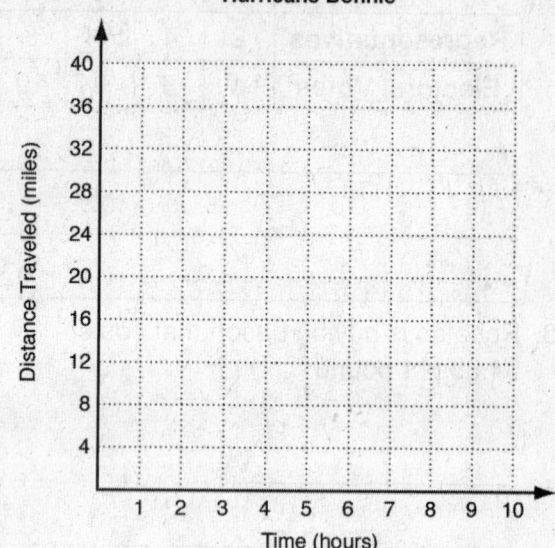

3. Use the graph to estimate how far Hurricane Bonnie traveled in 3.5 hours.

_____

Select the correct answer.

4. The graph below shows the relation between the cost of an item and the sales tax due. Which function is graphed below?

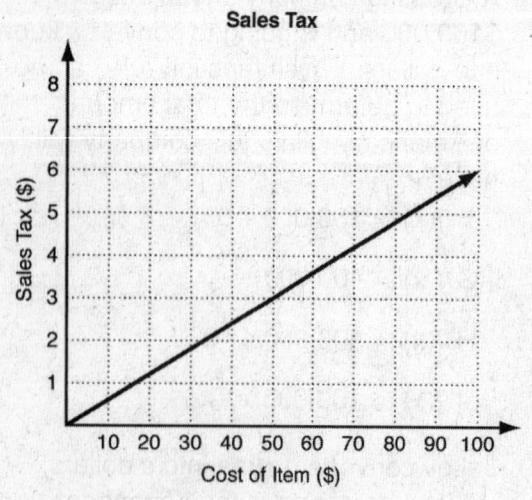

A $y = \dfrac{6}{x}$ C $y = \dfrac{x}{6}$

B $y = 0.06x$ D $y = 6x$

5. The graph below shows the relation between Jeremy's age and the number of times per year he refused to eat his brussel sprouts. Which function is graphed for the domain {1, 2, 3, 4, 5}?

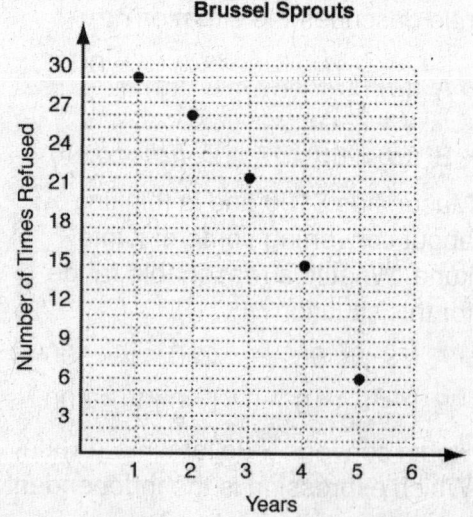

F $y = 30 - x$ H $y = 30 - x^2$

G $y = x + 28$ J $y = 29x$

Name _____ Date _____ Class _____

LESSON 4-5 Problem Solving
Scatter Plots and Trend Lines

Fawn is trying to improve her reading skills by taking a speed-reading class. She is measuring how many words per minute (wpm) she can read after each week of the class.

1. Graph a scatter plot using the given data.

Weeks	1	2	3	4	5
wpm	220	230	260	260	280

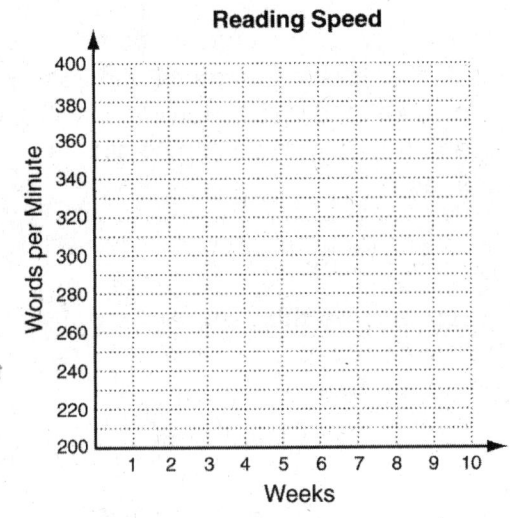

2. Describe the correlation illustrated by the scatter plot.

   _____

   _____

3. Draw a trend line and use it to predict the number of words per minute that Fawn will read after 8 weeks of this class.

   _____

4. Fawn is paying for this class each week out of her savings account. Identify the correlation between the number of classes and Fawn's account balance.

   _____

   _____

Choose the scatter plot that best represents the described relationship.

5. the distance a person runs and how physically tired that person is
   - A Graph 1
   - B Graph 2
   - C Graph 3
   - D Graph 4

6. the price of a new car and the number of hours in a day
   - F Graph 1
   - G Graph 2
   - H Graph 3
   - J Graph 4

7. a person's age and the amount of broccoli the person eats
   - A Graph 1
   - B Graph 2
   - C Graph 3
   - D Graph 4

8. the number of cats in a barn and the number of mice in that barn
   - F Graph 1
   - G Graph 2
   - H Graph 3
   - J Graph 4

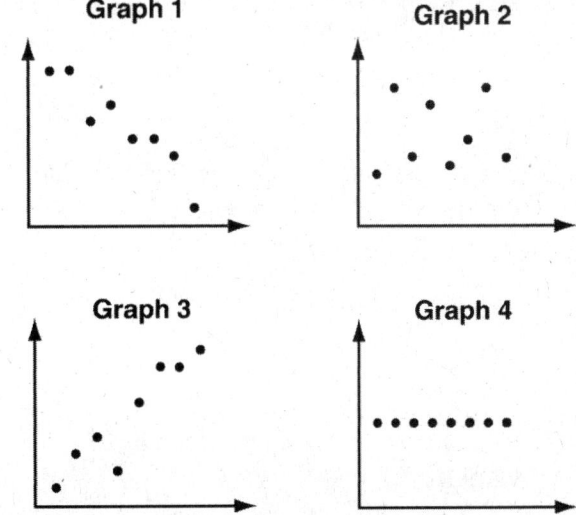

Original content Copyright © by Holt McDougal. Additions and changes to the original content are the responsibility of the instructor.

Problem Solving
4-6 Arithmetic Sequences

Find the indicated term of each arithmetic sequence.

1. Darnell has a job and his saving his paychecks each week.

Weeks	1	2	3	4
Savings	$130	$260	$390	$520

   How much will Darnell have saved after 11 weeks?

   _____

2. A tube containing 3 ounces of toothpaste is being used at a rate of 0.15 ounces per day. How much toothpaste will be in the tube after one week?

   _____

3. A new car costs $13,000 and is depreciating by $900 each year. How much will the car be worth after 4 years?

   _____

4. Jessie is playing an arcade game that costs 50¢ for the first game and 25¢ to continue if she loses. How much will she spend on the game if she continues 9 times?

   _____

Use the graph below to answer questions 5–9. The graph shows the size of Ivor's ant colony over the first four weeks. Assume the ant population will continue to grow at the same rate. Select the best answer.

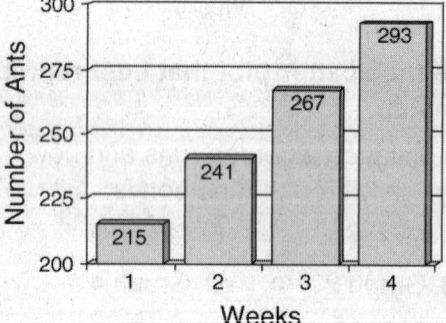

5. Which of the following shows how many ants Ivor will have in the next three weeks?

   A 315, 341, 367
   B 317, 343, 369
   C 318, 334, 350
   D 319, 345, 371

6. Which rule can be used to find how large the colony will be in *n* weeks?

   F $a_n = 215 + 26n$
   G $a_n = 215n + 26$
   H $a_n = 215(n-1) + 26$
   J $a_n = 215 + 26(n-1)$

7. How many ants will Ivor have in 27 weeks?

   A 891   C 5616
   B 917   D 5831

8. Ivor's ants weigh 1.5 grams each. How many grams do all of his ants weigh in 13 weeks?

   F 660.5   H 722
   G 683   J 790.5

9. When the colony reaches 1385 ants, Ivor's ant farm will not be big enough for all of them. In how many weeks will the ant population be too large?

   A 45   C 47
   B 46   D 48

Name _____ Date _____ Class _____

LESSON 5-1 Problem Solving
Identifying Linear Functions

Write the correct answer.

1. A daycare center charges a $75 enrollment fee plus $100 per week. The function $f(x) = 100x + 75$ gives the cost of daycare for x weeks. Graph this function and give its domain and range.

   _____

   _____

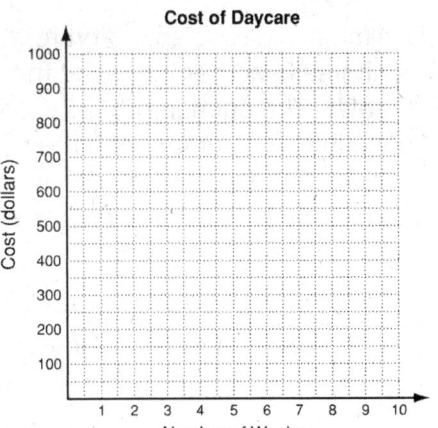

2. A family swimming pool holds 60 m³ of water. The function $f(x) = 60 - 0.18x$ gives the cubic meters of water in the pool, taking into account water lost to evaporation over x days. Graph this function and give its domain and range.

   _____

   _____

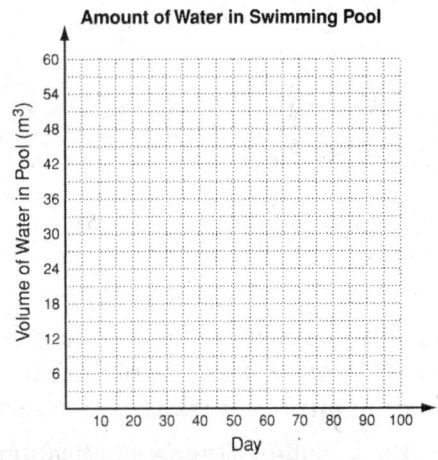

Elijah is using a rowing machine. The table shows how many Calories he can burn for certain lengths of time. Select the best answer.

Time (min)	Calories
2	24
4	48
6	72
8	96
10	120

3. Which function could be used to describe the number of Calories burned after x minutes?

   F $y = 12 + x$ H $xy = 12$
   G $x + y = 12$ J $y = 12x$

4. What is the domain of the function?

   A {0, 1, 2, 3, ...}   C $x \varepsilon 0$
   B {2, 4, 6, ...}   D $x \varepsilon 2$

5. What is the range of the function?

   F {0, 12, 24, 36, ...}   H $y \varepsilon 0$
   G {24, 48, 72, ...}   J $y \varepsilon 24$

6. Elijah graphed the function in problem 4. Which best describes the graph?

   A It is a line that increases from left to right.
   B It is a line that decreases from left to right.
   C It forms a U-shape.
   D It forms a V-shape.

Name _____ Date _____ Class _____

LESSON 5-2
Problem Solving
Using Intercepts

Write the correct answer.

1. Naima has $40 to spend on refreshments for herself and her friends at the movie theater. The equation $5x + 2y = 40$ describes the number of large popcorns x and small drinks y she can buy. Graph this function and find its intercepts.

2. Turner is reading a 400-page book. He reads 4 pages every 5 minutes. The number of pages Turner has left to read after x minutes is represented by the function $f(x) = 400 - \frac{4}{5}x$. Graph this function and find its intercepts.

The graph shows the distance of an elevator at Chimney Rock, North Carolina, from its destination as a function of time. Use the graph to answer questions 3–6. Select the best answer.

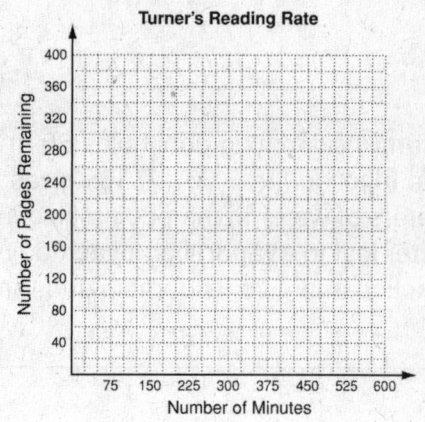

3. What is the x-intercept of this function?

   A 0   C 258

   B 30   D 300

4. What does the x-intercept represent?

   F the total distance the elevator travels

   G the number of seconds that have passed for any given distance

   H the number of seconds it takes the elevator to reach its destination

   J the distance that the elevator has traveled at any given time

5. What is the y-intercept for this function?

   A 0   C 258

   B 30   D 300

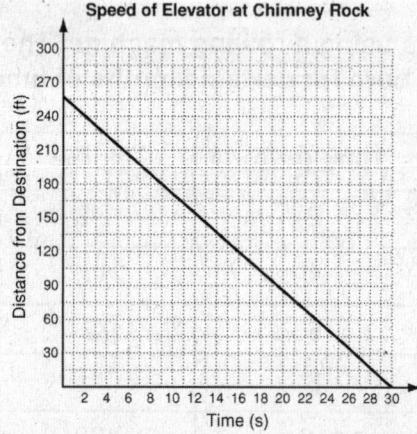

6. What does the y-intercept represent?

   F the total distance the elevator travels

   G the number of seconds that have passed for any given distance

   H the number of seconds it takes the elevator to reach its destination

   J the distance that the elevator has traveled at any given time

Name _____ Date _____ Class _____

LESSON 5-3 Problem Solving
Rate of Change and Slope

Write the correct answer.

1. The table shows the cost per pound of Granny Smith apples.

Weight (lb)	1	2	3	4
Cost ($)	1.49	2.98	4.47	5.96

   Describe the rate(s) of change shown by the data.

   _____

   _____

2. The table shows Gabe's height on his birthday for five years. Find the rate of change during each time interval.

Age	9	11	12	13	15
Height (in.)	58	59.5	61.5	65	69

   _____

   _____

   When did the greatest rate of change occur? _____

   When was the rate of change the least?

   _____

3. The table shows the distance of a courier from her destination.

Time (p.m.)	2:15	2:30	2:45	3:00
Distance (mi)	5.4	5.5	5.0	0.5

   What is the rate of change from 2:15 p.m. to 2:30 p.m.? What does this rate of change mean?

   _____

   _____

   During which two time periods were the rates of change the same?

   _____

The graph below tracks regular gasoline prices from July 2004 to December 2004. Use the graph to answer questions 5–8. Select the best answer.

4. What is the slope of the line from November to December?

   A −4   C −0.04
   B −1   D −0.01

5. During which time interval did the cost decrease at the greatest rate?

   F Jul to Aug   H Sep to Oct
   G Aug to Sep   J Oct to Nov

6. During which time interval was the slope positive?

   A Jul to Aug   C Sep to Oct
   B Aug to Sep   D Oct to Nov

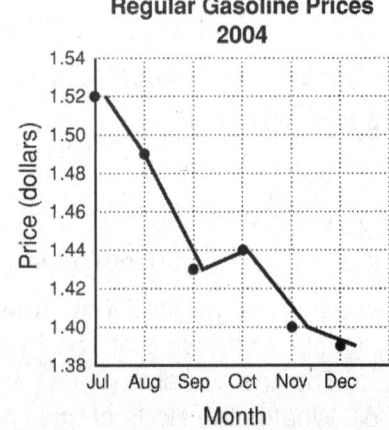

Regular Gasoline Prices 2004

7. What was the rate of change from October to December?

   F −0.05   H 0.025
   G −0.025   J 0.05

Name _____ Date _____ Class _____

LESSON 5-4
Problem Solving
The Slope Formula

Write the correct answer.

1. The graph shows the number of emergency kits assembled by volunteers over a period of days. Find the slope of the line. Then tell what the slope represents.

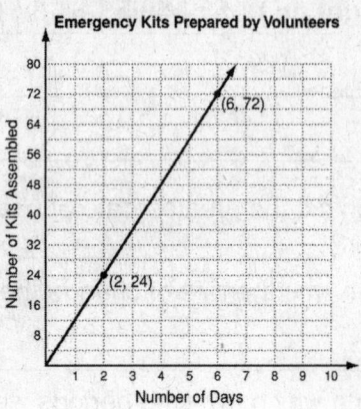

_____
_____

2. The graph shows how much flour is in a bag at different times. Find the slope of the line. Then tell what the slope represents.

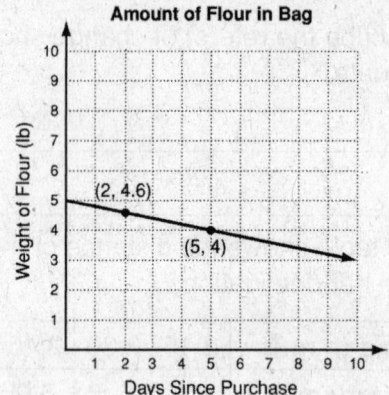

_____
_____

3. The function $20x - y = 250$ describes the profit y Bridget can make from selling x pairs of earrings. The graph of this function is a line. Find its slope. _____

The graph below shows the cost of membership at Fabulously Fit. Use the graph to answer questions 4–7. Select the best answer.

4. What is the slope of the line?

   A 24 C 50
   B 35 D 70

5. What does the slope represent?

   F the enrollment fee
   G the late payment fee
   H the total cost of membership
   I the monthly membership fee

6. A second line is graphed that shows the cost of membership at The Fitness Studio. The line contains (0, 35) and (5, 85). What is the slope of this line?

   A 10 C 45
   B 20 D 50

7. How much greater is the monthly fee at Fabulously Fit than The Fitness Studio?

   F $15   H $35
   G $25   I $40

Name _____ Date _____ Class _____

LESSON 5-5

Problem Solving
The Midpoint and Distance Formulas

Write the correct answer.

1. From base camp, a hiker walks 3.5 miles west and 1.5 miles north. Another hiker walks 2 miles east and 0.5 miles south. To the nearest tenth of a mile, how far apart are the hikers?

   _____

2. A ramp begins at the end of a sidewalk and rises 15 vertical feet over a horizontal distance of 150 feet. Find the length of the ramp to the nearest tenth of a foot. (Hint: Use (0, 0) for the end of the sidewalk.)

   _____

3. From school, George walked 8 blocks north and 3 blocks east. Pedro walked 6 blocks south and 1 block west. If they decide to meet each other at the exact halfway point, describe the shortest route Pedro could take to get there.

   _____

4. A belt on an assembly line rises 35 feet over a horizontal distance of 100 feet. When the belt jammed, an item on the belt was at the halfway point. How high above the ground was the item?

   _____

A police department sketch artist drew a map of the St. Petersburg, Florida, area on a coordinate grid on the main wall of their office. Coordinates of four locations are shown in the table. Choose the letter of the best answer.

Brandon	(11.2, 14.6)
Clearwater	(1, 15)
Treasure Island	(2.2, 11)
Ruskin	(8.5, 9.9)

5. Each unit represents 3 miles. What is the distance from Clearwater to Treasure Island?

   A about 4.2 miles
   B about 5.4 miles
   C about 12.5 miles
   D about 16.3 miles

6. An emergency occurs midway between Ruskin and Brandon. Where on the grid does the officer place a tack to show this location?

   F at about (1, 2)
   G at about (5, 5)
   H at about (5, 8)
   I at about (10, 12)

7. An officer wants to connect Treasure Island and Brandon with a string. If each unit on the wall is 1 foot long, how much string does he need?

   A about 4 feet
   B about 4.7 feet
   C about 9.2 feet
   D about 9.7 feet

8. A police helicopter flies directly from Clearwater to Ruskin. Each unit represents 4.5 kilometers. How far did the helicopter travel?

   F about 41 kilometers
   G about 27 kilometers
   H about 10 kilometers
   I about 8 kilometers

Name _____ Date _____ Class_____

LESSON 5-6
Problem Solving
Direct Variation

Write the correct answer.

1. Wesley earns $6.50 per hour at the bookstore. The total amount of his paycheck varies directly with the number of hours he works. Write a direct variation equation for the amount of money y Wesley earns for working x hours.

   _____

2. The equation $-4x + y = 0$ relates the number of pages in a photo album y to the number of pictures in the album x. Tell whether the relationship is a direct variation. Explain your answer.

   _____

3. The formula $9x - 5y = -160$ relates the temperature in degrees Fahrenheit y to the temperature in degrees Celsius x. Tell whether the relationship is a direct variation. Explain your answer.

   _____

4. The number of miles driven varies directly with the number of gallons of gas used. Erin drove 297 miles on 9 gallons of gas. How far would she be able to drive on 14 gallons of gas?

   _____

Select the best answer.

5. The table shows the relationship between the number of lemons purchased and their cost.

Lemons x	1	2	3	4
Cost y	0.1	0.2	0.3	0.4

   Is the relationship a direct variation?

   A Yes; it can be written as $y = 0.1x$.
   B Yes; it can be written as $y = 10x$.
   C No; it cannot be written as $y = kx$.
   D No; the relationship is not a function.

6. The table shows the relationship between the hours since sunrise and the temperature in degrees Celsius.

Hour x	1	2	3	4
Temp. y	25	26	28	32

   Is the relationship a direct variation?

   F Yes; it can be written as $y = 25x$.
   G Yes; it can be written as $y = 8x$.
   H No; it cannot be written as $y = kx$.
   J No; the relationship is not a function.

7. The Diaz family is driving at a constant speed on the highway so their distance varies directly with their speed. They traveled 17.5 miles in 15 minutes. How far did they travel in 2 hours?

   A 50 miles   C 140 miles
   B 70 miles   D 262.5 miles
                  (17.5 times 15)

8. On July 26, 2005, it rained a record 37 inches in Mumbai, India, in a 24-hour period. Which equation of direct variation relates the number of inches of rain y to the number of hours x?

   F $y = \dfrac{24}{37}x$ H $y = 24x$

   G $y = \dfrac{37}{24}x$ J $y = 37x$

Name _____ Date _____ Class _____

LESSON 5-7 Problem Solving
Slope-Intercept Form

The cost of food for an honor roll dinner is $300 plus $10 per student. The cost of the food as a function of the number of students is shown in the graph. Write the correct answer.

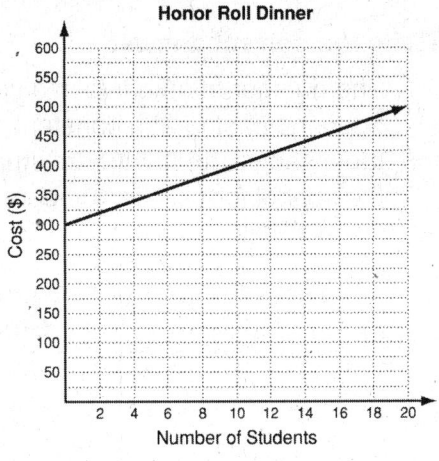

1. Write an equation that represents the cost as a function of the number of students.

   _____

2. Identify the slope and y-intercept and describe their meanings.

   _____

   _____

3. Find the cost of the food for 50 students.   _____

Laura is on a two-day hike in the Smoky Mountains. She hiked 8 miles on the first day and is hiking at a rate of 3 mi/h on the second day. Her total distance as a function of time is shown in the graph. Select the best answer.

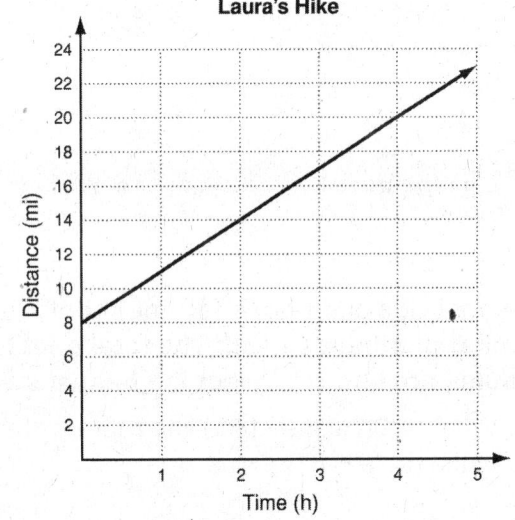

4. Which equation represents Laura's total distance as a function of time?

   A $y = 3x$ C $y = 3x + 8$
   B $y = 8x$ D $y = 8x + 3$

5. What does the slope represent?

   F Laura's total distance after one day
   G Laura's total distance after two days
   H the number of miles Laura hiked per hour on the first day
   J the number of miles Laura hikes per hour on the second day

6. What does the y-intercept represent?

   A Laura's total distance after one day
   B Laura's total distance after two days
   C the number of miles Laura hiked per hour on the first day
   D the number of miles Laura hikes per hour on the second day

7. What will be Laura's total distance if she hikes for 6 hours on the second day?

   F 14 miles   H 26 miles
   G 18 miles   J 28 miles

Name _____ Date _____ Class _____

LESSON 5-8
Problem Solving
Point-Slope Form

Write the correct answer.

1. The number of students in a school has been increasing at a constant rate. The table shows the number of students in the school for certain numbers of years since 1995.

Years Since 1995	Number of Students
0	118
5	124
10	130

   Write an equation in point-slope form that represents this linear function.

   _____

   Write the equation in slope-intercept form.

   _____

   Assuming the rate of change remains constant, how many students will be in the school in 2010?

   _____

2. Toni is finishing a scarf at a constant rate. The table shows the number of hours Toni has spent knitting this week and the corresponding number of rows in the scarf.

Toni's Knitting	
Hours	Rows of Knitting
2	38
4	44
6	50

   Write an equation in slope-intercept form that represents this linear function.

   _____

3. A photo lab manager graphed the cost of having photos developed as a function of the number of photos in the order. The graph is a line with a slope of $\frac{1}{10}$ that passes through (10, 6). Write an equation in slope-intercept form that describes the cost to have photos developed. How much does it cost to have 25 photos developed?

   _____

The cost of a cell phone for one month is a linear function of the number of minutes used. The total cost for 20, 35, and 40 additional minutes are shown. Select the best answer.

4. What is the slope of the line represented in the table?

   A 0.1 C 2
   B 0.4 D 2.5

5. What would be the monthly cost if 60 additional minutes were used?

   F $64 H $84
   G $72 I $150

Cell-Phone Costs			
Number of Additional Minutes	20	35	40
Total Cost	$48	$54	$56

6. What does the y-intercept of the function represent?

   A total cost of the bill
   B cost per additional minute
   C number of additional minutes used
   D cost with no additional minutes used

Original content Copyright © by Holt McDougal. Additions and changes to the original content are the responsibility of the instructor.

Name _____ Date _____ Class _____

LESSON 5-9 Problem Solving
Slopes of Parallel and Perpendicular Lines

Write the correct answer.

1. Hamid is making a stained-glass window. He needs a piece of glass that is a perfect parallelogram. Hamid lays a piece of glass that he has cut on a coordinate grid. Show that the glass is in the shape of a parallelogram.

   _____
   _____
   _____
   _____

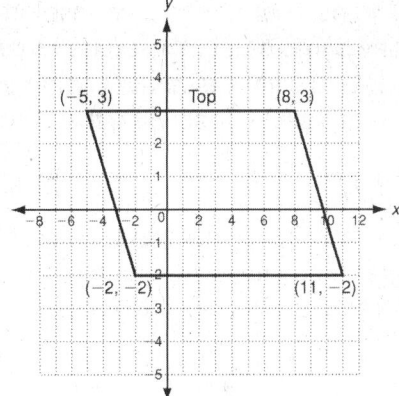

2. Norelle's garden is shown at right. Is her garden in the shape of a right triangle? Justify your answer.

   _____
   _____
   _____
   _____

Norelle's Garden

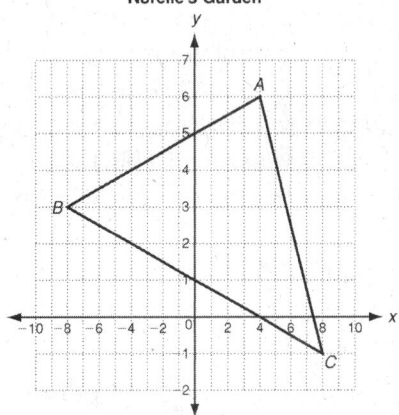

**The graph shows a street map.
Use it to answer questions 3–5.**

3. The district plans to add Industrial Road next year. It will run perpendicular to Smith Ave. and pass through (−14, 2). What equation will describe the location of Industrial Road?

   A $y = 14 - x$ C $y = -14$
   B $y = x - 14$ D $x = -14$

4. In two years, the business district plans to add Stock Street. It will run parallel to Market Blvd. and pass through (−1, 5). What equation will describe the location of Stock Street?

   F $y = -7x + 12$ H $y = \dfrac{1}{7}x + \dfrac{34}{7}$
   G $y = -7x - 2$ J $y = \dfrac{1}{7}x + \dfrac{36}{7}$

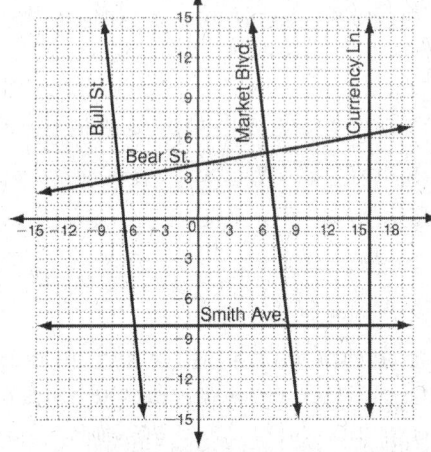

5. What is the slope of a street parallel to Bear Street?

   A −7
   B $-\dfrac{1}{7}$
   C $\dfrac{1}{7}$
   D 7

Original content Copyright © by Holt McDougal. Additions and changes to the original content are the responsibility of the instructor.

Name _____ Date _____ Class _____

LESSON 5-10
Problem Solving
Transforming Linear Functions

Write the correct answer.

1. The number of camp counselors at a day camp must include 1 counselor for every 8 campers, plus 3 camp directors. The function describing the number of counselors is $f(x) = \frac{1}{8}x + 3$ where x is the number of campers. How will the graph change if the number of camp directors is reduced to 2?

   _____

2. A city water service has a base cost of $12 per month plus $1.50 per hundred cubic feet (HCF) of water. Write a function $f(x)$ to represent the cost of water as a function of x, amount used. Then write a second function $g(x)$ to represent the cost if the rate rises to $1.60 per HCF.

   _____

   How would the graph of $g(x)$ compare to the graph of $f(x)$?

   _____

3. Owen earns a base salary plus a commission that is a percent of his total sales. His total weekly pay is described by $f(x) = 0.15x + 325$, where x is his total sales in dollars. What is the change in Owen's salary plan if his total weekly pay function changes to $g(x) = 0.20x + 325$?

   _____

An attorney charges $250 per hour. The graph represents the cost of the attorney as a function of time. Select the best answer.

4. When a traveling fee is added to the attorney's rate for cases outside the city limits, the graph is translated up 50 units. What function $h(x)$ would describe the attorney's rate with the traveling fee?

   A $h(x) = 250x - 50$
   B $h(x) = 250x + 50$
   C $h(x) = 200x$
   D $h(x) = 300x$

5. The attorney's paralegal has an hourly rate of $150. How would you transform the graph of $f(x)$ into a graph for the paralegal's rate?

   F Reflect it over the y-axis.
   G Translate it down 100 units.
   H Translate it to the left 100 units.
   J Rotate it clockwise about (0, 0).

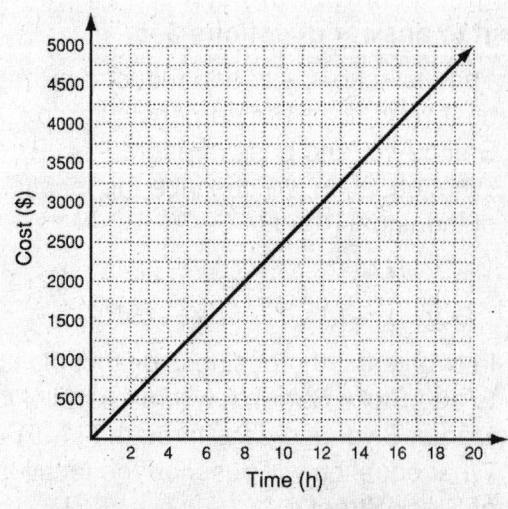

6. Which hourly rate would NOT make the attorney's graph steeper?

   A $225   C $300
   B $275   D $325

Name _____ Date _____ Class _____

LESSON 6-1 Problem Solving
Solving Systems by Graphing

Write the correct answer.

1. Mr. Malone is putting money in two savings accounts. Account A started with $200 and Account B started with $300. Mr. Malone deposits $15 in Account A and $10 in Account B each month. In how many months will the accounts have the same balance? What will that balance be?

   _____

2. Tom currently has 5 comic books in his collection and has subscribed to receive 5 new comic books each month. His uncle has 145 comic books, but sends 5 to each of his 3 nieces each month. In how many months will they have the same number of comic books? How many books will that be?

   _____

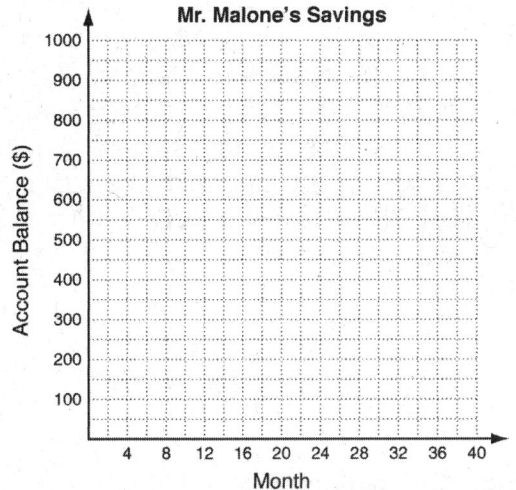
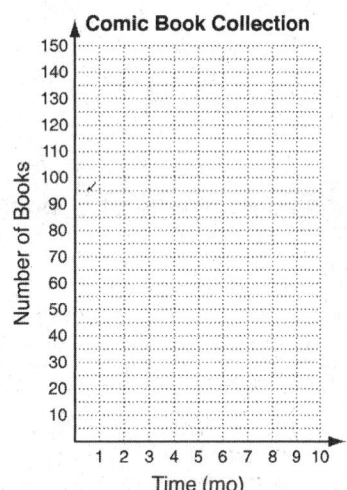

The graph below compares the heights of two trees. Use the graph to answer questions 3–5. Select the best answer.

3. How many years after planting will the trees be the same height?

   A 1 years   C 4 years
   B 2 years   D 6 years

4. Which system of equations is represented by the graph?

   F $\begin{cases} y = x+2 \\ y = 0.5x+2 \end{cases}$ H $\begin{cases} y = 2x+4 \\ y = x+4 \end{cases}$

   G $\begin{cases} y = x+2 \\ y = 0.5x+4 \end{cases}$ J $\begin{cases} y = 4x-2 \\ y = 2x+2 \end{cases}$

5. How fast does the tree that started at 2 feet tall grow?

   A 0.5 ft/yr   C 1.5 ft/yr
   B 1 ft/yr   D 2 ft/yr

6. How fast does the tree that started at 4 feet tall grow?

   F 0.5 ft/yr   H 1.5 ft/yr
   G 1 ft/yr   J 2 ft/yr

LESSON 6-2

Problem Solving
Solving Systems by Substitution

Write the correct answer.

1. Maribel has $1.25 in her pocket. The money is in quarters and dimes. There are a total of 8 coins. How many quarters and dimes does Maribel have in her pocket?

   _____

   _____

2. Fabulously Fit offers memberships for $35 per month plus a $50 enrollment fee. The Fitness Studio offers memberships for $40 per month plus a $35 enrollment fee. In how many months will the fitness clubs cost the same? What will the cost be?

   _____

3. Vong grilled 21 burgers at a block party. He grilled the same number of pounds of turkey burgers as hamburgers. Each turkey burger weighed $\frac{1}{4}$ pound and each hamburger weighed $\frac{1}{3}$ pound. How many of each did Vong grill?

   _____

   _____

4. Kate bought 3 used CDs and 1 used DVD at the bookstore. Her friend Joel bought 2 used CDs and 2 used DVDs at the same store. If Kate spent $20 and Joel spent $22, determine the cost of a used CD and a used DVD.

   _____

   _____

Use the chart below to answer questions 5–8. Select the best answer. The chart compares the quotes that the Masons received from four different flooring contractors to tear out and replace a floor.

5. Which expression shows the total cost if the work is done by Dad's Floors?

   A 8 + 150x   C 150(8x)
   B 150 + 8x   D 158x

6. How many square feet would the Masons need to have installed to make the total cost of V.I.P. Inc. the same as the total cost of Floorshop?

   F 10 sq ft   H 100 sq ft
   G 200 sq ft   J 350 sq ft

7. When the total costs of V.I.P. Inc. and Floorshop are the same, what is the total cost?

   A $1125.00   C $1950.00
   B $1900.00   D $3187.50

Contractor	Cost to tear out old floor	Cost of new floor per square foot
Smith & Son	$250	$8.00
V.I.P. Inc.	$350	$7.75
Dad's Floors	$150	$8.00
Floorshop	$300	$8.25

8. How many square feet would the Masons need to have installed to make the total cost of Smith & Son the same as the total cost of V.I.P. Inc.?

   F 80 sq ft   H 400 sq ft
   G 100 sq ft   J 1000 sq ft

Name _____ Date _____ Class _____

LESSON 6-3
Problem Solving
Solving Systems by Elimination

Write the correct answer.

1. Mr. Nguyen bought a package of 3 chicken legs and a package of 7 chicken wings. Ms. Dawes bought a package of 3 chicken legs and a package of 6 chicken wings. Mr. Nguyen bought 45 ounces of chicken. Ms. Dawes bought 42 ounces of chicken. How much did each chicken leg and each chicken wing weigh?

   _____

   _____

2. Jayce bought 2 bath towels and returned 3 hand towels. His sister Jayna bought 3 bath towels and 3 hand towels. Jayce's bill was $5. Jayna's bill was $45. What are the prices of a bath towel and a hand towel?

   _____

   _____

3. The Lees spent $31 on movie tickets for 2 adults and 3 children. The Macias spent $26 on movie tickets for 2 adults and 2 children. What are the prices for adult and child movie tickets?

   _____

   _____

4. Last month Stephanie spent $57 on 4 allergy shots and 1 office visit. This month she spent $9 after 1 office visit and a refund for 2 allergy shots from her insurance company. How much does an office visit cost? an allergy shot?

   _____

   _____

Use the chart below to answer questions 5–6. Select the best answer.
The chart shows the price per pound for dried fruit.

Dried Fruit Price List			
Pineapple	Apple	Mango	Papaya
$7.50/lb	$7.00/lb	$8.00/lb	$7.25/lb

5. A customer bought 5 pounds of mango and papaya for $37.75. How many pounds of each fruit did the customer buy?

   A 2 lbs mango and 3 lbs papaya

   B 3 lbs mango and 2 lbs papaya

   C 1 lb mango and 4 lbs papaya

   D 4 lbs mango and 1 lb papaya

6. A store employee made two gift baskets of dried fruit, each costing $100. The first basket had 12 pounds of fruit x and 2 pounds of fruit y. The second basket had 4 pounds of fruit x and 9 pounds of fruit y. Which two fruits did the employee use in the baskets?

   F pineapple and apple

   G apple and mango

   H mango and papaya

   J papaya and pineapple

LESSON 6-4 Problem Solving
Solving Special systems

Write the correct answer.

1. Tyra and Charmian are training for a bike race. Tyra has logged 256 miles so far and rides 48 miles per week. Charmian has logged 125 miles so far and rides 48 miles per week. If these rates continue, will Tyra's distance ever equal Charmian's distance? Explain.

   _____

   _____

2. Metroplexpress and Local Express are courier companies. Metroplexpress charges $15 to pick up a package and $0.50 per mile. Local Express charges $10 to pick up a package and $0.55 per mile. Classify this system and find its solution, if any.

   _____

   _____

3. The Singhs start savings accounts for their twin boys. The accounts earn 5% annual interest. The initial deposit in each account is $200. Classify this system and find its solution, if any.

   _____

   _____

4. Frank earns $8 per hour. Madison earns $7.50 per hour. Frank started working after Madison had already earned $300. If these rates continue, will Frank's earnings ever equal Madison's earnings? If so, when?

   _____

   _____

Select the best answer.

5. A studio apartment at The Oaks costs $400 per month plus a $350 deposit. A studio apartment at Crossroads costs $400 per month plus a $300 deposit. How many solutions does this system have?

   A no solutions
   B 1 solution
   C 2 solutions
   D an infinite number of solutions

6. Jane and Gary are both landscape designers. Jane charges $75 for a consultation plus $25 per hour. Gary charges $50 for a consultation plus $30 per hour. For how many hours will Jane's charges equal Gary's charges?

   F never
   G after 2 hours
   H after 5 hours
   J always

7. A tank filled with 75 liters of water loses 0.5 liter of water per hour. A tank filled with 50 liters of water loses 0.1 liter of water per hour. How would this system be classified?

   A inconsistent
   B dependent
   C consistent and independent
   D consistent and dependent

8. Simon is 3 years older than Renata. Five years ago, Renata was half as old as Simon is now. How old are Simon and Renata now?

   F Simon is 13 and Renata is 10.
   G Simon is 15 and Renata is 10.
   H Simon is 16 and Renata is 8.
   J Simon is 16 and Renata is 13.

LESSON 6-5 Problem Solving
Solving Linear Inequalities

Write the correct answer.

1. Shania would like to give $5 gift cards and $4 teddy bears as party favors. Sixteen people have been invited to the party. Shania has $100 to spend on party favors. Write and graph an inequality to find the number of gift cards x and teddy bears y Shania could purchase.

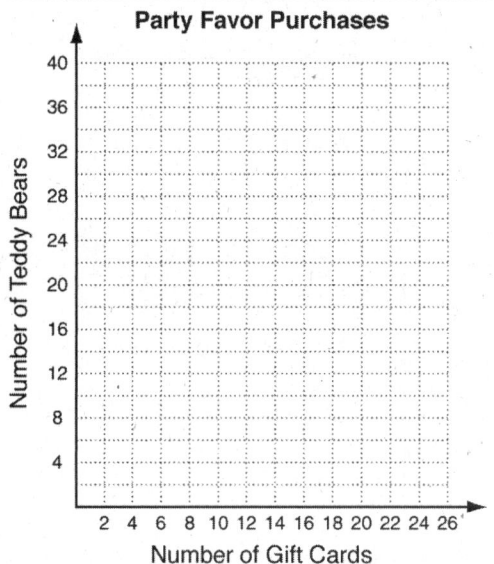

2. Hank has 20 yards of lumber that he can use to build a raised garden. Write and graph a linear inequality that describes the possible lengths and widths of the garden. If Hank wants the dimensions to be whole numbers only, what dimensions would produce the largest area?

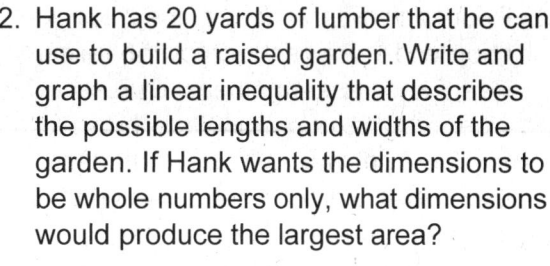

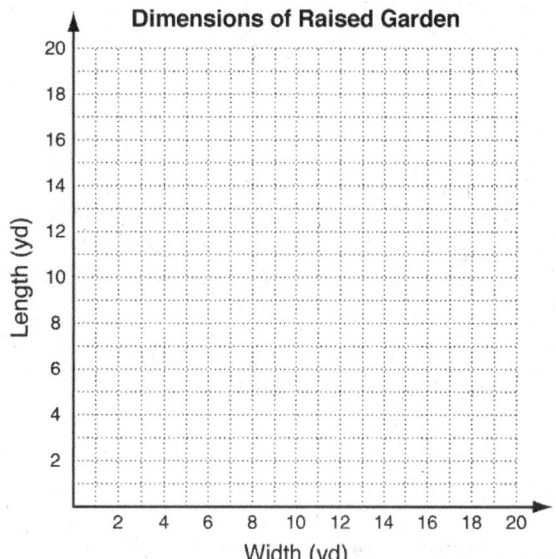

Select the best answer.

3. The royalties for the high school play are $250. Tickets to the play cost $5 for students and $8 for nonstudents. What linear inequality describes the number of student and nonstudent tickets that need to be sold so that the drama class can pay the royalties?

   A $5x + 8y \geq 250$ C $5xy + 8 < 250$
   B $5x + 8y > 250$ D $5xy + 8 \geq 250$

5. A baker is making chocolate and lemon pound cakes. He can make at most 12 cakes at one time. Which inequality describes the situation?

   A $x + y > 12$ C $x + y \leq 12$
   B $x + y \geq 12$ D $x + y < 12$

4. The inequality $x + y \leq 8$ describes the amounts of two juices Annette combines to make a smoothie. Which is a solution to the inequality?

   F (3, 6) H (7, 2)
   G (6, 1) J (0, 10)

6. Erasmus is the master gardener for a university. He wants to plant a mixture of purple and yellow pansies at the west entrance to the campus. From past experience, Erasmus knows that fewer than 350 pansies will fit in the planting area. Which inequality describes the situation?

   F $x + y \geq 350$ H $x + y \leq 350$
   G $x + y > 350$ J $x + y < 350$

Name _____ Date _____ Class _____

LESSON 6-6 Problem Solving
Solving Systems of Linear Inequalities

Write the correct answer.

1. Paul earns $7 per hour at the bagel shop and $12 per hour mowing lawns. Paul needs to earn at least $120 per week, but he must work less than 30 hours per week. Write and graph the system of linear inequalities that describes this situation.

   _____

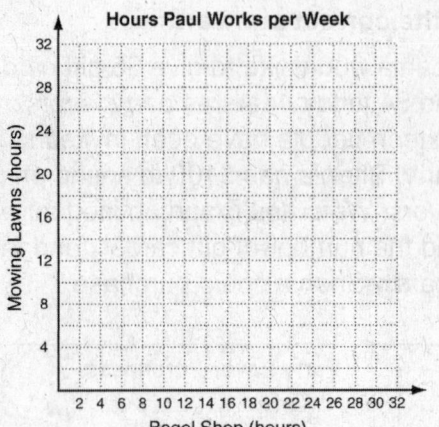

2. Zoe plans to knit a scarf. She wants the scarf to be more than 1 but less than 1.5 feet wide, and more than 6 but less than 8 feet long. Graph all possible dimensions of Zoe's scarf. List two possible combinations.

   _____

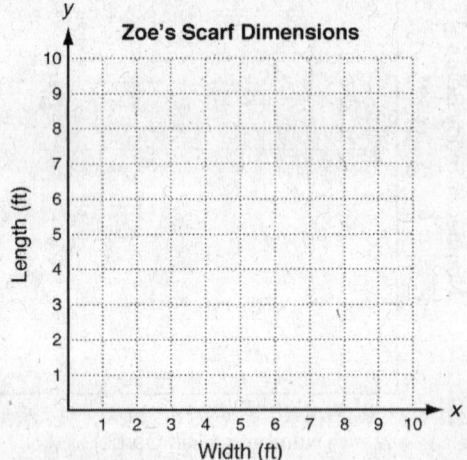

The graph shows the numbers of two types of custom wood tables that can be made to fit a client's needs. Select the best answer.

3. Which system of linear inequalities represents the graph?

   A $\begin{cases} x + y \leq 15 \\ y \geq 12 - \frac{4}{3}x \end{cases}$ C $\begin{cases} x + y \geq 15 \\ y \geq \frac{4}{3}x - 12 \end{cases}$

   B $\begin{cases} y \leq x + 15 \\ y \geq 12 - \frac{4}{3}x \end{cases}$ D $\begin{cases} y \leq 15 - x \\ y \leq \frac{4}{3}x - 12 \end{cases}$

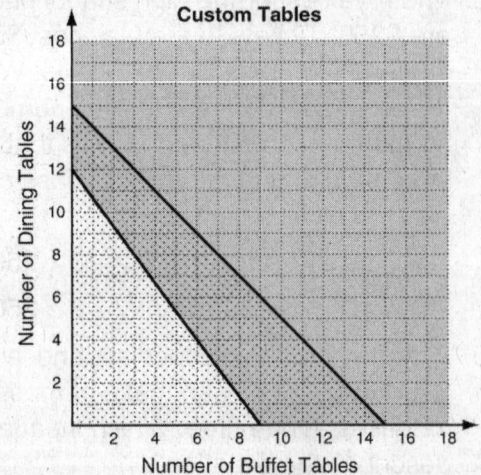

4. If 6 buffet tables are built, which can NOT be the number of dining tables built?

   F 4   H 8
   G 6   J 10

Name _____ Date _____ Class _____

LESSON 7-1 Problem Solving
Integer Exponents

Write the correct answer.

1. At the 2005 World Exposition in Aichi, Japan, tiny mu-chips were embedded in the admissions tickets to prevent counterfeiting. The mu-chip was developed by Hitachi in 2003. Its area is $4^2(10)^{-2}$ square millimeters. Simplify this expression.

2. Despite their name, Northern Yellow Bats are commonly found in warm, humid areas in the southeast United States. An adult has a wingspan of about 14 inches and weighs between $3(2)^{-3}$ and $3(2)^{-2}$ ounces. Simplify these expressions.

3. Saira is using the formula for the area of a circle to determine the value of π. She is using the expression Ar^{-2} where $A = 50.265$ and $r = 4$. Use a calculator to evaluate Saira's expression to find her approximation of the value of π to the nearest thousandth.

4. The volume of a freshwater tank can be expressed in terms of x, y, and z. Expressed in these terms, the volume of the tank is $x^3y^{-2}z$ liters. Determine the volume of the tank if $x = 4$, $y = 3$, and $z = 6$.

Alison has an interest in entomology, the study of insects. Her collection of insects from around the world includes the four specimens shown in the table below. Select the best answer.

Insect	Mass
Emperor Scorpion	2^{-5} kg
African Goliath Beetle	11^{-1} kg
Giant Weta	2^{-4} kg
Madagascar Hissing Cockroach	5^{-3} kg

5. Cockroaches have been found on every continent, including Antarctica. What is the mass of Alison's Madagascar Hissing Cockroach expressed as a quotient?

   A $-\dfrac{1}{125}$ kg   C $\dfrac{1}{15}$ kg

   B $\dfrac{1}{125}$ kg   D 125 kg

6. Many Giant Wetas are so heavy that they cannot jump. Which expression is another way to show the mass of the specimen in Alison's collection?

   F $-(2)4$ kg   H $\dfrac{1}{2 \cdot 2 \cdot 2 \cdot 2}$ kg

   G $\left(\dfrac{1}{2}\right)^{-4}$ kg   J $4\dfrac{1}{2}$ kg

7. Scorpions are closely related to spiders and horseshoe crabs. What is the mass of Alison's Emperor Scorpion expressed as a quotient?

   A $-\dfrac{1}{32}$ kg   C $\dfrac{1}{32}$ kg

   B $\dfrac{1}{25}$ kg   D 32 kg

Problem Solving

Powers of 10 and Scientific Notation

LESSON 7-2

Write the correct answer

1. Insects can multiply rapidly during the summer. A pair of houseflies could potentially grow to a population of 1.91×10^{20}. If all the descendants of a female cabbage aphid lived, the population could increase to 1.56×10^{24}. Which population would be larger?

2. The graph shows the gross domestic product (GDP) for several countries around the world. Identify the country whose GDP is twice that of another country. Write the GDPs of both countries in standard form.

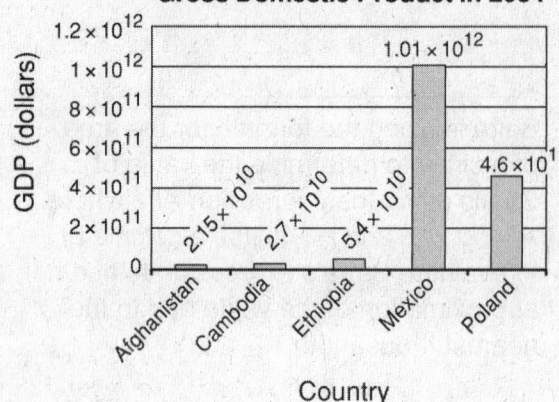

3. The 2005 population estimates of five countries are listed below.

Brazil	1.86×10^8
India	1.08×10^9
Kenya	3.38×10^7
Philippines	8.79×10^7
United Kingdom	6.04×10^7

   List the countries in order of population size from least to greatest.

The table shows astronomical data about several planets.
Use the table to answer questions 4–7. Select the best answer.

4. An AU is an astronomical unit. One AU equals 150,000,000 km. What is that measure in scientific notation?

   A 1.50×10^8 km   C 1.50×10^{10} km
   B 1.50×10^9 km   D 1.50×10^{11} km

5. Suppose the mass of Mars were written in standard form. How many digits would be to the *left* of the decimal?

   F 23   H 25
   G 24   J 26

6. Which of these is the distance from the Sun to Mercury expressed in scientific notation?

   A 0.38 AU   C 3.8×10^{-1} AU
   B 3.8×10^1 AU   D 38×10^{-2} AU

7. What is the diameter of the Earth in scientific notation?

   F 1.28×10^2 km   H 1.28×10^4 km
   G 1.28×10^3 km   J 1.28×10^5 km

Astronomical Data for the First Five Planets

Planet	Avg. Distance from Sun (AU)	Diameter (Km)	Mass (kg)
Mercury	0.38	4,880	3.20×10^{23}
Venus	0.72	12,100	4.87×10^{24}
Earth	1	12,800	5.97×10^{24}
Mars	1.52	6,790	6.42×10^{23}
Jupiter	5.20	143,000	1.90×10^{27}

Problem Solving
7-3 Multiplication Properties of Exponents

Write the correct answer.

1. In the mid-nineteenth century, several landowners in Australia released domestic rabbits into the wild. Suppose 100 rabbits were released. By 1950, the population had increased about 6×10^6 times. Determine the wild rabbit population in 1950.

2. Barnard's star is the fifth closest star to the Earth, after the Sun and the stars in the Alpha Centauri system. It takes 1.86×10^8 seconds for light from Barnard's star to reach the Earth. Light travels at a speed of 1.86×10^5 miles per second. Calculate the distance from Barnard's star to the Earth.

3. Saturn's smallest moon, Tethys, has a diameter of about 6.5×10^2 miles. The diameter of Jupiter's largest moon, Ganymede, is 5 times that of Tethys. Determine the diameter of Ganymede. Write your answer in standard form and in scientific notation.

4. Delaware and Montana have roughly the same population. Delaware's area is 2.49×10^3 square miles. Montana is 59 times larger. Determine the area of Montana. Write your answer in standard form and in scientific notation.

Select the best answer.

5. The formula for the volume of a cylinder is $V = 2\pi r^2 h$ where r is the radius and h is the height. What is the volume of the cylinder shown below?

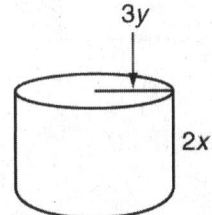

A $12\pi xy$ cm^3 C $24\pi x^2 y$ cm^3
B $12\pi xy^2$ cm^3 D $36\pi xy^2$ cm^3

6. What is the volume of the cube shown below?

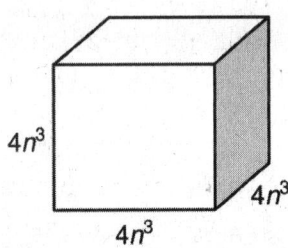

F $12n^6$ in^3 H $64n^9$ in^3
G $12n^9$ in^3 J $256n^9$ in^3

7. Belize borders Mexico and Guatemala in Central America. It has an area of 2.30×10^4 square kilometers. Russia borders fourteen countries and is 7.43×10^2 times larger than Belize. What is the area of Russia?

A 1.71×10^6 sq km   C 1.71×10^8 sq km
B 1.71×10^7 sq km   D 1.71×10^9 sq km

8. In 1989, Voyager 2 discovered six moons that orbit Neptune. The smallest of these is Naiad, which orbits Neptune in a brief 7.2 hours, or 8.22×10^{-4} years. Neptune's orbit of the Sun takes 2×10^5 times longer than Naiad's. How long does Neptune's orbit take?

F 10.2 years   H 102 years
G 16.4 years   J 164 years

Name _____ Date _____ Class _____

LESSON 7-4

Problem Solving
Division Properties of Exponents

Write the correct answer.

1. Kudzu is a fast-growing vine that has become a nuisance in the southeastern United States. It covers 2.5×10^5 acres in Alabama. In 2004 the population of Alabama was estimated to be 4.45×10^6 people. How many acres of kudzu are there for each person in Alabama?

2. A cylindrical water tank has a volume of $6\pi x^2 y^4$ cubic meters. The formula for the volume of a cylinder is $\pi r^2 h$. The water tank has a radius of xy meters. What is its height?

3. Voyager 2 was launched in 1979 to explore the planets of the outer solar system. The spacecraft travels an average of 4.68×10^6 kilometers in one year. Determine the speed of Voyager 2 in kilometers per hour. (*Hint*: 1 year = 8760 hours)

4. The population of Laos is 6.22×10^6. In 2004 its gross domestic product (GDP) was $\$1.13 \times 10^{10}$. The population of Norway is 4.59×10^6. In 2004 its GDP was $\$1.83 \times 10^{11}$. What is the GDP per capita, or per person, of Laos and Norway?

Select the best answer.

5. A rectangular parking lot has an area of $10a^3 b^6$ square yards. What is the width of the parking lot?

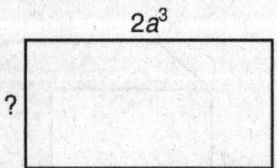

  A $5b^2$ yards   C $5b^6$ yards
  B $5b^3$ yards   D $25b^6$ yards

6. A storage chest is shaped like a cube. What is the volume of the storage chest?

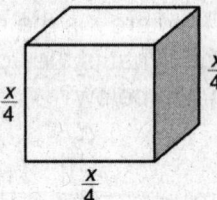

  F $\dfrac{x^3}{64}$ cubic units   H $\dfrac{32}{x^3}$ cubic units
  G $\dfrac{x^3}{32}$ cubic units   J $64x^3$ cubic units

7. The wavelengths of electromagnetic radiation vary greatly. Green light has a wavelength of about 5.1×10^{-7} meters. The wavelength of a U-band radio wave is 2.0×10^{-2} meters. About how much greater is the wavelength of a U-band radio wave than that of green light?

  A 2.55×10^{-9} C 3.92×10^4
  B 2.55×10^{-5} D 3.92×10^5

8. Puerto Rico has an area of 5.32×10^3 square miles and a population of 3.89×10^6. What is the population density of Puerto Rico in persons per square mile?

  F 1.37×10^{-3} H 7.31×10^2
  G 1.37×10^{-2} J 7.31×10^3

Name _____ Date _____ Class _____

LESSON 7-5

Problem Solving
Rational Exponents

Write the correct answer.

1. For a pendulum with a length of L meters, the time in seconds that it takes the pendulum to swing back and forth is approximately $2L^{\frac{1}{2}}$. About how long does it take a pendulum that is 9 meters long to swing back and forth?

   _____

2. The Beaufort Scale is used to measure the intensity of tornados. For a tornado with Beaufort number B, the formula $v = 1.9B^{\frac{3}{2}}$ may be used to estimate the tornado's wind speed in miles per hour. Estimate the wind speed of a tornado with Beaufort number 9.

   _____

3. Given a cube whose faces each have area A, the volume of the cube is given by the formula $V = A^{\frac{3}{2}}$. Find the volume of a cube whose faces each have an area of 64 in^2.

   _____

4. At a factory that makes cylindrical cans, the formula $r = \left(\dfrac{V}{12}\right)^{\frac{1}{2}}$ is used to find the radius of a can with volume V. What is the radius of a can whose volume is 192 cm^3?

   _____

Given an animal's body mass m, in grams, the formula $B = 1.8m^{\frac{3}{4}}$ may be used to estimate the mass b, in grams, of the animal's brain. The table shows the body mass of several birds. Use the table for questions 5–6. Select the best answer.

5. Which is the best estimate for the brain mass of a macaw?

   A 9 g   C 125 g
   B 45 g   D 225 g

6. How much larger is the brain mass of a barn owl compared to the brain mass of a cockatiel?

   F 189 g   H 388.8 g
   G 340.2 g   I 1215 g

7. An animal has a body mass given by the expression x^4. Which expression can be used to estimate the animal's brain mass?

   A $B = 1.8x^3$ C $B = 1.8x^{12}$
   B $B = 1.8x^{\frac{3}{4}}$ D $B = 1.8x$

Typical Body Masses of Birds	
Bird	Body Mass (g)
Cockatiel	81
Guam Rail	256
Macaw	625
Barn Owl	1296

Sources:
http://www.beyondveg.com/billings-t/comp-anat/comp-anat-appx2.shtml
http://www.sandiegozoo.org/animalbytes/index.html

LESSON 7-6 Problem Solving
Polynomials

Write the correct answer.

1. The surface area of a cylinder is given by the polynomial $2\pi r^2 + 2\pi rh$. A cylinder has a radius of 2 centimeters and a height of 5 centimeters. Find the surface area of the cylinder. Use 3.14 for π.

2. A firework is launched from the ground at a velocity of 180 feet per second. Its height after t seconds is given by the polynomial $-16t^2 + 180t$. Find the height of the firework after 2 seconds and after 5 seconds.

3. In the United Kingdom, transportation authorities use the polynomial $\frac{1}{20}v^2 + v$ for calculating the number of feet needed to stop on dry pavement. In the United States, many use the polynomial $0.096v^2$. Both formulas are based on speed v in miles per hour. Calculate the stopping distances for a car traveling 45 miles per hour in both the U.S. and the UK.

4. A piece of cardboard that measures 2 feet by 3 feet can be folded into a box if notches are cut out of the corners. The length of the side of the notch will be the same as the height h of the resulting box. The volume of the box is given by $4h^3 - 10h^2 + 6h$. Find the volume of the box for $h = 0.25$ and $h = 0.5$.

The height of a rocket in meters t seconds after it is launched is approximated by the polynomial $0.5at^2 + vt + h$ where a is always -9.8, v is the initial velocity, and h is the initial height. Use this information with the data in the chart for questions 5 – 7. Select the best answer.

5. A 300X was launched from a height of 10 meters. What was its height after 3 seconds?

   A 715.9 m   C 755.5 m
   B 745.3 m   D 760 m

6. Marie and Bob launched their rockets at the same time from a platform 5 meters above the ground. Marie launched the 4400i and Bob launched the Q99. How much higher was Marie's rocket after 2 seconds?

   F 35 meters   H 140 meters
   G 70 meters   J 320 meters

Model Number	Initial Velocity (m/s)
300X	250
Q99	90
4400i	125

7. The 4400i was launched from the ground at the same time the Q99 was launched from 175 meters above the ground. After how many seconds were the rockets at the same height?

   A 2 s   C 5 s
   B 4 s   D 6 s

Name _____ Date _____ Class _____

LESSON 7-7
Problem Solving
Adding and Subtracting Polynomials

Write the correct answer.

1. There are two boxes in a storage unit. The volume of the first box is $4x^3 + 4x^2$ cubic units. The volume of the second box is $6x^3 - 18x^2$ cubic units. Write a polynomial for the total volume of the two boxes.

   _____

   _____

2. The recreation field at a middle school is shaped like a rectangle with a length of $15x$ yards and a width of $10x - 3$ yards. Write a polynomial for the perimeter of the field. Then calculate the perimeter if $x = 2$.

   _____

3. Two cabins on opposite banks of a river are $12x^2 - 7x + 5$ feet apart. One cabin is $9x + 1$ feet from the river. The other cabin is $3x^2 + 4$ feet from the river. Write the polynomial that represents the width of the river where it passes between the two cabins. Then calculate the width if $x = 3$.

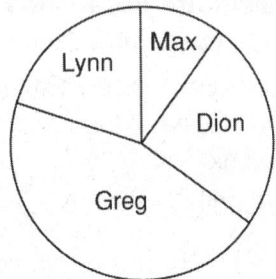

   _____

The circle graph represents election results for the president of the math team. Use the graph for questions 4–6. Select the best answer.

4. The angle value of Greg's sector can be modeled by $x^2 + 6x + 2$. The angle value of Dion's sector can be modeled by $7x + 20$. Which polynomial represents both sectors combined?

   A $x^2 + x + 18$ C $6x^2 + 7x + 18$
   B $x^2 + 13x + 22$ D $7x^2 + 6x + 22$

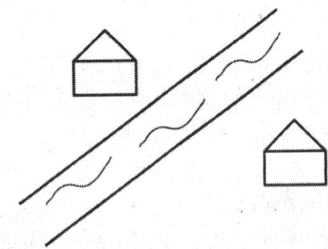

Math Team Election Results

5. The sum of Greg and Lynn's sectors is $2x^2 + 4x - 6$. The sum of Max and Dion's sectors is $10x + 26$. Which polynomial represents how much greater Greg and Lynn's combined sectors are than Max and Dion's?

   F $2x^2 + 6x + 32$ H $2x^2 - 6x - 32$
   G $2x^2 - 6x + 20$ J $2x^2 + 14x + 20$

6. The sum of Lynn's sector and Max's sector is $2x^2 - 9x - 2$. Max's sector can be modeled by $3x + 6$. Which polynomial represents the angle value of Lynn's sector?

   A $2x^2 - 6x + 4$ C $2x^2 - 12x + 8$
   B $2x^2 - 6x - 4$ D $2x^2 - 12x - 8$

Name _____ Date _____ Class_____

LESSON 7-8

Problem Solving
Multiplying Polynomials

Write the correct answer.

1. A bedroom has a length of $x + 3$ feet and a width of $x - 1$ feet. Write a polynomial to express the area of the bedroom. Then calculate the area if $x = 10$.

   _____

2. The length of a classroom is 4 feet longer than its width. Write a polynomial to express the area of the classroom. Then calculate the area if the width is 22 feet.

   _____

3. Nicholas is determining if he can afford to buy a car. He multiplies the number of months m by $i + p + 30f$ where i represents the monthly cost of insurance, p represents the monthly car payment, and f represents the number of times he fills the gas tank each month. Write the polynomial that Nicholas can use to determine how much it will cost him to own a car both for one month and for one year.

   _____

4. A seat cushion is shaped like a trapezoid. The shorter base of the cushion is 3 inches greater than the height. The longer base is 2 inches shorter than twice the height. Write the polynomial that can be used to find the area of the cushion. (The area of a trapezoid is represented by $\frac{1}{2}h(b_1+b_2)$.)

   _____

The volume of a pyramid can be found by using $\frac{1}{3}Bh$ where B is the area of the base and h is the height of the pyramid. The Great Pyramid of Giza has a square base, and each side is about 300 feet longer than the height of the pyramid. Select the best answer.

5. Which polynomial represents the approximate area of the base of the Great Pyramid?

   A $h + 90,000$
   B $2h + 90,000$
   C $h^2 + 600h + 90,000$
   D $2h^2 + 600h + 90,000$

6. Which polynomial represents the approximate volume of the Great Pyramid?

   F $\frac{1}{3}h^3 + 200h^2 + 30,000h$
   G $\frac{1}{3}h^2 + 200h + 30,000$
   H $h^3 + 600h^2 + 90,000h$
   J $3h^3 + 600h^2 + 90,000h$

7. The original height of the Great Pyramid was 485 feet. Due to erosion, it is now about 450 feet. Find the approximate volume of the Great Pyramid today.

   A 562,500 ft³   C 84,375,000 ft³
   B 616,225 ft³   D 99,623,042 ft³

Name _____ Date _____ Class _____

LESSON 7-9 Problem Solving
Special Products of Binomials

Write the correct answer.

1. This week Kyara worked $x + 4$ hours. She is paid $x - 4$ dollars per hour. Write a polynomial for the amount that Kyara earned this week. Then calculate her pay if $x = 12$.

   _____

   _____

2. A museum set aside part of a large gallery for a special exhibit.

   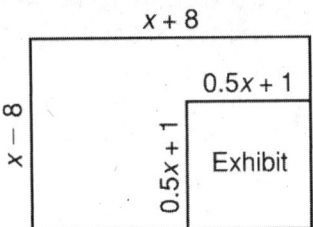

   Write a polynomial for the area of the gallery that is not part of the exhibit. Then calculate the area of that section if $x = 60$.

   _____

3. Gary is building a square table for a kitchen. In his initial sketch, each side measured x inches. After rearranging some furniture, he realized he would have to add one foot to the length and remove one foot from the width and have a rectangular table instead. Write a polynomial to represent the area of the rectangular table.

   _____

A fountain is in the center of a square garden. The radius of the fountain is $x - 2$ feet. The length of the garden is $2x + 4$ feet. Use this information and the diagram for questions 4 – 7. Select the best answer.

4. Which polynomial represents the area of the fountain?

   A $2\pi x - 4\pi$ C $\pi x^2 - 4\pi$
   B $\pi x^2 - 4\pi x - 4\pi$ D $\pi x^2 - 4\pi x + 4\pi$

5. Which polynomial represents the area of the garden, including the fountain?

   F $4x^2 + 8$ H $4x^2 + 16$
   G $4x^2 + 16x + 16$ J $4x^2 + 8x + 16$

6. Which polynomial represents the area of the garden *outside* the fountain? (Use 3.14 for π.)

   A $0.86x^2 + 28.56x + 3.44$
   B $0.86x^2 + 3.44x + 28.56$
   C $7.14x^2 + 28.56x + 3.44$
   D $7.14x^2 + 3.44x + 28.56$

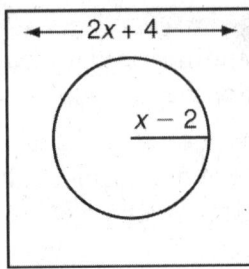

7. A 3-ft wide path is built around the garden. Which expression represents the area of the path?

   F $12x + 33$ H $4x^2 + 28x + 29$
   G $24x^2 + 84$ J $4x^2 + 40x + 100$

Name _____ Date _____ Class _____

LESSON 8-1
Problem Solving
Factors and Greatest Common Factors

Write the correct answer.

1. Eloise saved all her awards from school. She has 18 athletic awards and 27 academic awards. Eloise wants to display the two types separately but in rows of equal length. Determine the greatest number of awards Eloise can put in each row. Then determine the total number of rows.

   _____

   _____

2. Parker is preparing snacks for the children at a day camp. He has 48 carrot sticks and 36 apple slices. Find the number of identical snacks he can prepare if he puts as much food into each snack as possible without any leftovers. Then describe the snack.

   _____

3. Matías and Hannah are responsible for the centerpieces on the buffet tables at the school dance. They have 6 dozen carnations, 80 lilies, and 64 rosebuds. All the centerpieces must be identical. Determine the greatest number of centerpieces Matías and Hannah can make if they use all the flowers. Then describe the centerpiece.

   _____

   _____

4. Ms. Thompson has 120 same-sized tiles with which to make a rectangular design on her patio floor. 54 of the tiles are green; the rest are blue. To keep the rectangular shape, all rows must have the same number of tiles. If she wants each row to have the same number of blue and green tiles, how many rows will there be if she wants to use all the tiles and wants the rows to be as long as possible?

   _____

Part of an ad for interlocking foam squares is shown below. Use it to answer questions 5–7. Select the best answer.

5. A class arranges one package into a rectangle with dimensions other than those shown. Which could have been the dimensions?

   A 2 × 18   C 4 × 8
   B 3 × 16   D 5 × 6

Each package comes with 36 foam squares that interlock for a safe, colorful floor mat! You can make a ...

square   rectangle   or any shape
                             you want!

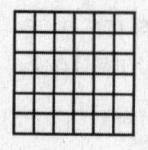 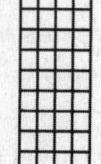 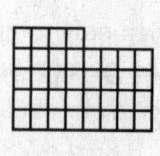

6. A teacher has 2 packages of red, 6 packages of blue, and half a package of yellow squares. He wants to build a rectangle so that each row is the same color. What can be the maximum number of squares per row?

   F 2   H 18
   G 6   J 36

7. In problem 6, how many rows will be blue?

   A 2   C 6
   B 3   D 12

Name _____ Date _____ Class _____

LESSON 8-2
Problem Solving
Factoring by GCF

Write the correct answer.

1. The area of a rug, which is shaped like a rectangle, is $4x^2 + 4x$ square feet. Factor this polynomial to find expressions for the dimensions of the rug.

   _____

2. The number of customers visiting a local museum since the year 2000 can be modeled by the expression $-3x^2 - 27x + 825$, where x is the number of years since 2000. Factor this polynomial.

   _____

3. The perimeter of a rhombus is $12x + 28$ feet. Factor this expression. Then find the length of one side if $x = 8$. (*Hint:* A rhombus is a parallelogram with four congruent sides.)

   _____

4. The foundation for a new high school building is rectangular in shape, and the area is $5x^3 + 4x^2 - 10x - 8$ square meters. Factor by grouping to find expressions for the dimensions of the building.

   _____

The diagram shows four sections of an herb garden. Use the figure to answer questions 5–8. Select the best answer.

5. The section where rosemary grows is square and has an area of $4x^2$ square feet. What is the length of one side?

   A x feet   C $2x$ feet
   B x^2 feet   D $4x$ feet

6. Rosemary and mint cover $6x^2 - 2x$ square feet. Assuming the length is adjacent to rosemary, what is the width of the mint section?

   F $2x$ feet   H $2x - 2$ feet
   G $x - 1$ feet J $3x - 1$ feet

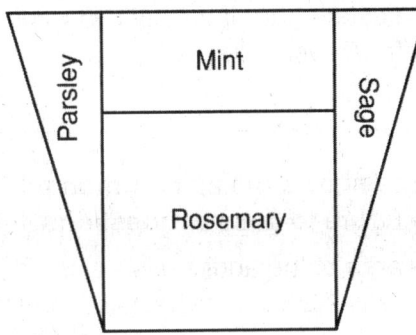

7. The parsley and sage sections each have an area of $\frac{1}{2}(3x^2 - 6x - x + 2)$ square feet. Factor $3x^2 - 6x - x + 2$. What are the base and height of each triangular section?

   A $2x - 3$ feet; $x + 1$ feet
   B $2x - 3$ feet; $x^2 + 1$ feet
   C $3x - 1$ feet; $x - 2$ feet
   D $3x - 1$ feet; $x^2 - 2$ feet

8. Assuming the side adjacent to mint and rosemary is the base, what is the height of each triangle on which parsley and sage grow?

   F $x - 2$ feet
   G $x + 1$ feet
   H $x^2 + 1$ feet
   J $2x$ feet

Name _____ Date _____ Class _____

LESSON 8-3 Problem Solving
Factoring $x^2 + bx + c$

Write the correct answer.

1. A plot of land is rectangular and has an area of $x^2 - 5x - 24$ m². The length is $x + 3$ m. Find the width of the plot.

   _____

2. An antique Persian carpet has an area of $(x^2 + x - 20)$ ft² and a length of $(x + 5)$ feet. The rug is displayed on a wall in a museum. The wall has a width of $(x + 2)$ feet and an area of $(x^2 + 17x + 30)$ ft². Write expressions for the length and width of both the rug and wall. Then find the dimensions of the rug and the wall if $x = 20$ feet.

3. The area of a poster board is $x^2 + 3x - 10$ inches. The width is $x - 2$ inches.

   a. Write an expression for the length of the poster board.

   _____

   b. Find the dimensions of the poster board when $x = 14$.

   _____

   c. Write a polynomial for the area of the poster board if one inch is removed from each side.

   _____

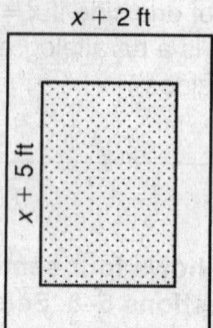

The figure shows the plans for an addition on the back of a house.
Use the figure to answer questions 4–6. Select the best answer.

4. The area of the addition is $(x^2 + 10x - 200)$ ft². What is its length?

   A $(x - 20)$ feet
   B $(x - 2)$ feet
   C $(x + 2)$ feet
   D $(x + 20)$ feet

5. What is the area of the original house?

   F $(x^2 - 10x - 200)$ ft²
   G $(x^2 + 8x - 20)$ ft²
   H $(x^2 + 12x + 200)$ ft²
   J $(x^2 + 30x + 200)$ ft²

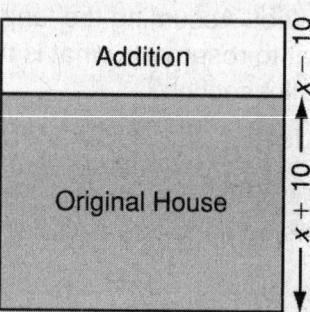

6. The homeowners decide to extend the addition. The area with the addition is now $(x^2 + 12x - 160)$ ft². By how many feet was the addition extended?

   A 1 foot   C 3 feet
   B 2 feet   D 4 feet

Name _____ Date _____ Class _____

LESSON 8-4 Problem Solving
Factoring $ax^2 + bx + c$

Write the correct answer.

1. A rectangular painting has an area of $(2x^2 + 8x + 6)$ cm². Its length is $(2x + 2)$ cm. Find the width of the painting.

2. A ball is kicked straight up into the air. The height of the ball in feet is given by the expression $-16t^2 + 12t + 4$, where t is time in seconds. Factor the expression. Then find the height of the ball after 1 second.

3. Instructors led an exercise class from a raised rectangular platform at the front of the room. The width of the platform was $(3x - 1)$ feet and the area was $(9x^2 + 6x - 3)$ ft². Find the length of this platform. After the exercise studio is remodeled, the area of the platform will be $(9x^2 + 12x + 3)$ ft². By how many feet will the width of the platform change?

4. A clothing store has a rectangular clearance section with a length that is twice the width w. During a sale, the section is expanded to an area of $(2w^2 + 19w + 35)$ ft². Find the amount of the increase in the length and width of the clearance section.

Select the best answer.

5. The area of a soccer field is $(24x^2 + 100x + 100)$ m². The width of the field is $(4x + 10)$ m. What is the length?

  A $(3x + 10)$ m C $(6x + 10)$ m
  B $(6x + 1)$ m   D $(8x + 2)$ m

6. A square parking lot has an area of $(4x^2 + 20x + 25)$ ft². What is the length of one side of the parking lot?

  F $(2x + 5)$ ft H $(5x + 4)$ ft
  G $(2x + 10)$ ft J $(5x + 2)$ ft

7. For a certain college, the number of applications received after x recruiting seminars is modeled by the polynomial $3x^2 + 490x + 6000$. What is this expression in factored form?

  A $(3x - 40)(x - 150)$
  B $(3x + 40)(x + 150)$
  C $(3x - 30)(x - 200)$
  D $(3x - 30)(x + 200)$

8. Jin needs to fence in his rectangular backyard. The fence will have one long section away from, but parallel to, the length of his house and two shorter sides connecting that section to the house. The length of Jin's house is $(3x + 4)$ yd and the area of his backyard is $(9x^2 + 15x + 4)$ yd². How many yards of fencing will Jin need?

  F $(6x + 2)$ yd H $(9x + 9)$ yd
  G $(9x + 6)$ yd J $(12x + 10)$ yd

Name _____ Date _____ Class _____

LESSON 8-5
Problem Solving
Factoring Special Products

Write the correct answer.

1. A rectangular fountain has an area of $(16x^2 + 8x + 1)$ ft². The dimensions of the rectangle have the form $ax + b$, where a and b are whole numbers. Write an expression for the perimeter of the fountain. Then find the perimeter when $x = 2$ feet.

   _____

   _____

2. A square tabletop has an area of $(9x^2 - 90x + 225)$ cm². The dimensions of the tabletop have the form $cx - d$, where c and d are whole numbers. Write an expression for the perimeter of the tabletop. Then find the perimeter when $x = 25$ centimeters.

   _____

   _____

3. The floor plan of a daycare center is shown.

   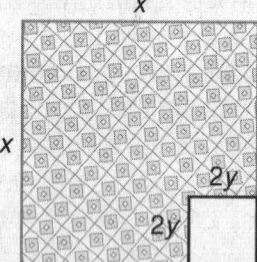

   The arts and crafts area in the lower right corner is not carpeted. The rest of the center is carpeted. Write an expression, in factored form, for the area of the floor that is carpeted.

   _____

4. A plate with a decorative border is shown.

   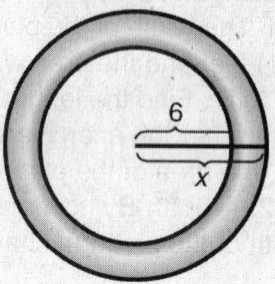

   Write an expression, in factored form, for the area of the border. (*Hint:* First factor out the GCF.)

   _____

Nelson is making open top boxes by cutting out corners from a sheet of cardboard, folding the edges up, and then taping them together. Select the best answer.

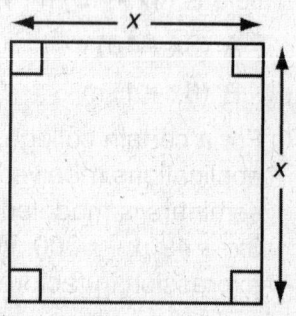

5. Nelson cut corners so that each corner was a square with side lengths of 4. What is the total area of the remaining piece of cardboard?

   A $x^2 - 8x + 16$ C $x^2 - 16x + 64$
   B $x^2 + 8x + 16$ D $x^2 + 16x + 64$

6. What are the dimensions of the square corners if the total remaining area is $x^2 - 4x + 4$?

   F 1 by 1   H 4 by 4
   G 2 by 2   J 8 by 8

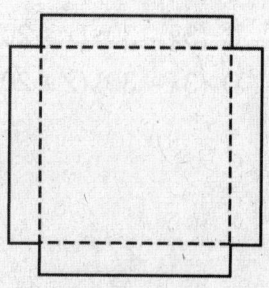

Name _____ Date _____ Class _____

LESSON 8-6 Problem Solving
Choosing a Factoring Method

Write the correct answer.

1. A rectangular stage set up in a theater has an area of $(15x^2 + 3x - 12)$ square feet. Factor the polynomial completely.

   _____

2. The area of a circular rug is $(16\pi k^2 - 16\pi k + 4\pi)$ m^2. Factor the expression completely. Then find the area of the rug if $k = 1$ meter.

   _____

   _____

3. An artist framed a picture. The dimensions of the picture and frame are shown below.

   Completely factor the expression for the area of the frame.

   _____

4. The attendance for a team's basketball game can be approximated with the polynomial $-5x^2 + 80x + 285$, where x is the number of wins the team had in the previous month. Factor the polynomial completely. Then predict the attendance when the team won 4 games in the previous month.

   _____

   _____

Select the best answer.

5. The volume of a box can be modeled by the expression $7x^4 - 28$. Which shows this expression completely factored?

   A $7(x^4 - 4)$
   B $7(x^2 - 2)^2$
   C $(7x^2 + 4)(x^2 - 7)$
   D $7(x^2 + 2)(x^2 - 2)$

6. The area of a Japanese rock garden is $(30x^2 + 3x - 6)$ square feet. Factor the polynomial completely.

   F $3(10x^2 + x - 2)$
   G $3(2x + 1)(5x - 2)$
   H $(6x + 3)(5x - 2)$
   J $(15x - 6)(2x + 1)$

7. The money made from the sales of x mountain bikes is approximated by $20x^2 + 10x + 90$. Factor the expression completely.

   A $2(10x + 9)(x + 5)$
   B $5(4x^2 + 2x + 18)$
   C $10(2x^2 + x + 9)$
   D The expression cannot be factored.

8. Kyle stood on a bridge and threw a rock up and over the side. The height of the rock, in meters, can be approximated by $-5t^2 + 5t + 24$, where t is the time in seconds after Kyle threw it. Completely factor the expression.

   F $-5(t^2 + t + 24)$
   G $(-5t + 3)(t + 8)$
   H $-1(5t + 8)(t + 3)$
   J The expression cannot be factored.

Problem Solving
9-1 Identifying Quadratic Functions

Write the correct answer.

1. During a softball game, Kay hit a fly ball. The function $f(x) = -16t^2 + 64t + 4$ describes the height of the softball in feet. Make a table of values for the function and then graph it.

x					
f(x)					

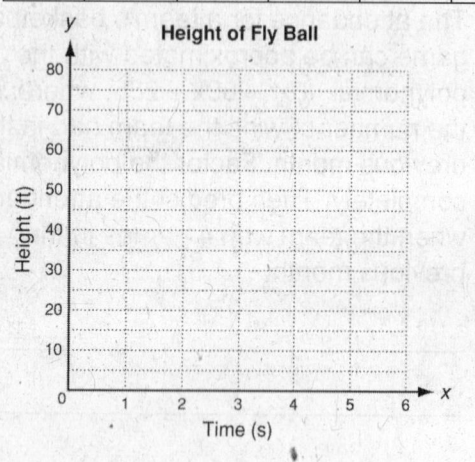

2. Jorge recorded the number of customers y that came to his store over a number of hours x. Does the data represent a quadratic function? Explain.

x	1	3	5	7	9
y	2	5	11	17	23

   _____

   _____

3. NASA has a plane that travels in a parabola to simulate zero-gravity. Its path can be modeled by the equation $y = -8.6x^2 + 560x + 24000$ where y is the altitude in feet and x is the time since it started the maneuver. What is a reasonable domain for this function?

   _____

Radio telescopes are built in the shape of a parabola. The graph below shows a radio telescope dish in cross-section. Select the best answer.

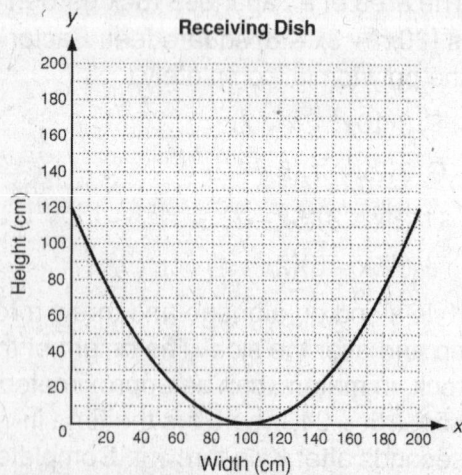

4. What is the vertex of this parabola?
   - A (0, 120)
   - B (100, 0)
   - C (200, 120)
   - D (100, 120)

5. What are the domain and range of this function?
   - F D: all real numbers
     R: all real numbers
   - G D: $x \geq 0$, R: $y \geq 0$
   - H D: $x \leq 200$ R: $y \leq 120$
   - J D: $0 \leq x \leq 200$ R: $0 \leq y \leq 120$

6. Which of the following could be the equation used by engineers to construct the radio telescope dish?
   - A $y = 1.2x + 120$
   - B $y = -1.2x + 120$
   - C $y = 0.012x^2 - 2.4x + 120$
   - D $y = -0.012x^2 - 2.4x + 120$

Name _____ Date _____ Class _____

LESSON 9-2
Problem Solving
Characteristics of Quadratic Functions

Write the correct answer.

1. A superhero is trying to leap over a tall building. The function $f(x) = -16x^2 + 200x$ gives the superhero's height in feet as a function of time. The building is 612 feet high. Will the superhero make it over the building? Explain.

   _____

   _____

   _____

2. The graph shows the height of an arch support for a pedestrian bridge.

   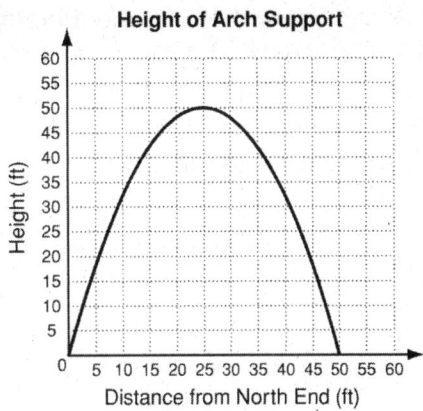

   Find the zeros (if any) and axis of symmetry of this parabola.

   _____

3. The distance between the cables suspending a bridge and the water below is given by the function $y = 0.02x^2 - 2x + 80$. Find the vertex of the graph.

   _____

After a heavy snowfall, Joe and Karin made an igloo. The dome of the igloo is in the shape of a parabola and the height of the igloo in inches is given by $f(x) = -0.03x^2 + 2.4x$. Select the best answer.

4. Joe wants to place a support in the middle of the igloo, along the axis of symmetry. How far from the edge of the igloo should he place the support?

   A 24 in.   C 48 in.
   B 40 in.   D 80 in.

5. Neither Joe nor Karin can stand up inside the igloo. How tall is the center of the igloo? (*Hint*: the top of the igloo is the vertex of the parabola.)

   F 24 in.   H 48 in.
   G 40 in.   J 80 in.

6. Karin graphs the parabola and looks at the zeros to see how wide the igloo is. What are the zeros of this parabola?

   A −80 and 80   C 0 and 80
   B −40 and 40   D 40 and 80

7. What is the vertex of the parabola that Karin graphed?

   F (20, 36)   H (48, 40)
   G (40, 48)   J (80, 0)

8. Which graph below is the graph that Karin made?

   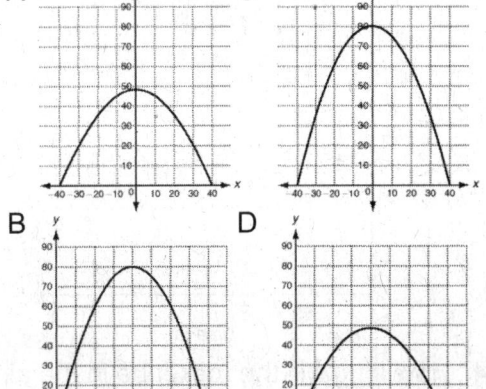

Holt McDougal Algebra 1

Problem Solving
Graphing Quadratic Functions

LESSON 9-3

Write the correct answer.

1. An Olympic diver is competing for a medal. His height in feet above the water can be modeled by the function $f(x) = -3x^2 + 6x + 24$, where x is the time in seconds after he begins the dive. Graph the function. Then find how long it takes the diver to reach the water.

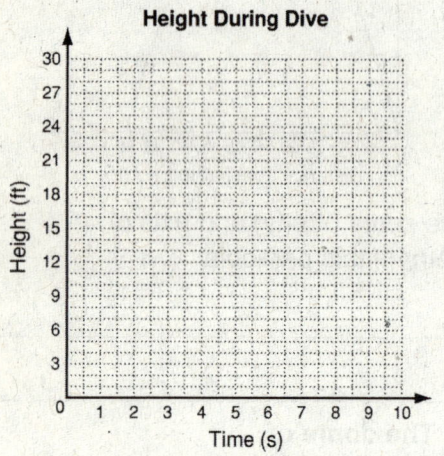

2. Tanisha kicks a soccer ball during a game. The height of the ball, in feet, can be modeled by the function $f(x) = -16x^2 + 48x$, where x is the time in seconds after she kicks the ball. Graph the function. Find the maximum height of the ball and how long it takes the ball to reach that height.

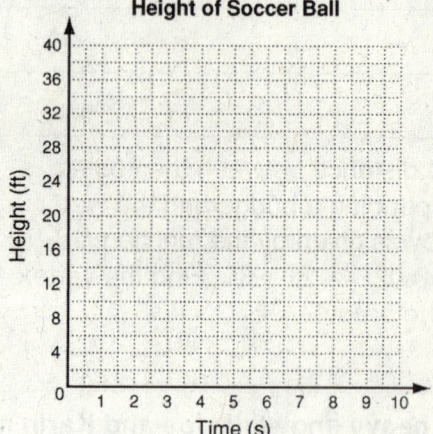

A model rocket is launched from a platform into the air. Keona records its height at different times until it reaches its peak at 259 ft. Her graph of these points is shown below. Use this graph to answer questions 3–5.

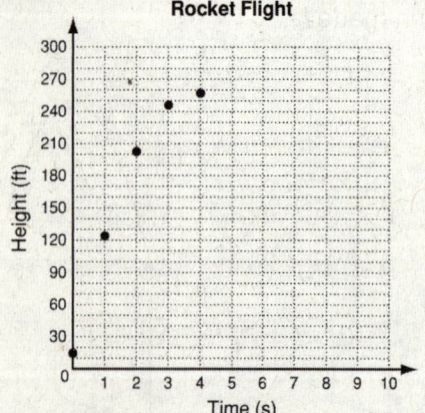

4. How long will the rocket be in the air?

   A 4 seconds   C 8 seconds
   B 6 seconds   D 10 seconds

3. Keona wants to complete her graph by plotting the heights of the rocket as it descended. Which of the following points will she graph?

   F (4, 180)   H (6, 200)
   G (5, 150)   J (10, 0)

5. Which of the following equations models the flight of the ball where x is the time in seconds and y is the height in feet?

   A $16x^2 + 15x + 125$
   B $16x^2 + 125x + 15$
   C $-16x^2 + 125x + 15$
   D $-16x^2 + 15x + 125$

Name _____ Date _____ Class _____

LESSON 9-4 Problem Solving
Transforming Quadratic Functions

Write the correct answer.

1. Two construction workers working at different heights on a skyscraper dropped their hammers at the same time. The first was working at a height of 400 ft, the second at a height of 160 ft. Write the two functions that describe the heights of the hammers.

   _____

   _____

2. Graph the two functions you found in problem 1 on the grid below.

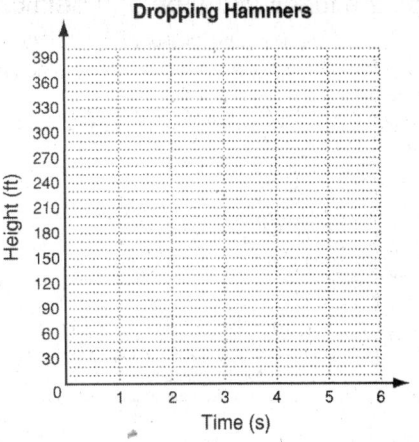

3. Based on the graphs you drew in problem 2, how long will it take each hammer to reach the ground?

   _____

   _____

The pull of gravity varies from planet to planet. The graph shows the height of objects dropped from 500 ft on the surface of four planets. Use this graph to answer questions 4–6. Select the best answer.

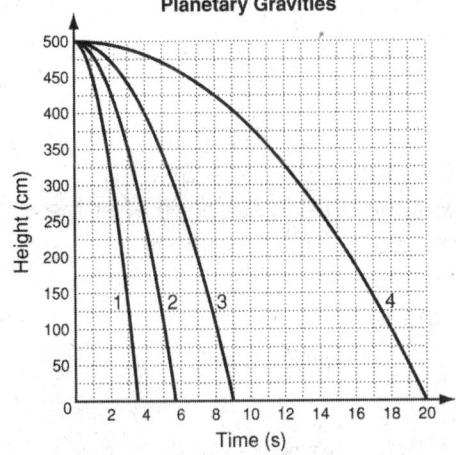

4. Of the four planets, Jupiter has the strongest gravity. Which of the four graphs represents the height of the object dropped on Jupiter?

   F Graph 1   H Graph 3
   G Graph 2   J Graph 4

6. Due to its small size, Pluto has a very weak pull of gravity. Which of the equations below represents the graph of the object dropped on Pluto?

   A $h(t) = -41x^2 + 500$
   B $h(t) = -16x^2 + 500$
   C $h(t) = -6x^2 + 500$
   D $h(t) = -1.25x^2 + 500$

5. Which of the graphs represents an object dropped on Earth?

   A Graph 1   C Graph 3
   B Graph 2   D Graph 4

Original content Copyright © by Holt McDougal. Additions and changes to the original content are the responsibility of the instructor.

Holt McDougal Algebra 1

Name _____ Date _____ Class _____

LESSON 9-5

Problem Solving
Solving Quadratic Equations by Graphing

The path of a certain firework in the air is modeled by the parabolic function $y = -16x^2 + 256x - 624$ where x is the number of seconds after the fuse is lit. Write the correct answer.

1. Graph the function on the grid below.

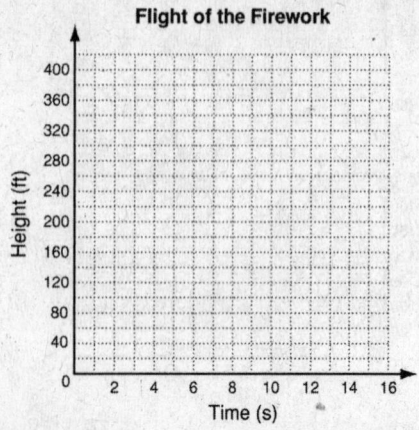

Flight of the Firework

2. The firework will explode when it reaches its highest point. How long after the fuse is lit will the firework explode and how high will the firework be?

   _____

   _____

3. Based on the graph of the firework, what are the two zeros of this function?

   _____

   _____

4. What is the meaning of each of the zeros you found in problem 3?

   _____

   _____

   _____

Select the best answer.

5. The quadratic function $f(x) = -16x^2 + 90x$ models the height of a baseball in feet after x seconds. How long is the baseball in the air?

   A 2.8125 s   C 11.25 s
   B 5.625 s   D 126.5625 s

6. The height of a football y in feet is given by the function $y = -16x^2 + 56x + 2$ where x is the time in seconds after the ball was kicked. This function is graphed below. How long was the football in the air?

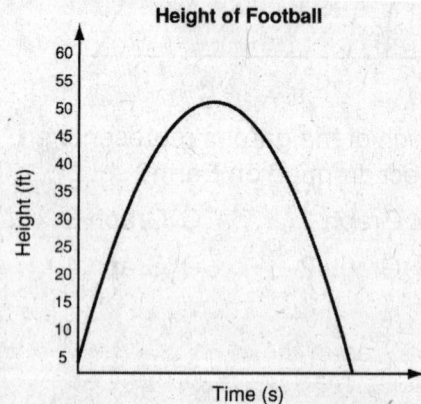

Height of Football

   A 0.5 seconds   C 2 seconds
   B 1.75 seconds   D 3.5 seconds

7. The function $y = -0.04x^2 + 2x$ models the height of an arch support for a bridge, where x is the distance in feet from where the arch supports enter the water. How many real solutions does this function have?

   F 0   H 2
   G 1   J 3

Name _____ Date _____ Class _____

LESSON 9-6

Problem Solving
Solving Quadratic Equations by Factoring

Write the correct answer.

1. The height of an acorn falling out of a tree is $h = -16t + 25$ where h is height in feet and t is time in seconds. Determine how long it takes the acorn to reach the ground. Check your answer by graphing the function.

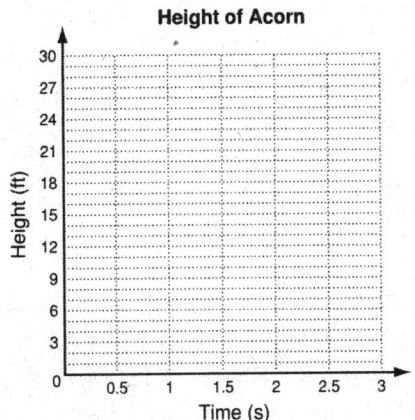

2. An architect is designing a building with a right triangular footprint.

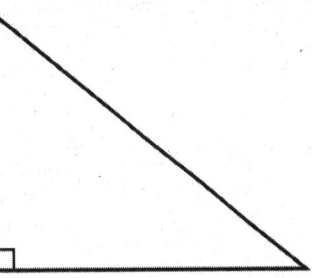

The hypotenuse of the triangle is 80 feet longer than one leg of the triangle and 40 feet longer than the other leg. Use the Pythagorean Theorem to find the dimensions of the footprint of the building.

3. Robert threw a rock off a bridge into the river. The distance from the rock to the river is modeled by the equation $h = -16t^2 - 16t + 60$, where h is the height in feet and t is the time in seconds. Find how long it took the rock to enter the water.

4. During a game of golf, Kayley hits her ball out of a sand trap. The equation $h = -16t^2 + 20t - 4$ models the height of the golf ball in feet in relation to the number of t seconds since it was hit. Find how long it takes Kayley's golf ball to reach to green.

A new store is being built in the shape of a rectangle with a parking lot in the shape of an isosceles trapezoid. The parking lot and the store will share a side as shown. Select the best answer.

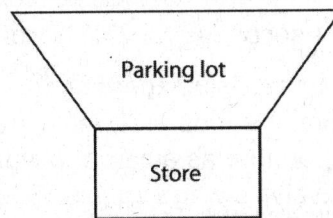

5. The parking lot will have an area of 160 square meters. The shorter base is 4 m longer than the height of the trapezoid, and the longer base is 8 m longer than the height. What is the length of the shorter base?

   F 10 meters   H 18 meters
   G 14 meters   J 20 meters

6. The area of the store is to be 154 square meters. If the depth is given as $\frac{1}{14}x^2 + \frac{15}{14}x$, what is the value of x?

   A 7   C 14
   B 11   D 28

7. What is the depth of the store in meters?

   F 7   H 14
   G 11   J 28

LESSON 9-7

Problem Solving
Solving Quadratic Equations by Using Square Roots

A furniture maker has designed a bookcase with the proportions shown in the diagram below. Write the correct answer.

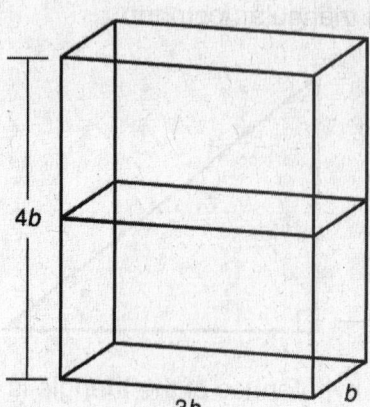

1. A customer has requested a bookcase with the two shelves having a total area of 864 square inches. What should b equal to meet the customer's specifications?

2. Barnard has a stain on his wall and would like to cover it up with a bookcase. What should b equal in order for the back of the bookcase to cover an area of 4800 square inches?

3. Bria would like to display her collection of soap carvings on top of her bookcase. The collection takes up an area of 400 square inches. What should b equal for the top of the bookcase to have the correct area? Round your answer to the nearest tenth of an inch.

4. Eliana would like to cover the side panels with silk. She has 1600 square inches of silk. What should b equal so that she can use all of her silk to completely cover the sides? Round your answer to the nearest tenth of an inch.

Select the best answer.

5. Carter plans to wallpaper the longest wall in his living room. The wall is twice as long as it is high and has an area of 162 square feet. What is the height of the wall?

   A 8 feet C 12 feet
   B 9 feet D 18 feet

6. An apple drops off the apple tree from a height of 8 feet. How long does it take the apple to reach the ground? Use the function $f(x) = -16x^2 + c$, where c is the initial height of a falling object, to find the answer.

   F 0.5 seconds   H 1 second
   G 0.71 seconds J 2.23 seconds

7. Trinette cut a square tablecloth into 4 equal pieces that she used to make two pillow covers. The area of the tablecloth was 3600 square inches. What is the side length of each piece Trinette used to make the pillow covers?

   A 20 inches C 60 inches
   B 30 inches D 90 inches

8. Elton earns x dollars per hour at the bookstore. His mother, Evelyn, earns x^2 dollars per hour as a career counselor. Twice Evelyn's wage equals $84.50. What is Elton's hourly wage? Round your answer to the nearest cent.

   F $4.60   H $9.19
   G $6.50   J $13.00

Name _____ Date _____ Class _____

LESSON 9-8 Problem Solving
Completing the Square

The Ward family is redecorating several rooms of their house. Write the correct answer.

1. The Wards decided to use carpet tiles in the family room. The room has an area of 176 square feet and is 5 feet longer than it is wide. Find the dimensions of the family room.

2. Angelique wants to have a rug that is 9 feet long and 7 feet wide in her bedroom. The rug will cover the whole floor except a border that is x feet wide. The area of her room is 167 square feet.

   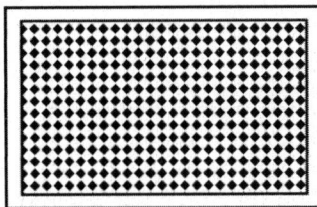

   Find the width of the border, x. Round your answer to the nearest tenth of a foot.

3. Giselle is going to frame a portrait of the family and place it on the mantle in the family room. The portrait is 10 inches longer than it is tall and will take up a total area of 1344 square inches once it is inside the 2 inch thick frame. Find the dimensions and area of the unframed portrait.

Select the best answer.

4. The landing for the steps leading up to a county courthouse is shaped like a trapezoid. The area of the landing is 1500 square feet. The shorter base of the trapezoid is 15 feet longer than the height. The longer base is 5 feet longer than 3 times the height. What is the length of the longer base?

   A 25 feet   C 80 feet
   B 40 feet   D 95 feet

5. The height of a pumpkin launched from a cannon is given by the function $h = -16t^2 + 240t + 16$ where t is the time in seconds. How many seconds is the pumpkin in the air? Round your answer to the nearest tenth of a second.

   F 7.5 seconds   H 16 seconds
   G 15.1 seconds   J 32 seconds

6. Georgia works part-time at a daycare while she is going to college. She earned $160 last week. Georgia worked 12 more hours than the amount she is paid per hour. What is Georgia's hourly pay rate?

   A $6.00   C $12.00
   B $8.00   D $20.00

7. Part of the set for a play is a triangular piece of plywood. The area of the triangle is 20 square feet. The base is 3 feet longer than the height. What is the height of the triangle? Round your answer to the nearest tenth of a foot.

   F 3 feet   H 3.9 feet
   G 3.2 feet   J 5 feet

Original content Copyright © by Holt McDougal. Additions and changes to the original content are the responsibility of the instructor.

Holt McDougal Algebra 1

Problem Solving
LESSON 9-9: The Quadratic Formula and the Discriminant

Write the correct answer.

1. Theo's flying disc got stuck in a tree 14 feet from the ground. Theo threw his shoe up at the disc to dislodge it. The height in feet h of the shoe is given by the equation $h = -16t^2 + 25t + 6$, where t is the time in seconds. Determine whether the shoe hit the disc. Use the discriminant to explain your answer.

   _____

   _____

2. A picture frame holds a 4-in. by 6-in. photograph. The frame adds a border x inches wide around three sides of the photo. On the fourth side the frame forms a border that is $3x - 0.5$ in. wide.

   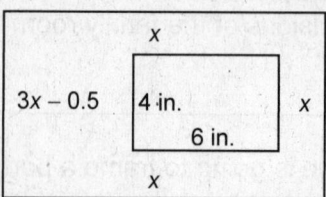

   The combined area of the photograph and the frame is 80.5 in^2. Write a quadratic equation for the combined area. Then use the quadratic formula to find x.

   _____

   _____

3. The manager of a park enclosed an area for small dogs to play. He made the length 15 feet longer than the width and enclosed an area covering 1350 square feet. What are the dimensions of the dogs' play area?

   _____

The equation $-5x^2 + 72x + 378$ models the number of students enrolled in a school where x is the number of years since the school first opened in 1990. Select the best answer.

4. How many students did the school have when it opened?
   - A 68
   - B 72
   - C 378
   - D 445

5. Which equation can be used to find the year in which 502 students were enrolled?
   - F $-5x^2 + 72x + 502 = 0$
   - G $-5x^2 + 72x - 124 = 0$
   - H $-5x^2 + 72x - 502 = 0$
   - J $-5x^2 + 72x + 124 = 0$

6. In which year were 502 students enrolled?
   - A 1992
   - B 1996
   - C 1998
   - D 2002

7. In which year were 598 students enrolled?
   - F 1995
   - G 1998
   - H 2000
   - J 2010

8. Which statement is true?
   - A Enrollment exceeded 650 students at one point.
   - B Enrollment never exceeded 650 students.
   - C The highest enrollment of any year was exactly 650 students.
   - D There were two years where 650 students were enrolled.

Problem Solving

10-1 Organizing and Describing Data

The table below gives the top five ringtone genres reported during a survey of cell phone subscribers in August, 2005.

Ringtone genre	Males (millions)	Females (millions)
Hip Hop or Rap	2.232	2.472
Rock or Alternative	2.219	2.082
Pop	1.044	2.069
TV/Movie/Game Themes	1.161	1.371
Classic Rock	0.949	0.918

1. Use the data to make a graph below. Explain why you chose that type of graph.

   _____

   _____

   _____

2. From the graph (*not* the table), explain how you can tell that the Pop genre is nearly twice as popular with females as males.

   _____

   _____

In 2000, there were approximately 27 million people 18–24 years old in the United States. The circle graph below shows the highest level of education for that population. Use the graph to select the best answers for questions 3–5.

3. Which level of education was least represented?

   A Less than high school graduate

   B Some college or associate degree

   C High school graduate

   D Bachelor's degree or higher

4. How many 18–24 year-olds had attained a bachelor's degree or higher?

   F 2.16 million   H 10.26 million

   G 8 million   J 12.42 million

5. How many 18–24 year-olds never attended college?

   A 6.75 million   C 12.42 million

   B 7.83 million   D 14.58 million

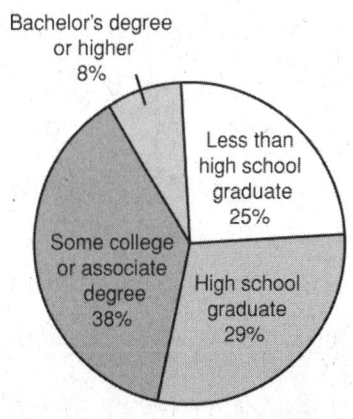

Educational Attainment of the Population 18–24 Years Old, 2000

Name _____ Date _____ Class _____

LESSON 10-2 Problem Solving
Frequency and Histograms

The heights in inches of the 2005 NBA All-Star Game players are given below.

Players' Heights (in.)											
75	78	80	87	72	80	81	83	85	78	76	81
77	78	83	83	78	82	79	80	75	84	82	90

1. Use the data to make a frequency table with intervals. Use an interval of 5.

Players' Heights	
Heights (in.)	Frequency

2. Use your frequency table to make a histogram for the data.

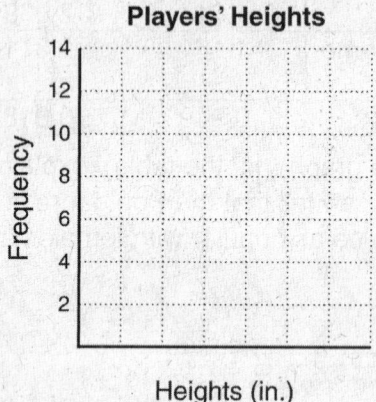

Select the best answer.

3. The stem-and-leaf plot below gives the file sizes of the songs on two albums after being converted to mp3 files. What is the largest file size for Album 1?

MP3 File Sizes (megabytes)

Album 1		Album 2
0	5	0 1 2 4 5 5 8
6 6 5 3 1	6	0 6 7
7 3 0	7	3 6 8
3 1	8	6
8 7 2 0	9	9

Key: | 8 | 6 means 8.6 MB
1 | 8 | means 8.1 MB

A 6.6 MB   C 9.8 MB
B 8.9 MB   D 9.9 MB

4. The cumulative frequency table below gives the scores of 100 students on a standardized mathematics test. How many students scored between 400 and 499?

Standardized Test Scores	
Scores	Cumulative Frequency
200–299	1
300–399	3
400–499	19
500–599	50
600–699	85
700–799	100

F 15   H 19
G 16   J 31

Name _____ Date _____ Class _____

LESSON 10-3
Problem Solving
Data Distributions

Write the correct answer.

1. While window shopping, Sandra recorded the prices of shoes she would like to try on. The prices were $48, $63, $52, $99, and $58. Find the mean, median, and mode of the prices. Which best represents the typical shoe she looked at? Why?

   _____

   _____

2. The number of cans Xavier recycled each week for eight weeks is 24, 33, 76, 42, 35, 33, 45, and 33. Find the mean, median, and mode of the numbers of cans. How do the mean and median change when the outlier is removed?

   _____

   _____

3. The amounts due on the Harvey's electric bill, rounded to the nearest dollar, for the past six months were $64, $83, $76, $134, $76, and $71. Find the mean, median, and mode of the amounts. Which value should Mr. Harvey tell his family to convince them to cut down on electric use?

   _____

4. A manager at a bowling alley surveys adult patrons about their shoes sizes. He records sizes 11, 12, 8, 4, 8, 5, 8, 7, 9, 10, 8, 9, 8, and 10. Find the mean, median, and mode of the sizes. Which is most important to the manager when ordering new rental shoes?

   _____

The number of traffic citations given daily by two police departments over a two-week period is shown in the box-and-whisker plots. Choose the letter of the best answer.

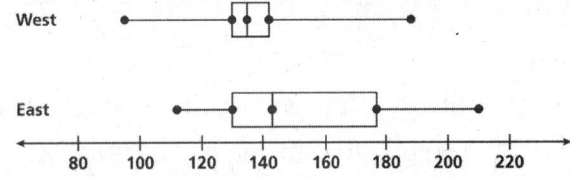

5. What is the best estimate of the difference in the greatest number of citations given by each department in one day?

   A 10   B 20
   C 30   D 35

6. What is the difference in the median number of citations between the two departments?

   F about 8
   G about 15
   H about 22
   I about 40

7. Which statement is NOT true?

   A The East department gave the greatest number of citations in one day.

   B The East department gave the least number of citations in one day.

   C The East department has a greater IQR than the West department.

   D The East department has the greater median number of citations in one day.

LESSON 10-4 Problem Solving
Misleading Graphs and Statistics

Analyze these misleading graphs.

1. This graph shows the years in which the world population reached, or is projected to reach, integer multiples of 1 billion people.

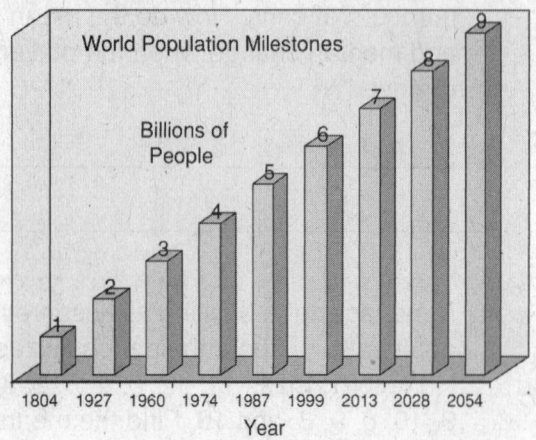

   a. Explain why the graph is misleading.

   _____

   _____

   b. What might someone believe because of the graph?

   _____

   _____

2. This graph shows dog registrations with the American Kennel Club.

   Dog Breeds Registered with the American Kennel Club, 2004

   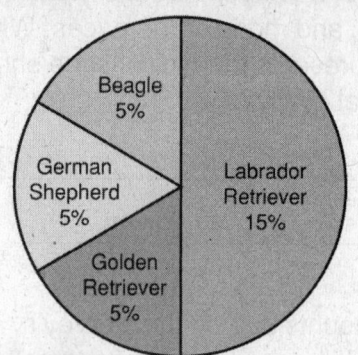

   a. Explain why the graph is misleading.

   _____

   _____

   b. Who might want to use this graph, and why?

   _____

   _____

Use the graph to select the best answer.

3. The graph is misleading because of which scale(s)?

   A horizontal only   C both
   B vertical only   D neither

4. Which statement is certainly true?

   F The average house price increased every year between 1995 and 2004.

   G The average house prices have increased $80,000 between 1995 and 2004.

   H The average house price in 2001 was about $160,000.

   J None of the above.

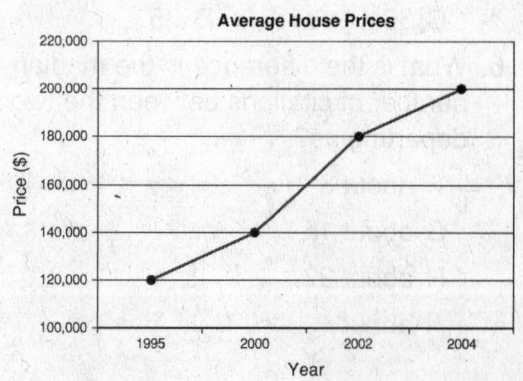

Name _____ Date _____ Class _____

LESSON 10-5
Problem Solving
Experimental Probability

Write the correct answer.

1. A manufacturer of bottled juices has a contest where prizes are printed on the inside of the bottle caps. 2 million caps are printed with "Sorry"; 1.5 million say "Free Bottle"; 0.4 million say "T-Shirt"; and 0.1 million say "CD."

   a. Identify the sample space.

   _____

   b. If Tammy buys one bottle, is it impossible, unlikely, as likely as not, likely, or certain that she will get a cap that says "Sorry"?

   _____

   c. If Eagle buys one bottle, is it impossible, unlikely, as likely as not, likely, or certain that he will get a cap that says "CD"?

   _____

2. At the end of the 2005 season, Major League Baseball player Andruw Jones had 1408 hits out of 5271 times at bat during his entire career.

   a. What is the experimental probability that Andruw Jones will have a hit during any time at bat? (This statistic is called his *batting average* and is usually stated as a decimal rounded to the thousandths.)

   _____

   b. If Andruw has 570 at-bats during a season, predict the number of hits he will have during the season.

   _____

A pharmaceutical company tests the effectiveness of a diabetes screening test by administering it to several volunteers who actually know whether or not they have diabetes. The results are summarized in the table below. Select the best answer.

3. What is the experimental probability that this screening test will *not* identify someone who actually does have diabetes? (This type of result is called a false negative.)

   A 2.9 %   C 20%
   B 16.6%   D 28.6%

4. If this test is used on 1000 patients who do not know whether or not they have diabetes, about how many patients would the test predict *do* have diabetes?

   F 66   H 92
   G 79   J 101

		Volunteer _____ have diabetes.	
		does	does not
Test predicts that the person _____ have diabetes.	does	10	4
	does not	2	136

173 Holt McDougal Algebra 1

Name _____ Date _____ Class _____

LESSON 10-6 Problem Solving
Theoretical Probability

Mahjong is a classic Chinese game frequently played with tiles. Each tile has numbers, pictures, or characters on them. Similar to a deck of playing cards, most of the tiles can be grouped into suits. From a certain set of mahjong tiles, the odds *in favor* of selecting a tile from the bamboo suit is 1:3.

1. What is the probability of selecting a tile from the bamboo suit?

2. What is the probability of selecting a tile that is *not* from the bamboo suit?

3. Any set of mahjong tiles has 36 tiles in the bamboo suit. How many tiles are in the entirety of this set? (*Hint:* Set up a proportion using your answer from question 1.)

4. This set of mahjong tiles also has 8 special tiles that represent flowers or seasons. What are the odds *against* selecting a tile that represents a flower or a season?

At a carnival game, you drop a ball into the top of the machine shown below. As the ball falls, it goes either left or right as it hits each peg. In total, the ball can follow 16 different paths. (See if you can find all 16 paths.) The ball eventually lands in one of the bins at the bottom and you win that amount of money. (One path to $0 is shown.) Select the best answer.

5. What is the probability of wining $2?

   A $\frac{1}{16}$ C $\frac{1}{4}$

   B $\frac{1}{8}$ D $\frac{1}{2}$

6. What is the probability of wining $1?

   F $\frac{1}{8}$ H $\frac{1}{4}$

   G $\frac{3}{16}$ J $\frac{3}{8}$

7. What are the odds in favor of winning nothing ($0)?

   A 1:1   C 1:3
   B 1:2   D 1:4

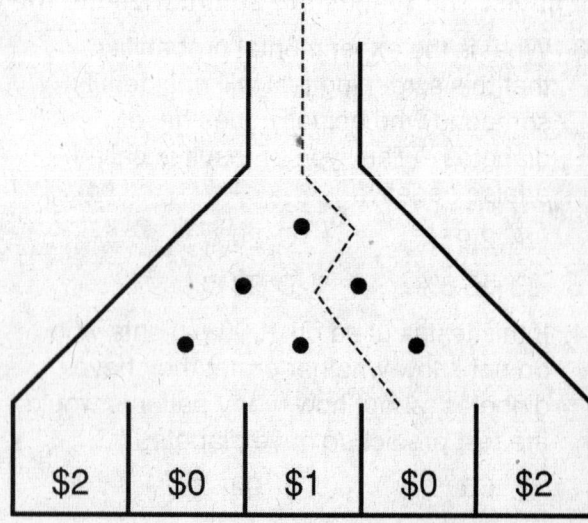

Problem Solving
10-7 Independent and Dependent Events

Janeesa's backpack has 4 pens and 6 pencils in the front pocket. She reaches in, grabs one, and removes it. Then she reaches in again, grabs another, and removes it. Write the correct answer.

1. Are these two events independent or dependent? Explain.

2. What is the probability that Janeesa removes two pens?

3. What is the probability that Janeesa removes two pencils?

4. What is the probability that Janessa removes a pencil and then a pen?

5. What is the probability that she removes a pen and then a pencil?

6. Your answers to questions 4 and 5 should be numerically identical. Does that mean that the events are identical? Explain.

On a game show, a contestant tries to win a car by randomly picking tiles from a bag. Some of the tiles are printed with the digits in the price of the car and some are printed with strikes (red X's). Select the best answer.

7. When the prices of cars only had four digits, the game was played with 7 tiles—4 digits and 3 strikes. Whenever you picked a strike, it was removed from the bag. In this old version of the game, what was the probability of picking three strikes in a row?

  A $\frac{1}{343}$ C $\frac{6}{343}$
  B $\frac{1}{210}$ D $\frac{1}{35}$

8. When the prices of cars began to have five digits, the game was modified to use 6 tiles—5 digits and 1 strike. Whenever you picked a strike, it was put back in the bag. In this new version of the game, what is the probability of picking three strikes in a row?

  F $\frac{1}{216}$ H $\frac{1}{36}$
  G $\frac{1}{120}$ J $\frac{1}{20}$

Holt McDougal Algebra 1

Problem Solving

Lesson 10-8: Combinations and Permutations

Write the correct answer.

1. In 1963, the United States Postal Service started using ZIP (Zone Improvement Plan) codes. Each ZIP code is a sequence of five digits. How many different U.S. ZIP codes are possible?

   _____

2. In the early 1970's, Canada Post started using six-character postal codes. Each postal code uses three letters and three digits in an alternating pattern. How many different Canadian postal codes are possible?

   _____

3. A band's new album contains 12 songs. The record company decides to promote the album at a music festival by giving away CD samplers that contain 3 songs from the album.

   a. Does this situation involve combinations or permutations? Explain.

   _____
   _____
   _____

   b. How many different ways can the band select songs for the sampler?

   _____

4. A 12-person jury is being selected for a court trial. After lengthy interviews, the attorney's have narrowed the candidates down to 14 people that they both think are fair and unbiased.

   a. Does this situation involve combinations or permutations? Explain.

   _____
   _____
   _____

   b. How many different ways can the attorneys select the jury?

   _____

Select the best answer.

5. Myra works Monday to Thursday as a waitress. She has 6 short-sleeve shirts that are appropriate for her to wear as part of her uniform. If she doesn't wear the same shirt twice, how many different ways can she wear her shirts during a 4-day work week?

   A 15   C 360
   B 24   D 720

6. At Cold Marble Ice Cream, you create your own ice cream flavor by choosing from a list of 10 "add-ins" that can be mixed into vanilla ice-cream. If you can pick one add-in, any combination of two add-ins, or any combination of three add-ins, how many different flavors are possible?

   F 120   H 210
   G 175   J 820

Name _____ Date _____ Class _____

LESSON 11-1 Problem Solving
Geometric Sequences

Write the correct answer.

1. A ball is dropped from 400 feet. The table shows the height of each bounce.

Bounce	Height (ft)
1	280
2	196
3	137.2

   Find the height of the ball on the 6th bounce. Round your answer to the nearest tenth of a foot.

   _____

2. A plant starts with 1 branch. Every year, each branch becomes 3 branches. A sketch of the plant for the first 3 years is shown. How many branches will the plant have in year 10?

   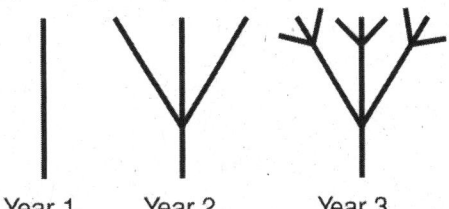

   Year 1   Year 2   Year 3

   _____

   How many branches would the plant have in year 10 if the plant had 5 branches the first year? (Each branch still becomes 3 branches every year.)

   _____

3. Jeanette started selling bagels to offices in her area. Her sales for the first 3 months are shown in the table.

Month	Sales ($)
1	$200.00
2	$230.00
3	$264.50

   If this trend continues, find the amount of Jeanette's sales in Month 8.

   _____

The table shows the number of houses in a new subdivision. Use the table to answer questions 4–7. Select the best answer.

Month	Houses
1	3
2	6
3	12
4	24

4. The number of houses forms a geometric sequence. What is r?

   A 0.5   C 3
   B 2   D 6

5. Assuming that the trend continues, how many houses would be in the subdivision in Month 6?

   F 36   H 60
   G 48   J 96

6. Management decides the subdivision is complete when the number of houses reaches 48. When will this happen?

   A Month 5   C Month 7
   B Month 6   D Month 8

7. Suppose the number of houses tripled every month. How many more houses would be in the subdivision in Month 4? (The number of houses in Month 1 is still 3.)

   F 48   H 72
   G 57   J 81

LESSON 11-2

Problem Solving
Exponential Functions

Write the correct answer.

1. The function $f(x) = 6(1.5)^x$ models the length of a photograph in inches after the photo has been enlarged by 50% x times.

   a. What is the length of the photograph after it has been enlarged 4 times?

   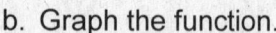

   b. Graph the function.

   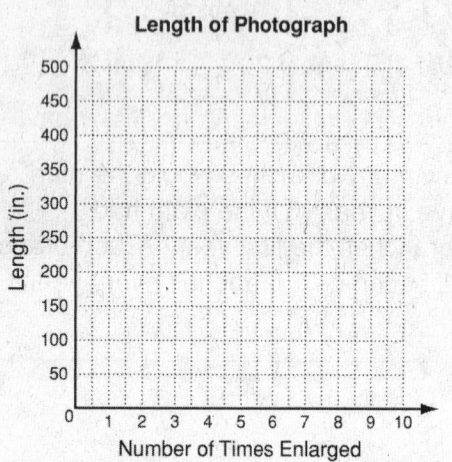

2. A population of 550 rabbits is increasing by 2.5% each year. The function $y = 5.5(1.025)^x$ gives the population of rabbits, in hundreds, x years from now. About how long will it take the population to reach 600 rabbits? 1200 rabbits?

   _____

   _____

3. The function $y = 200(1.0004)^x$ models the balance on a customer's line of credit x days after the end of the grace period (the time when no interest accumulates). If Jack does not make any payments, determine Jack's balance 30 days after the grace period ends.

   _____

4. The function $f(x) = 2300(0.995)^x$ models enrollment in a high school, where x is the number of years after 2005. Use the model to estimate the enrollment in 2013. _____

A lake was stocked with fish in early April. Select the best answer.

5. The function $f(x) = 300(0.85)^x$ models the number of landlocked salmon in the lake x months after the lake was stocked. Which is the best estimate of the number of landlocked salmon in early July?

   A 157   C 217
   B 184   D 255

7. The function $f(x) = 400(1.05)^x$ models the number of bass x months after the lake was stocked. During what month will the population reach 600?

   F September   H November
   G October   J December

6. The function $f(x) = 75(1.2)^x$ models the number of rainbow trout in the lake x years after 2005. Likewise, the function $f(x) = 105(1.08)^x$ models the number of perch in the lake for the same time period. Which statement is NOT true?

   A The population of perch will reach 120 before the population of rainbow trout does.

   B In 2009, the number of rainbow trout will exceed the number of perch.

   C In 2007, the number of rainbow trout will be less than 100.

   D In 10 years, there will be at least twice as many rainbow trout as perch.

Problem Solving
11-3 Exponential Growth and Decay

Write the correct answer.

1. A condo in Austin, Texas, was worth $80,000 in 1990. The value of the condo increased by an average of 3% each year. Write an exponential growth function to model this situation. Then find the value of the condominium in 2005.

2. Markiya deposited $500 in a savings account. The annual interest rate is 2%, and the interest is compounded monthly. Write a compound interest function to model this situation. Then find the balance in Markiya's account after 4 years.

3. The population of a small Midwestern town is 4500. The population is decreasing at a rate of 1.5% per year. Write an exponential decay function to model this situation. Then find the number of people in the town after 25 years.

4. Twelve students at a particular high school passed an advanced placement test in 2000. The number of students who passed the test increased by 16.4% each year thereafter. Find the number of students who passed the test in 2004.

Half-lives range from less than a second to billions of years. The table below shows the half-lives of several substances. Select the best answer.

5. About how many grams of a 500 g sample of Technetium-99 is left after 2 days?
   - A 1.95 g
   - B 7.81 g
   - C 31.25 g
   - D 62.5 g

Half-Lives	
Nitrogen-16	7 s
Technetium-99	6 h
Sulfur-35	87 days
Tritium	12.3 yr
Uranium-238	4.5 billion yrs

6. Which equation can be used to find how much of a 50 g sample of Nitrogen-16 is left after 7 minutes?
   - F $A = 50(0.5)^1$
   - G $A = 50(0.5)^7$
   - H $A = 50(0.5)^{42}$
   - J $A = 50(0.5)^{60}$

7. How many billions of years will it take 1000 grams of Uranium-238 to decay to just 125 grams?
   - A 0.125
   - B 3
   - C 9
   - D 13.5

8. A researcher had 37.5 g left from a 600 g sample of Sulfer-35. How many half-lives passed during that time?
   - F 4
   - G 5
   - H 7
   - J 16

9. Look at problem 8. How many days passed during that time?
   - A 7
   - B 16
   - C 348
   - D 435

Problem Solving
Lesson 11-4: Linear, Quadratic, and Exponential Models

Write the correct answer.

1. The table shows the height of a baseball for different times after it was thrown. Graph the data. Which kind of model best describes the data?

Height of Baseball

Time (s)	0	1	2	3	4
Height (ft)	5	53	69	53	5

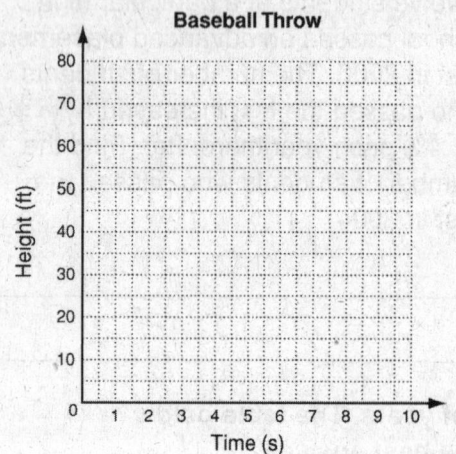

2. The table shows the cost of peaches. Look for a pattern and determine which kind of model best describes the data. Then write a function that models the data.

Cost of Peaches

Pounds	1	2	3	4
Cost ($)	1.29	2.58	3.87	5.16

_____

3. The table shows the number of computers in a school for your years.

Number of Computers

Year	'00	'01	'02	'03
Computers	14	28	56	112

Write a function to model the data. Then use the function to predict how many computers the school will have in 2006 if the pattern continues.

_____

The chart shows the ticket sales for movies on two different screens at one theater over four days. Select the best answer.

	Screen 1	Screen 2
Day 1	400	3000
Day 2	440	2400
Day 3	480	1920
Day 4	520	1536

4. Which kind of model best describes the ticket sales for the movie on screen 1?
   - A linear
   - B quadratic
   - C exponential
   - D none of these

5. Which function describes the data for screen 1?
   - F $y = 40x^2$
   - G $y = 40x + 400$
   - H $y = 400x$
   - J $y = 400(40)^x$

6. Which kind of model best describes the ticket sales for the movie on screen 2?
   - A linear
   - B quadratic
   - C exponential
   - D none of these

7. Which function describes the data for screen 2?
   - F $y = -600x + 3000$
   - G $y = 600x^2 + 2400$
   - H $y = 3000(0.8)^x$
   - J $y = 3000(1.25)^x$

Name _____ Date _____ Class _____

LESSON 11-5 Problem Solving
Square-Root Functions

Write the correct answer.

1. Use the formula $r = \sqrt{\dfrac{A}{\pi}}$ to find the radius of a circular fountain with an area of 200 square feet. Use 3.14 for π. Round your answer to the nearest foot.

   _____

2. The manager of a magazine gives a rating to each article written using $y = \sqrt{10x}$ where x is the number of positive responses received about that article. What rating would the manager give an article if it received 21 positive responses? (Round to the nearest tenth.)

   _____

3. The distance to the horizon (in km) from an aircraft can be roughly approximated using $y = 4\sqrt{x}$ where x is the aircraft's altitude in meters. Graph this function.

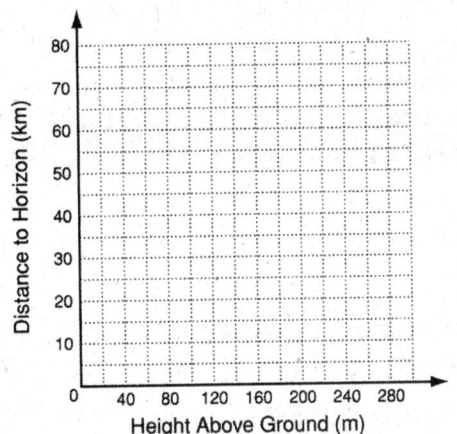

4. The amount of water flowing through a hose in gallons per minute is given by $y = 35\sqrt{x}$ where x is the nozzle pressure in pounds per square inch. What is the water flow in the hose if the pressure is 25 pounds per square inch?

   _____

Select the best answer.

5. The diameter of a can of tuna is found by $d = 2\sqrt{\dfrac{V}{\pi h}}$ where V is volume and h is height. To the nearest cm, what is the radius of a tuna can with a volume of 150 cm³ and a height of 3 cm?

   A 2 cm   C 8 cm
   B 4 cm   D 16 cm

6. The side length of the base of a square pyramid can be found by $s = \sqrt{\dfrac{3V}{h}}$ where V is volume and h is height. To the nearest meter, what is the side length of the base of a square pyramid if its volume is 13,653 m³ and its height is 40 m?

   F 3 m   H 32 m
   G 18 m   J 55 m

7. The radius of a ball is found by $r = \sqrt{\dfrac{S}{4\pi}}$ where S is surface area. To the nearest tenth of an inch, what is the radius of a ball with a surface area of 154 in²?

   A 3.5 in.   C 7.0 in.
   B 6.2 in.   D 12.3 in.

Name _____ Date _____ Class _____

LESSON 11-6
Problem Solving
Radical Expressions

Write the correct answer.

1. Annalise walks 200 meters from her house, turns a corner, and then walks another 100 meters to the bus stop. She wants to know how much shorter her walk would be if she cut across the field. Find the distance across the field from Annalise's house to the bus stop. Give your answer as a radical expression in simplest form. Then find the difference in the two routes to the nearest meter.

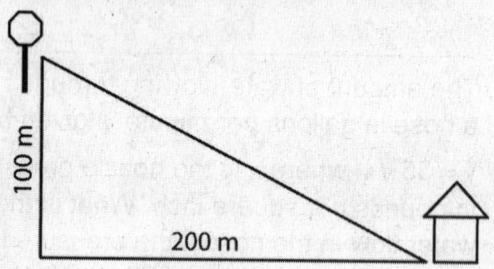

_____

2. A construction worker drops a nail from some scaffolding 192 feet from the ground. The nail is in freefall. The time t in seconds for an object in freefall to reach the ground is $t = \sqrt{\dfrac{d}{16}}$, where d is the distance in feet that it falls. The speed v in feet per second of an object in freefall is modeled by $v = 8\sqrt{d}$. Determine how long it takes the nail to reach the ground. Also find the speed the nail is traveling at 192 feet. Give your answers as radical expressions in simplest form. Then estimate the time to the nearest second and the speed to the nearest foot per second.

_____

Police officers determine the speed a car was traveling when the driver slammed on the brakes by measuring the length of skid marks left by the tires. On dry concrete, $f(x) = \sqrt{24x}$ gives the speed in mi/h when the length of the skid marks is x feet. The graph shows lengths of skid marks from several cars. Select the best answer.

3. Which shows the speed of car A in simplest radical form?

   A $\sqrt{3360}$ mi/h   C $4\sqrt{210}$ mi/h
   B $2\sqrt{840}$ mi/h   D $16\sqrt{210}$ mi/h

4. Which shows the speed of car B in simplest radical form?

   F $2\sqrt{78}$ mi/h   H $8\sqrt{78}$ mi/h
   G $4\sqrt{78}$ mi/h   J $16\sqrt{78}$ mi/h

5. Which shows the speed of car C in simplest radical form?

   A $2\sqrt{540}$ mi/h   C $12\sqrt{15}$ mi/h
   B $4\sqrt{135}$ mi/h   D $16\sqrt{135}$ mi/h

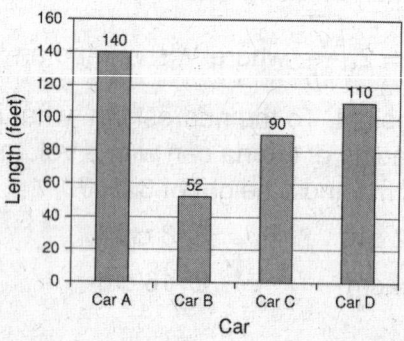

6. The driver of car D claims his skid marks were really only 60% as long as officers claim they were. If the driver is telling the truth, what was his speed in simplest radical form?

   F $\sqrt{66}$ mi/h   H $2\sqrt{396}$ mi/h
   G $\sqrt{1584}$ mi/h   J $12\sqrt{11}$ mi/h

Name _____ Date _____ Class _____

LESSON 11-7 Problem Solving
Adding and Subtracting Radical Expressions

Write the correct answer as a radical expression in simplest form.

1. The parks department is installing a fence along a scenic overlook. The area to be fenced has 3 sides measuring $4\sqrt{5}$ feet, $3\sqrt{5}$ feet, and $5\sqrt{5}$ feet. Find the total amount of fencing that needs to be installed.

   _____

2. A rectangular laundry room has a length of $\sqrt{54}$ feet and a width of $\sqrt{48}$ feet. Find the perimeter of the laundry room.

   _____

3. Mr. Lansberry bought four watermelons for a family reunion. The watermelons weighed $\sqrt{75}$ pounds, $\sqrt{108}$ pounds, $\sqrt{125}$ pounds, and $\sqrt{80}$ pounds. How many pounds of watermelon did Mr. Lansberry bring to the reunion?

   _____

4. Travon is hanging the same wallpaper border in two rooms. One room is a perfect square with an area of 120 square feet. The other room, a rectangle, has a width of $\sqrt{30}$ feet and a length of 8 feet. How much wallpaper border does Travon need to go around the perimeter of the two rooms?

   _____

Select the best answer.

5. A cafeteria tray is shaped like an isosceles trapezoid. The bases measure $\sqrt{180}$ in. and $\sqrt{320}$ in. The legs measure $\sqrt{80}$ in. Find the perimeter of the tray.

   A $2\sqrt{145}$ in.   C $18\sqrt{5}$ in.
   B $2\sqrt{165}$ in.   D $22\sqrt{5}$ in.

6. Jack, Aislinn, Mercedes, and Dae are a team participating in a relay at a fall festival. Jack's time was $7\sqrt{2}$ seconds, Aislinn's was $12\sqrt{2}$ seconds, Mercedes's was $6\sqrt{2}$ seconds, and Dae's was $9\sqrt{2}$ seconds. What was the team's total time?

   F 24 s   H $34\sqrt{2}$ s
   G $24\sqrt{2}$ s   J 68 s

7. Lily has two picture frames she is replacing. The first frame is shaped like a regular octagon, and all sides measure $\sqrt{12}$ in. The second frame is shaped like a rectangle; the length and width are $\sqrt{60}$ in. and $\sqrt{12}$ in. respectively. How much total framing will she need?

   A $2\sqrt{6} + 2\sqrt{15}$ in.
   B $4\sqrt{3} + 2\sqrt{15}$ in.
   C $16\sqrt{3} + 4\sqrt{15}$ in.
   D $20\sqrt{3} + 4\sqrt{15}$ in.

8. A triangular pennant has two sides that measure $28\sqrt{3}$ centimeters and a third side that measures $7\sqrt{3}$ centimeters. Mrs. Kwan is sewing 2 rows of gold ribbon around the perimeter of the pennant. How much ribbon does she need?

   F $63\sqrt{3}$ cm   H $126\sqrt{3}$ cm
   G $70\sqrt{3}$ cm   J 189 cm

LESSON 11-8

Problem Solving
Multiplying and Dividing Radical Expressions

Write each correct answer as a radical expression in simplest form.

1. The expression $\sqrt{\dfrac{W}{R}}$ models the electrical current in amperes, where W is power in watts and R is resistance in ohms. How much electrical current is running through an appliance with 500 watts of power and 16 ohms of resistance?

   _____

2. The diagram shows the dimensions of a dining table. With a leaf in place, the table expands to seat eight people.

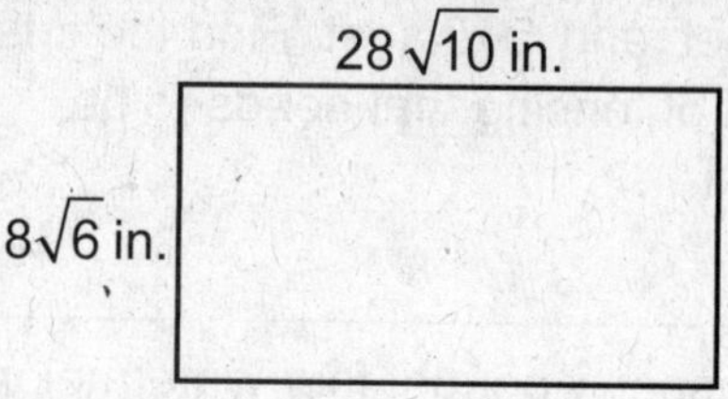

   [Rectangle: $28\sqrt{10}$ in. by $8\sqrt{6}$ in.]

   Find the area of the table.

   _____

3. Riley's new bedroom is a perfect square. Each side measures $2\sqrt{3}$ meters. Find the area and perimeter of Riley's bedroom.

   _____

   Find the area of the table with the addition of a leaf that measures $8\sqrt{6}$ inches by $18\sqrt{3}$ inches.

   _____

Select the best answer.

4. R.J. lives in a studio apartment. The apartment is rectangular with a width of $10 + 4\sqrt{2}$ feet and a length of $20 + 11\sqrt{2}$ feet. What is the area of R.J.'s apartment?

   A 60 ft²
   B 288 ft²
   C 200 + 190$\sqrt{2}$ ft²
   D 288 + 190$\sqrt{2}$ ft²

5. The volume of water in a lake, in gallons, can be represented by $x\sqrt{2}$. Heavy rains are forecast. The volume of water is expected to increase $\sqrt{2}$ times. How many gallons of water are expected in the lake after the rain?

   F $\dfrac{x}{2}$ gallons
   G x gallons
   H $x\sqrt{2}$ gallons
   J $2x$ gallons

6. The area of a rectangular window is 40 square feet. The length is $\sqrt{20}$ feet. What is the width of the window?

   A $\sqrt{2}$ feet   C $4\sqrt{5}$ feet
   B 2 feet   D $4\sqrt{10}$ feet

7. The height of a triangle can be found using $h = \dfrac{2A}{b}$ where A is the area and b is the base of the triangle. Which shows the height of a triangle with an area of $\sqrt{90}$ cm² and a base of $\sqrt{5}$ cm written in simplest form?

   F $2\sqrt{18}$ cm   H $6\sqrt{2}$ cm
   G $3\sqrt{18}$ cm   J $18\sqrt{2}$ cm

Name _____ Date _____ Class _____

LESSON 11-9
Problem Solving
Solving Radical Equations

Write the correct answer.

1. The perimeter of the marching band's practice field is 360 yards. Its length and width are shown in the diagram.

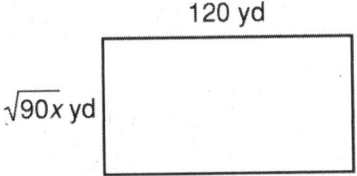

   Find the value of x and the width of the field. Then calculate the area of the field.

   _____

   _____

   _____

2. The formula $v = \dfrac{\sqrt{2Em}}{m}$ describes the relationship between an object's mass m in kilograms, its velocity v in meters per second, and its kinetic energy E in joules. A bowling ball with a mass of 5 kg is thrown with a velocity of 8 meters per second. Determine the kinetic energy of the bowling ball.

   _____

3. An office has a storage closet with an area of 48 square feet. The length of the closet is 8 feet. The width is $2\sqrt{11-x}$ feet. Find the value of x and the width of the closet.

   _____

   _____

Select the best answer.

4. The equation $v = \sqrt{2.5r}$ describes the relationship between the radius r in feet of an unbanked curve and the maximum velocity v in miles per hour that a car can safely go around the curve. A primary road with a speed limit of 35 miles per hour curves through a residential area. What is the radius of the unbanked curve?

   A 14 feet   C 450 feet
   B 49 feet   D 490 feet

6. A building sits on a lot that is shaped like a triangle with a base of 120 feet and a height of $\sqrt{5000x}$ feet. The area of the lot is 12,000 square feet. Which length represents the height of the triangle?

   A 8 feet   C 200 feet
   B 100 feet   D 400 feet

5. The remains of a structure on an archeological site are laid out in the shape of a rectangle. The area of the rectangle is 12 square meters. The width is 3 meters and the length is $\sqrt{x+6}$ meters. What is the value of x?

   F 4   H 12
   G 10   J 16

7. Gretchen mixes her own bubble bath using essential oils. She uses a jar that holds $\sqrt{33}$ ounces. Gretchen fills the jar with $\sqrt{x-4}$ ounces of bubble solution and oils. What is the value of x?

   F 37   H 1089
   G 39   J 1093

LESSON 12-1 Problem Solving
Inverse Variation

The number of gallons of gasoline that Isaac can afford y varies inversely as the price per gallon x. Isaac can afford 12 gal when the price is $2.50 per gallon.

1. Write an inverse variation for this situation.

   _____

2. Determine a reasonable domain and range.

   _____

3. Complete this table of ordered pairs and graph the inverse variation.

x		2.50	3.00		10.00
y	20	12		6	

4. Use the graph to estimate the number of gallons Isaac can afford when the price is $3.49 per gallon.

   _____

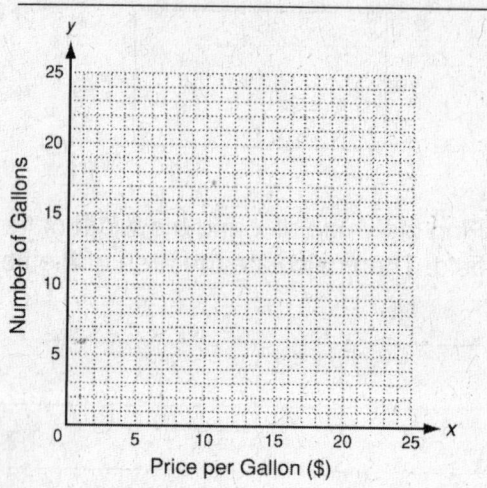

Select the best answer.

5. The inverse variation $xy = 9$ relates the current x in amps to the resistance y in ohms of a circuit attached to a 9-volt battery. What is the resistance of the circuit when the current is 1.8 amps?

   A 0.2 ohms   C 10.8 ohms
   B 5 ohms   D 16.2 ohms

6. Boyle's law states that the pressure of a quantity of gas x varies inversely as the volume of the gas y. The volume of air inside a bicycle pump is 6.1 in^3, and the pressure is 18.3 psi. Which equation represents this situation?

   F $y = 3x$ H $y = 111.63x$
   G $y = \dfrac{3}{x}$ J $y = \dfrac{111.63}{x}$

7. The time it takes to drive between two cities varies inversely as speed. Dolores can drive between Houston, Texas, and San Antonio, Texas, in 3.5 h at 60 mi/h. How long will the trip take if she drives 70 mi/h? (Round your answer to the nearest tenth.)

   A 2.3 h   C 3 h
   B 2.6 h   D 4.1 h

8. On a balanced lever, weight varies inversely as the distance from the fulcrum. Angie weighs 120 lb. When she sits $2\dfrac{1}{2}$ ft from the fulcrum of a seesaw, she balances with her brother, who weighs 80 lb. How far is her brother from the fulcrum of the seesaw?

   F $\dfrac{4}{15}$ ft   H $1\dfrac{2}{3}$ ft
   G $\dfrac{3}{5}$ ft   J $3\dfrac{3}{4}$ ft

Name _____ Date _____ Class _____

LESSON 12-2 Problem Solving
Rational Functions

Gabrielle saves $100 and decides to join a CD Club. As a member, she gets 12 CDs free and then must buy the rest at the regular price of x dollars. The number of CDs y she can buy is $y = \dfrac{100}{x} + 12$.

1. Determine a reasonable domain and range.

   _____

   _____

2. Identify the vertical and horizontal asymptotes.

   _____

3. Complete this table of ordered pairs and graph the rational function.

x	5	10	20	25
y				

4. Gabrielle learns that the regular price of a CD is $17.90. How many CDs can she buy through the Club with $100?

   _____

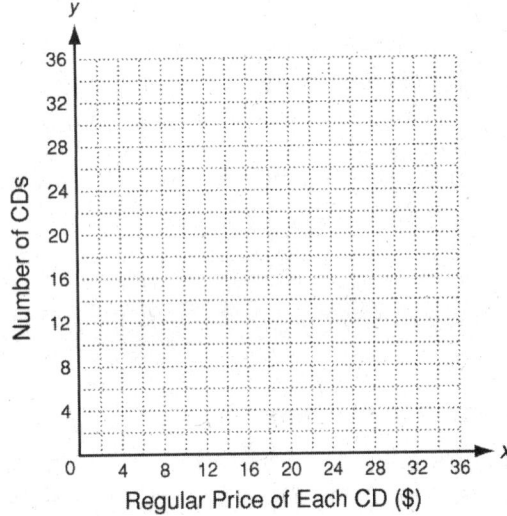

Regular Price of Each CD ($)

Select the best answer. For 5–6, refer to the situation above.

5. Before joining the CD Club, Gabrielle learns about the Student Savings Card. If she buys a card for $20, she gets $5 off every CD she buys at the local record store. If each CD costs x dollars at the local record store, then the number of CDs y she can buy is $y = \dfrac{100-20}{x-5}$. The average price of each CD at the local record store is $14.95. How many CDs can she buy with the Card and $100?

   A 4   C 10
   B 8   D 12

6. Gabrielle realizes she must pay $2.95 for shipping and handling on every CD from the club, including the 12 free CDs. That changes the function for the club to $y = \dfrac{100 - 2.95(12)}{x + 2.95} + 12$. If the regular price is still $17.90, how many CDs can she buy through the Club?

   F 3   H 16
   G 15   J 18

7. At x meters away from a very loud stereo speaker, the intensity of the sound y in Watts per square meter is given by $y = \dfrac{0.0016}{x^2}$. What is the intensity when you stand 4 meters away?

   A 0.0001 W/m²   C 0.0004 W/m²
   B 0.0002 W/m²   D 0.0008 W/m²

Name _____ Date _____ Class _____

LESSON 12-3 Problem Solving
Simplifying Rational Expressions

A food company is considering two types of cylindrical cans for a new trail mix. The company wants a can that uses the least material for the greatest volume. For a cylinder, $S = 2\pi r^2 + 2\pi rh$ and $V = \pi r^2 h$.

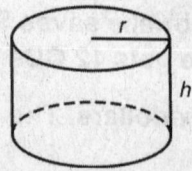

1. What is the surface-area-to-volume ratio for any cylinder?

   _____

2. Can A has radius 2 in. and height 3 in. What is the surface-area-to-volume ratio for Can A?

   _____

3. Can B has radius 1.5 in. and height 4 in. What is the surface-area-to-volume ratio for Can B?

   _____

4. Which can should the company choose? Explain.

   _____

   _____

Select the best answer.

5. For any circle with radius r, $P = 2\pi r$ and $A = \pi r^2$. Which expression represents the perimeter-to-area ratio?

   A $2r$ C $\dfrac{r}{2}$

   B $\dfrac{2}{r}$ D $\dfrac{1}{2r}$

6. Tyrone takes an 8-by-8 square piece of cardboard and cuts x-by-x squares out of each corner. (All units are inches.) He then folds up the sides to form a box with no top. Which expression represents the surface-area-to-volume ratio? (*Hint:* For the surface area, find the area of the entire piece of cardboard and subtract the squares that were removed.)

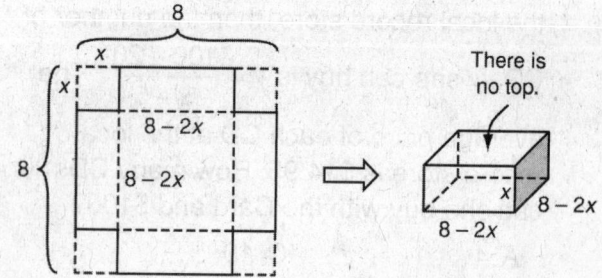

7. In 2000, there are x mountain lions (predators) and x deer (prey) in a wildlife preserve. In 2005, the populations level off at $3x$ mountain lions and $4x$ deer, for a predator-to-prey ratio of $\dfrac{3}{4}$. If the wildlife preserve adds 12 more deer in 2007, how many mountain lions should also be added to keep the predator-to-prey ratio equivalent to $\dfrac{3}{4}$?

   A 9   C 16

   B 12   D 20

   F $\dfrac{1}{x}$ H $\dfrac{8}{x(4-x)}$

   G $\dfrac{1}{2x(1-16x)}$ J $\dfrac{4+x}{x(4-x)}$

Name _____ Date _____ Class _____

LESSON 12-4 Problem Solving
Multiplying and Dividing Rational Expressions

A bag contains 5 more red marbles than blue marbles. Janis is going to pick two marbles out of the bag without looking, and without replacing the first marble. Let x represent the number of blue marbles.

1. Write and simplify an expression that represents the probability that Janis will pick two blue marbles.

   _____

2. Is the probability that Janis picks a red marble and then a blue marble the same as the probability that she picks a blue and then a red? Explain.

   _____
   _____
   _____

3. Write and simplify an expression that represents the probability that Janis will pick two red marbles. Then find the probability of picking two red marbles if the bag contains 20 blue marbles.

   _____
   _____
   _____

A square dart board has three regions, A, B, and C, as shown. Units are in inches. Select the best answer.

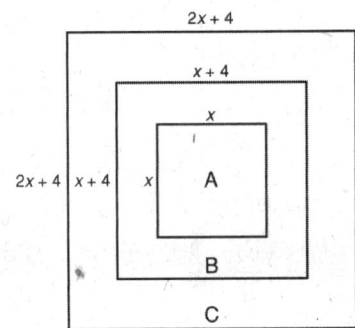

4. Which expression represents the probability of throwing two darts that land in region A and then region B?

   A $\dfrac{2x^2}{x+2}$ C $\dfrac{(x+4)^2}{16(x+2)^4}$

   B $\dfrac{x^2}{2(x+2)^3}$ D $\dfrac{x^2(x+4)^2}{4(x+2)^2}$

5. Divide two rational expressions to find how many times greater the probability of a dart landing in region C is than the probability of a dart landing in region A.

   F $\dfrac{3x+8}{x}$ H $\dfrac{4(x+2)^2}{x^2}$

   G $\dfrac{x}{2(x+1)}$ J $\dfrac{x(3x+8)}{8(x+2)}$

6. Which expression represents the probability of throwing two darts that both land in region B?

   A $\dfrac{4}{(x+2)^2}$

   B $\dfrac{x^2}{(x+4)^2}$

   C $\dfrac{(x+4)^4}{16(x+2)^4}$

   D $\dfrac{64(x+2)^2}{x^2(3x+8)^2}$

7. If $x = 2$ in., what is the probability of throwing two darts that both land in region A?

   F $\dfrac{1}{4}$ H $\dfrac{1}{32}$

   G $\dfrac{1}{16}$ J $\dfrac{1}{256}$

Name _____ Date _____ Class _____

LESSON 12-5

Problem Solving
Adding and Subtracting Rational Expressions

Adib is kayaking on the Peconic River in Long Island, New York. He paddles his kayak at an average rate of 3 mi/h, but does not know the rate of the river's current. Adib plans to kayak upstream 2 mi and then back downstream to his starting point.

1. Let x represent the rate of the current in the Peconic River in miles per hour. Write and simplify an expression for the total time of Adib's round trip.

2. If the rate of the river's current is 2 mi/h, how long will it take Adib to kayak round trip?

3. If the rate of the river's current is 3 mi/h, how long will it take Adib to kayak round trip? Explain what your answer could mean in this context.

_____

_____

Select the best answer.

4. Terry drives 2 mi on city streets, and 20 mi on the highway. Her speed on the highway is three times her speed on the city streets r, in miles per hour. Write and simplify and expression that represents the length of Terry's trip in hours.

   A $\dfrac{13}{3r}$ C $\dfrac{26}{3r}$

   B $\dfrac{22}{4r}$ D $\dfrac{62}{3r}$

5. Nahuel walks 1 km to school at a rate of w km/h. When he gets to school, he realizes that he forgot his math book, so he jogs back home and back to school at a rate 4 km/h faster than his walking rate. Write and simplify an expression that represents the length of Nahuel's entire trip to school in hours.

   F $\dfrac{3}{2w}$ H $\dfrac{2(w+1)}{w(w+2)}$

   G $\dfrac{3}{2(w+2)}$ J $\dfrac{3w+4}{w(w+4)}$

6. A test consists of 4 free response questions and 50 multiple choice questions. The test's writers assume an average student can do x free response questions per hour, and four times as many multiple choice questions per hour. If an average student can do 6 free response questions per hour, how long is the test?

   A $1\dfrac{4}{5}$ h   C $3\dfrac{3}{8}$ h

   B $2\dfrac{3}{4}$ h   D $5\dfrac{2}{3}$ h

7. In a carnival game, Beth runs 100 m to a table, picks up water balloons, and runs back to the starting line. Beth originally runs to the table at a rate of y m/s, but runs 1 m/s slower when she carries the balloons. If Beth originally runs 5 m/s, how long, to the nearest second, does it take her to finish?

   F 10 s   H 37 s

   G 22 s   J 45 s

Name _____ Date _____ Class _____

LESSON 12-6
Problem Solving
Dividing Polynomials

Write the correct answer.

1. The area of a rectangle is $x^2 + 2x - 8 m^2$, and the width is $x - 2$ m. Find the length.

2. On the dartboard below, the area of the outside ring is the difference between the area of the two largest circles, or $\pi(x+4)^2 - \pi(x+2)^2$ in^2. The area of the bull's-eye is πx^2 in^2. Expand and divide $[\pi(x+4)^2 - \pi(x+2)^2] \div \pi x^2$ to find the ratio of the area of the outside ring to the bull's-eye.

3. The area of a rectangular piece of paper is $4n^2 - 4n - 9$ cm^2. Then a triangle with area $2n + 6$ cm^2 is cut from one corner of the paper. What is the ratio of the area of the paper that remains to the area of the triangle that was removed? (*Hint:* First subtract to find the area of the paper that remains.)

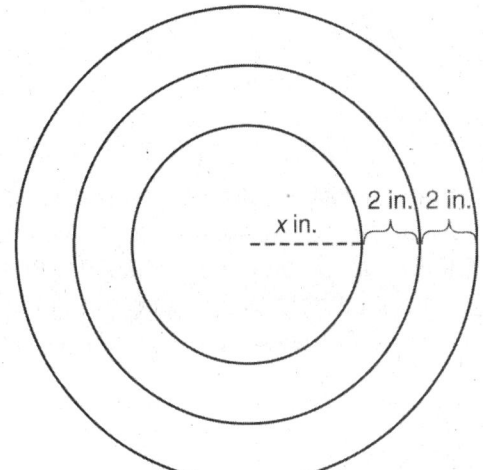

Select the best answer.

4. The area of a triangle is $8a^2 - 10a$ ft^2, and the height is $4a$ ft. Find the base.
   (*Hint:* Solve $A = \frac{1}{2}bh$ for b.)

   A $a - \dfrac{5a}{4}$ ft   C $4a - \dfrac{5a}{2}$ ft

   B $2a - \dfrac{5a}{2}$ ft   D $4a - 5$ ft

5. The volume of a rectangular prism is $2x^3 + 9x^2 - 11x - 30$ cm^3, and the height is $x + 5$ cm. Find the area of the base. ($V = BH$, where B is the area of the base and H is the height.)

   F $2x^2 - x - 6$ cm^2

   G $2x^2 - x - 16 + \dfrac{-110}{x+5}$ cm^2

   H $2x^2 - 4x - 16 + \dfrac{-35}{x+5}$ cm^2

   J $2x^2 + 19x + 84 + \dfrac{390}{x+5}$ cm^2

6. The volume of a cylinder is $V = \pi r^2 h$, where r is the radius and h is the height. The volume of a certain cylinder is $\pi(n^3 - 6n^2 - 36n + 216)$ in^3, and the radius is $n - 6$ in. Find the height. (*Hint:* To divide by r^2, divide by r twice.)

   A n in.   C $n + 6$ in.

   B $n - 6$ in.   D $n^2 - 36$ in.

Name _____ Date _____ Class _____

LESSON 12-7 Problem Solving
Solving Rational Equations

Write the correct answer.

1. Alex can remodel a bathroom in 2 days. Abraham can remodel the same bathroom in 4 days. How long will it take them to remodel the bathroom if they work together?

2. When only the cold faucet is fully turned on, a bathtub fills in 8 minutes. When only the hot faucet is fully turned on, the same bathtub fills in 12 minutes. If both the cold and hot faucets are fully turned on, how long will it take to fill the bathtub?

3. 100 mL of a solution contains 30 mL of acid; this is called a 30% acid solution because $\frac{part}{whole} = \frac{30}{100} = 0.30$. How many milliliters of acid x would need to be added to the solution to turn it into a 50% acid solution? (*Hint*: Adding acid increases both the volume of acid and the volume of the complete solution.)

4. Markus jogs 4 mi around a track at an average rate of *r* mi/h. Then he cools down by walking 1 mi at a rate 3 mi/h slower. His whole workout lasts 1 h. At what rates did Markus jog and walk?

Select the best answer.

5. Ms. Spinoni can prepare a mass-mailing of 500 letters in 10 hours. Mr. Harris can prepare a mass-mailing of 500 letters in 15 hours. How long will it take them to prepare a mass-mailing of 1000 letters if they work together? (*Hint:* The complete job is twice as big.)

   A 6 h
   B 12 h
   C $12\frac{1}{2}$ h
   D 25 h

6. At a cafeteria, the automatic ice machine can completely fill itself in 20 minutes. During lunch time, customers can completely empty the ice machine in 30 minutes. At the start of lunch time, the ice machine is completely empty and it starts making ice at the same time that customers start taking ice. How long will it take for the machine to be completely full? (*Hint:* The customers *take away* ice.)

   F 12 min
   G 20 min
   H 30 min
   J 60 min

7. To attend a family reunion, Beth drives 100 mi from Fresno and Clara drives 220 mi from San Jose. Both women drive the same speed in miles per hour, but Clara's drive takes 2 h longer than Beth's. Find the length of Beth's drive.

   A 1 h
   B $1\frac{2}{3}$ h
   C $2\frac{1}{5}$ h
   D $3\frac{2}{3}$ h